ELEMENTS

OF

DESCRIPTIVE GEOMETRY,

WITH

THEIR APPLICATION

TO

SPHERICAL TRIGONOMETRY, SPHERICAL PROJECTIONS,
AND WARPED SURFACES.

BY CHARLES DAVIES, LL.D.

AUTHOR OF ARITHMETIC, ELEMENTARY ALGEBRA, ELEMENTARY GEOMETRY, PRACTICAL GEOMETRY, ELEMENTS OF SURVEYING, ELEMENTS OF DESCRIPTIVE AND ANALYTICAL GEOMETRY, ELEMENTS OF DIFFERENTIAL AND INTEGRAL CALCULUS, AND A TREATISE ON SHADES, SHADOWS, AND PERSPECTIVE.

NEW YORK:
A. S. BARNES & Co., 111 & 113 WILLIAM STREET,
(CORNER OF JOHN STREET.)
SOLD BY BOOKSELLERS, GENERALLY, THROUGHOUT THE UNITED STATES.

1868.

DAVIES'
COURSE OF MATHEMATICS.

DAVIES' FIRST LESSONS IN ARITHMETIC,
DESIGNED FOR BEGINNERS.

DAVIES' ARITHMETIC,
DESIGNED FOR THE USE OF ACADEMIES AND SCHOOLS.

KEY TO DAVIES' ARITHMETIC.

DAVIES' ELEMENTARY ALGEBRA:
Being an introduction to the Science.

KEY TO DAVIES' ELEMENTARY ALGEBRA.

DAVIES' ELEMENTARY GEOMETRY.
This work embraces the elementary principles of Geometry. The reasoning is plain and concise, but at the same time strictly rigorous.

DAVIES' PRACTICAL GEOMETRY,
Embracing the facts of Geometry, with applications in ARTIFICER'S WORK, MENSURATION, and MECHANICAL PHILOSOPHY.

DAVIES' BOURDON'S ALGERRA,
Being an abridgment of the work of M. Bourdon, with the addition of practical examples.

DAVIES' LEGENDRE'S GEOMETRY AND TRIGONOMETRY,
Being an abridgment of the work of M. Legendre, with the addition of a Treatise on MENSURATION OF PLANES AND SOLIDS, and a Table of LOGARITHMS and LOGARITHMIC SINES.

DAVIES' SURVEYING,
With a description and plates of, the THEODOLITE, COMPASS, PLANE-TABLE, and LEVEL—also, Maps of the TOPOGRAPHICAL SIGNS adopted by the Engineer Department—an explanation of the method of surveying the Public Lands, and an Elementary Treatise on NAVIGATION.

DAVIES' ANALYTICAL GEOMETRY,
Embracing the EQUATIONS OF THE POINT AND STRAIGHT LINE—of the CONIC SECTIONS—of the LINE AND PLANE IN SPACE—also, the discussion of the GENERAL EQUATION of the second degree, and of SURFACES OF THE SECOND ORDER.

DAVIES' DESCRIPTIVE GEOMETRY,
With its application to SPHERICAL PROJECTIONS.

DAVIES' SHADOWS AND LINEAR PERSPECTIVE.

DAVIES' DIFFERENTIAL AND INTEGRAL CALCULUS.

PREFACE.

THIS Treatise on Descriptive Geometry has been prepared for the use of the Cadets of the Military Academy. In submitting it to the public, the author prefers no claim to invention or discovery. It has been his object to furnish a useful text book; and if this end be attained, he will have no cause to regret his labours.

The study of the Mathematics, whether considered as introductory to its sister science, Mechanical Philosophy, or as a salutary and invigorating exercise of the mind, is equally worthy of attention. The useful and important results to which it leads, the mutual dependence of its parts, and the concise and satisfactory reasoning in the development of its principles, recommend this study, as well to the practical man, who learns only what he can successfully apply, as to the lover of science, who explores all its departments in search of new facts and interesting truths.

The subject of Descriptive Geometry, which is treated of in these Elements, has not, as yet, been considered in this country as a necessary part either of a polite or practical education. It has been taught in the Military Academy since 1817, but has not found its way into other Seminaries with a rapidity at all proportionate to its usefulness. The progress of science, like that of truth, is always slow; yet it compensates for its want of velocity in the steadiness of its advancement and the certainty of its success. In France, Descriptive Geometry is an important element of a scientific education; it is taught in most of the public schools, and is considered indispensable to the Architect and Engineer. Its intimate connexion with Civil Engineering and Architecture, and the facilities which it affords in all graphic operations, render its acquisition desirable to those who devote themselves to these pursuits.

The author is by no means indifferent to the reception which this work may meet with from the public; yet, he will not complain of a rigid criticism, if it shall appear that he has been instrumental in diffusing a knowledge of an interesting and useful branch of science.

MILITARY ACADEMY,
WEST POINT. December, 1826.

TABLE OF CONTENTS.

CHAPTER I.

CHAPTER II.

CHAPTER III.

CHAPTER IV.

CHAPTER V.

CHAPTER VI.

CHAPTER VII.

CHAPTER VIII.

CHAPTER IX.

CHAPTER X.

CHAPTER XI.

CHAPTER XII.

CHAPTER XIII.

COMPLEMENT.

ELEMENTS

OF

DESCRIPTIVE GEOMETRY.

CHAPTER I.

FIRST PRINCIPLES.

§ 1. The object of Descriptive Geometry is twofold: first, *to represent with accuracy all geometrical magnitudes on planes;* and secondly, *to construct all graphic problems involving three dimensions.*

§ 2. The representation of a geometrical magnitude on a plane is called *its projection,* and the plane on which the representation is made is named *the plane of projection.*

§ 3. In Descriptive Geometry two planes of projection are used, and to simplify the constructions, they are taken at right angles to each other.

§ 4. If one plane be taken horizontal, the other will be vertical, and this position of the planes enables us to conceive most readily how objects are situated in space when their projections are known.*

§ 5. The planes are called, respectively, *the horizontal plane* of projection, and *the vertical plane* of projection. Their line of intersection, which is horizontal, is called the *ground line,* or *common intersection;* and each plane is supposed to extend indefinitely in the direction of, and from this line of intersection.

* Space is indefinite extension, in which all bodies are situated. The *absolute* position of bodies cannot be determined, but their *relative* positions may be, either by referring them to each other, or to objects whose places are assumed In Descriptive Geometry all bodies are referred to the planes of projection.

§ 6. Pl. 1. Fig. 1. When, therefore, a line, as AB, is assumed for the common intersection of the planes of projection, it is the intention simply to point out the line, and not to limit its extension.

§ 7. Let AB be the ground line, and the plane of the paper the horizontal plane of projection. The vertical plane passes through AB, and is perpendicular to the plane of the paper.

Suppose the vertical plane of projection to be turned or revolved around AB as an axis, or hinge, till it coincides with the plane of the paper. There are two ways in which this revolution can be made: first, we can so revolve the vertical plane, that the part which is above the horizontal plane shall fall in front of the ground line AB; the part of the vertical plane which is below the horizontal plane will, in that case, fall beyond the ground line AB; or, secondly, it can be so revolved that the part which is above the horizontal plane shall fall beyond the ground line, the part which is beneath the horizontal plane will then fall in front of the ground line AB. The latter method will be used. The part of the paper which is beyond the ground line will then represent that part of the vertical plane of projection which is above the horizontal plane, and also, that part of the horizontal plane which is behind the vertical plane: and the part of the paper which is in front of the ground line will represent that part of the vertical plane which is below the horizontal plane, and that part of the horizontal plane which is in front of the vertical plane.

§ 8. There are four diedral angles formed by these planes. First, the angle above the horizontal, and in front of the vertical plane; second, the angle above the horizontal and behind the vertical plane; third, the angle behind the vertical, and beneath the horizontal plane; fourth, the angle beneath the horizontal, and in front of the vertical plane

§ 9. Any line of a plane, about which the plane is made to turn, or revolve, is called the *axis of revolution.*

§ 10. In revolving a plane about an axis, like a door, for example, on its hinges, all the points and lines of the plane *preserve their relative positions.*

§ 11. If from any point of a plane, a line be drawn perpendicular to the axis, and the plane be then revolved, the point will describe the circumference of a circle—the radius of this circle is equal to the perpendicular let fall on the axis, and the plane of the circle is perpendicular to the axis, since the axis is perpendicular to all the radii. If, therefore, through any point of a revolving plane, a plane be drawn perpendicular to the axis, the point will continue during the revolution in the perpendicular plane. All the points of the axis remain fixed during the revolution.

§ 12. If from any point in space, a perpendicular be let fall on the horizontal plane, the foot of the perpendicular is the *horizontal projection of the point.* If, in like manner, a perpendicular be drawn to the vertical plane, the foot of the perpendicular is the *vertical projection of the point.* These perpendiculars are called the *projecting lines of the point.*

§ 13. Pl. 1. Fig. 1. Let AB be the ground line, and C the horizontal projection of a point. Since the horizontal projection of a point is the foot of a perpendicular passing through the point (12), the point of which C is the horizontal projection is any point of the right line drawn perpendicular to the horizontal plane at C. Let C′ be the vertical projection of the same point. That the point may answer these two conditions at the same time, it must be in a line perpendicular to the horizontal plane at C, and in a line perpendicular to the vertical plane at C′, and these lines intersect, since they pass through the same point. Conceive a plane to be drawn through the projecting lines of this point. It will be perpendicular to both the planes of projection, since it contains lines respectively perpendicular to these planes; it will consequently be perpendicular to their intersection, that is, to the ground line. *This plane will then intersect the planes of projection in two lines at right angles to each other, and perpendicular to the ground line at the same point.* When the vertical plane is revolved about the ground line, to coincide with the horizontal plane, the vertical projection of the point continues at its distance from the xis, and in a third plane passing through the point perpendicular to the axis (11); and after the revolution, it will be found in the intersection of this third plane with the horizontal plane; that is, *in a line through* C *perpendicular to the ground line* AB. Hence, when the planes of projection are revolved to coincide, *the vertical and horizontal projections of a point, are in a line perpendicular to the common intersection, or ground line.*

§ 14 We may remark, that the distance from the vertical projection of a point to the ground line, is equal to the distance of the point in space from the horizontal plane, and that the distance from the horizontal projection to the ground line, is equal to the distance of the point in space from the vertical plane. That is, C′D is equal to the height of the point above the horizontal plane, and CD to its distance from the vertical plane.

§ 15. All points in the first and second angles are projected on the vertical plane above the ground line; and all points in the third and fourth angles, below it. Points situated in the first and fourth angles are horizontally projected on that part of the horizontal plane which is in front of the vertical plane; and points situated in the second and third angles are projected on that part of the horizontal plane which is behind the vertical plane.

§ 16. Let AB be the ground line, C the horizontal, and C′ the vertical projection of a point; C′D is its distance above the horizontal plane, and CD its distance from the vertical plane; the point is then in the first angle. If C be the vertical, and E the horizontal projection of a point, it is situated in the second angle, CD is its height above the horizontal plane, and DE its distance behind the vertical plane. If C″ be the horizontal, and C the vertical projection of a point, the point is in the third angle,—C″D is its distance behind the vertical plane, and CD its distance beneath the horizontal plane. If C‴ be the horizontal projection, and E the vertical projection of a point, the point is situated in the fourth angle, in front of the vertical plane a distance equal to DC‴, and beneath the horizontal plane a distance equal to DE.

§ 17 *All points situated in one of the planes of projection are their own projections on that plane, and are projected on the other plane into the ground line.*

§ 18. *The two projections of a point determine its position in space.* For, let C and C′ be the projections of a point. Erect at C a perpendicular to the horizontal plane, it will pass through the point of which C is the horizontal projection. Draw also at C′ a perpendicular to the vertical plane; this perpendicular will intersect the perpendicular to the horizontal plane, before drawn, and their point of intersection is the position of the point in space.

§ 19. When it is necessary to refer to a point in space, given in position by its projections, instead of saying, the point whose horizontal projection is C and vertical projection C′, we say, simply, the point (C, C′).

§ 20. Two lines which intersect, or are parallel, determine the position of a plane passing through them. If, then, the lines in which a plane intersects the planes of projection are known, the plane itself is given in position. It is by means of these lines, which are called *traces*, that we are enabled to show, on the planes of projection, the position which planes have with each other in space.

§ 21. The line in which a plane intersects the horizontal plane is called its *horizontal trace;* and the line in which it intersects the vertical plane, is called its *vertical trace.*

§ 22. If a plane be parallel to either of the planes of projection, it will have but one trace, which will be on that plane to which it is not parallel.

§ 23. If a plane be parallel to the ground line, and not to either plane of projection, it will have two traces, both of which will be parallel to the ground line, else they would meet it, in which case the plane itself would meet the ground line. If a plane be not parallel to the ground line, it will meet it in a point; this point is in the vertical trace of the plane, since it is in the vertical plane of projection; it is in the horizontal trace, since it is in the horizontal plane of projection; and hence, *when a plane is not parallel to the ground line, its traces will both intersect it at the same point.*

§ 24. *The horizontal projection of a right line is the horizontal trace of a plane passing through the line and perpendicular to the horizontal plane. The vertical projection of a right line is the vertical trace of a plane passing through the line and perpendicular to the vertical plane. These planes are called the projecting planes of the line.*

§ 25. The projection of a right line on either plane of projection, is made up of the projections of all the points of the line. For, if perpendiculars be drawn from all the points of a right line, to either plane of projection, they will be contained in the projecting plane of that line, and will pierce the plane of projection in the trace of the projecting plane which contains them.

§ 26. *The two projections of a line determine its position in space.*

Let NM (Pl. 1. Fig. 2.) be the ground line, AB the horizontal, and A′B′ the vertical projection of a right line. If a plane be drawn through AB perpendicular to the horizontal plane, it will be the projecting plane of the line, and will therefore contain it. If through A′B′ a plane be drawn perpendicular to the vertical plane, this plane, being the other projecting plane of the line, also contains it. Hence, the line of which AB, A′B′ are the projections, is the line of intersection of these two planes, and since the planes are determined in position, their intersection is also determined. If the horizonta projection only be given, the line is somewhere in a plane passing through the horizontal projection and perpendicular to the horizontal plane, but its position in this projecting plane is not determined. So, when the vertical projection only is given, the line may have any position in the plane passing through the projection and perpendicular to the vertical plane.

§ 27. *If a line be parallel to one of the planes of projection, its projection on the other plane is parallel to the ground line*, for the projecting plane of the line is parallel to that plane of projection to which the line is parallel.

§ 28. *If a line be perpendicular to one of the planes of projection, its projection on that plane is a point*; for, the projecting lines of all the points coincide with the given line. Art. 24 does not apply to this case.

§ 29. When we have occasion to refer to a line in space, instead of saying, the line of which AB is the horizontal, and A′B′ the vertical projection, we say, the line (AB, A′B′).

§ 30. *The projections on the same plane of parallel lines are parallel:* for, the projecting planes containing the given parallel lines, and being perpendicular to the same plane (24), are parallel; hence their intersections by the plane of projection are also parallel. But these intersections are the projections of the lines (24), therefore the projections on the same plane of parallel lines are parallel.

§ 31. Pl. 1. Fig. 3. Let AB be the horizontal, and A′B′ the vertical trace of an oblique plane. If this plane were perpendicular to the horizontal plane, and had the same horizontal trace AB, *the vertical trace would pass through* A, *and be perpendicular to the ground line.* If the plane were perpendicular to the vertical plane, and cut the ground line, *its horizontal trace would be perpendicular to the ground line.* If the plane were perpendicular to both planes of projection, *both its traces would be perpendicular to the ground line.* A line situated in such a plane is not determined in position by its two projections (26). When we wish to designate a plane whose horizontal trace is AB, and vertical trace AB′, we say the plane (AB, AB′).

CHAPTER II.

Of the conventional methods of making the projections of lines and the traces of planes in the different angles; how the given and required parts are distinguished from those which are used merely to aid in the construction. Solution of some of the principal problems on the right line and plane.

§ 32. In every projection there is some point at which the eye is supposed to be situated, and from which the projection, or drawing, should present the same appearance as is presented by the objects which it is made to represent.

§ 33. In the projection now used, which is named the Orthographic, or Orthogonal projection, the eye is supposed to be at an infinite distance from the plane on which the projection is made, and the drawing or representation is supposed to be viewed from that position of the eye.

§ 34. The position of the eye is generally taken in tne first angle; hence, all objects situated within this angle can be seen, but objects in either of the other angles are concealed by the planes of projection. Lines that are given, or required, are made full if they can be seen, but are dotted if concealed by other objects or by the planes of projection. *Auxiliary lines*, or lines used to aid in the construction of a problem, are always dotted.

§ 35. The traces of given or required planes are made full in the first angle, unless they pass under bodies which prevent them from being seen, in which case they are broken. But when, as in Fig. 3, the horizontal trace BA is produced behind the vertical plane, or the vertical trace B'A is produced below the horizontal plane, the parts AC, AC', so produced, are made broken, as in the figure. The traces of auxiliary planes are always broken.

§ 36 Right lines and planes are indefinite; and the projections and traces which are made in the figures, are only the parts intercepted between given points.

PROBLEM I.

A right line being given by its projections, it is required to determine the points in which it pierces the planes of projection.

§ 37. Pl. 1. Fig. 4. Let CF be the ground line, AB the horizontal, and A′B′ the vertical projection of the given line.

Produce the horizontal projection AB till it intersects the ground line at D. At the point D, erect in the vertical plane the perpendicular DD′ to the ground line—DD′ is the vertical trace of the plane which projects the line on the horizontal plane. Produce the vertical projection of the line till it intersects the perpendicular at D′, and this point of intersection is the point at which the line pierces the vertical plane. To find the point at which it pierces the horizontal plane, produce the vertical projection till it intersects the ground line at C. From this point, draw in the horizontal plane the perpendicular CC′ to the ground line—CC′ is the horizontal trace of the plane which projects the given line on the vertical plane; the point C′, in which it intersects the horizontal projection of the line produced, is the point at which the line pierces the horizontal plane.

First, to prove that the line pierces the vertical plane at D″ Every line of a plane pierces the planes of projection in the traces of the plane. The given line must then pierce the vertical plane somewhere in the line CB′, the vertical trace of the plane which projects it on the vertical plane, and somewhere in the line DD′, the vertical trace of the plane which projects it on the horizontal plane; hence, the line pierces the vertical plane at D′, their point of intersection. For the same reasons it follows, that the line must pierce the horizontal plane in CC′, the horizontal trace of the plane which projects the line on the vertical plane, and in BC′, the trace of the plane which projects the line on the horizontal plane—hence it pierces it at C′, their point of intersection. The point D′ is above the horizontal plane the distance DD′, and the point C′ is behind the vertical plane the distance CC′.

PROBLEM II.

To find the length of a line joining any two points in space, given by their projections.

§ 38. Pl. 2. Fig. 1. Let (A, A′) and (B, B′) be the given points.

If a line pass through a point in space, the projections of the line will pass through the projections of the point; therefore, AB is the horizontal, and A′B′ the vertical projection of the line joining the given points.

Revolve the plane which projects the line on the horizontal plane around its horizontal trace till it coincides with the horizontal plane of projection. The point (A, A′) will fall in a line drawn through A, perpendicular to AB (11), and at a distance from A equal to its height above the horizontal plane. The point (B, B′) also falls in a perpendicular to the trace AB, and at a distance from the point B equal to its height above the horizontal plane. Having made AD and BC respectively equal to the heights of the points above the horizontal plane, draw DC, which will be the length of the line sought. The point F, in which the line joining the points pierces the horizontal plane, being in the axis, remains fixed during the revolution; the line CD produced should, therefore, pass through this point. A similar construction might be made on the vertical plane.

§ 39. We may here remark, *that the projection of a line on either plane is less than the line itself*, unless *the line be parallel to the plane on which it is projected.* For, if through D a line DC′ be drawn parallel to AB, it will be less than DC, the length of the given line, and equal to AB, its projection on the horizontal plane; and the same may be shown when it is projected on the vertical plane.

Plate 1.

Fig. 1.
C′
C
C″
E
A
D
D
D
D
B
C
E
C
C‴
Fig. 2.
B′
A′
N
M
A
B
Fig. 3.
B′
C
N
A
M
C′
B
Fig. 4.
B′
A′
D′
C′
C
D
F
A
B

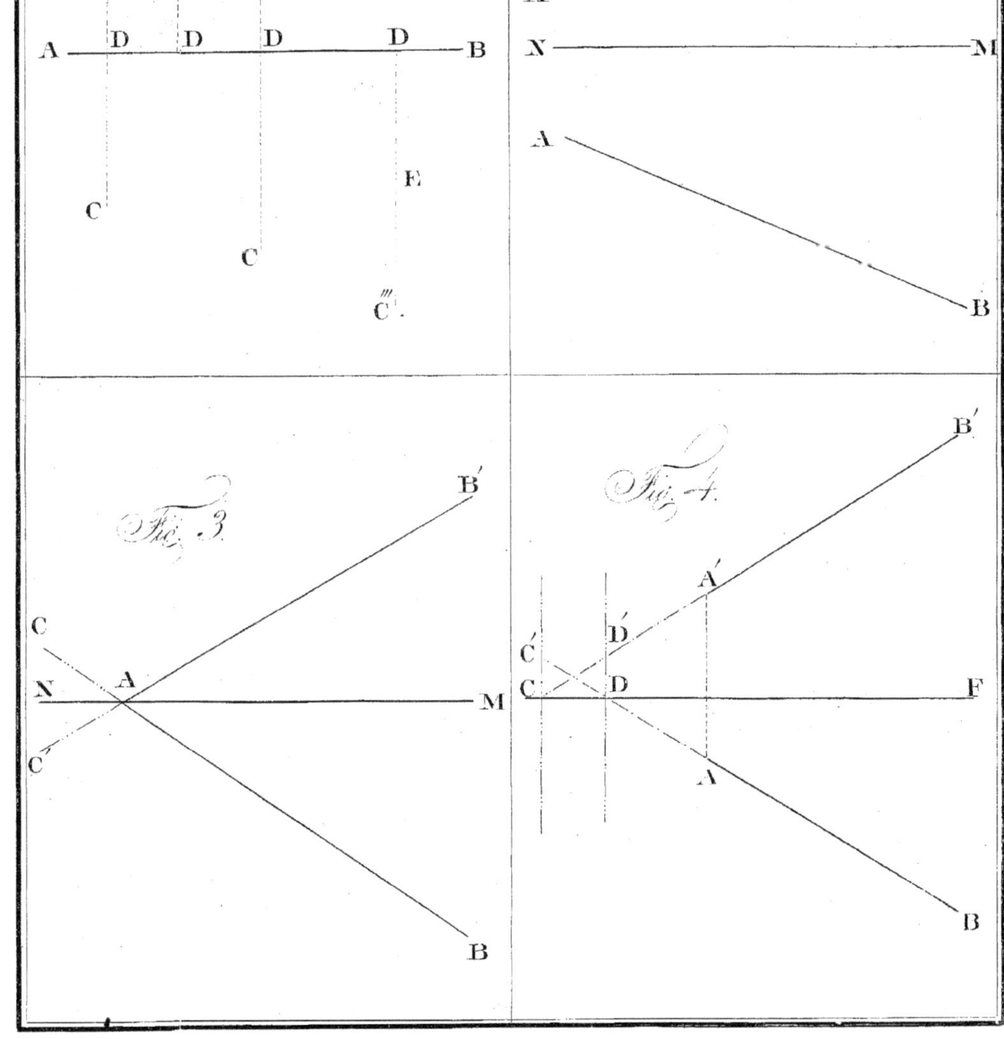

Since the angle formed by a line and plane is measured by the angle included between the line and its projection on the plane, the angle CFB, or its equal CDC′, is equal to the angle which the line (AB, A′B′) makes with the horizontal plane. *Hence, if a right-angled triangle be constructed, having the angle at the base equal to the angle which the line makes with the plane, the hypothenuse will be to the base, as the length of the line to the length of its projection.* We also conclude, that *the length of a line is equal to the hypothenuse of a triangle whose base is the projection of the line, and whose perpendicular is equal to the difference between the perpendiculars let fall from the two extremities of the line, on the plane of projection.*

§ 40. *If a line be parallel to a plane, its projection on such plane will evidently be equal to the line itself:* for the line, its projection, and the two projecting perpendiculars through its extremities form a rectangle, of which the line and its projection are opposite sides.

§ 41. The length of the line may also be determined from its projections, thus: Revolve the plane which projects the line on the horizontal plane, about the perpendicular to the horizontal plane at A, till it becomes parallel to the vertical plane: the line from this position will be projected on the vertical plane in its true length (40). In this revolution, all the points of the projecting plane describe, about the vertical axis, arcs of horizontal circles. The foot of the perpendicular to the horizontal plane at B describes the arc BG, on the horizontal plane, about A as a centre. Project the point G into the vertical plane, and erect at I the perpendicular IH to the ground line; IH will be the vertical projection, from its revolved position, of the perpendicular to the horizontal plane at B. But in the revolution the point (B,B′) neither approaches to, nor recedes from, the horizontal plane; its vertical projection must then be always found in a parallel to the ground line through B′. This parallel intersects the perpendicular IH at H; H is then the vertical projection of the point (B,B′) from the position which it has when the projecting plane of the line is revolved parallel to the vertical plane. The point (A,A′) re mains fixed, being in the axis, and A′H is the vertical projection of the given line from its revolved position. This line is evidently equal to CD.

PROBLEM III.

To pass a plane through three points in space, given by their projections; the points not being in the same right line.

§ 42. Pl. 2. Fig. 2. A plane can always be passed through three points, and this condition determines its position.

For, conceive two of the points to be joined by a right line, and through this line let any plane be drawn. Let the plane be revolved about this line until it embraces the third point; if the plane be revolved either way from this position, it will no longer contain the third point; hence, there is but one position in which it will pass through the three given points; or, in other words, *only one plane can be drawn through three points.*

Let FH be the ground line, (A,A′), (B,B′), (C,C′) the given points.

Conceive the points to be joined by the right lines (AB, A′B′), (AC, A′C′), (BC, B′C′), the projections of these lines will pass through the projections of the points respectively. Since these lines are lines of the required plane, the points in which they pierce the planes of projection are points of the traces of the required plane. Therefore, the point E, in which the line (AB, A′B′) pierces the vertical plane, is one point of the vertical trace; and the point D, in which the line (AC, A′C′) pierces the vertical plane, is a second point of the vertical trace; hence, DEF is the vertical trace of the required plane The line (BC, B′C′) pierces the horizontal plane at G, which is a point of the horizontal trace, and F is another point (23), therefore, GF is the horizontal trace of the required plane, and (FG, FD) is the plane containing the three given points. The point I, in which the line (BC, B′C′) pierces the vertical plane, is also a point of the vertical trace, and should be found in order to verify the construction. The points in which the lines (AB, A'B'), (AC, A'C') pierce the horizontal plane are points of the horizontal trace, and will be found in the trace FG, if the construction be correctly made.

PROBLEM IV.

Having given one projection of a point of an oblique plane, it is required to find the other projection, and the position of the point after the plane shall have been revolved to coincide with either plane of projection.

§ 43. Pl. 2. Fig. 3. Let AB be the ground line, (AE, AD') the given plane, and C the horizontal projection of the point.

Erect at C a perpendicular to the horizontal plane; the point in which this perpendicular pierces the oblique plane is the only point of that plane which is horizontally projected at C. Through the point in which the line pierces the oblique plane conceive a line to be drawn parallel to its horizontal trace. This parallel is a line of the oblique plane, is parallel to the horizontal plane, and its horizontal projection CD passes through C and is parallel to AE, the horizontal trace of the oblique plane (30).

Let DD' be drawn in the vertical plane, perpendicular to the ground line AB; the point D', in which it intersects the vertical trace of the oblique plane, is the point in which the line drawn parallel to the horizontal trace pierces the vertical plane, since it must pierce the vertical plane in the trace AD', and also in DD', the vertical trace of its projecting plane (37). The line D'C', drawn through D' parallel to the ground line, is the vertical projection of the line of which CD is the horizontal projection (27). The vertical projection of the required point is in the line C'D', it is also in the perpendicular from C to the ground line (13); hence it is at C', their point of intersection. If the vertical projection were given, the horizontal projection could be determined by a similar construction.

Let the oblique plane be revolved around AE till it coincides with the horizontal plane. The point (C,C') will fall in the trace of a plane drawn through it perpendicular to the axis AE (11), and at a distance from the point E equal to the hypothenuse of a triangle whose base is EC, and altitude the height of the point above the horizontal plane. Making CF, on the line CD, equal to this altitude, and joining E and F, gives EF for this hypothenuse. With E as a centre, and radius EF, describe a semicircle, and the points F′, F″, in which it intersects the trace F′F″, are the points sought. If the plane be revolved towards the vertical plane, the point (C,C′) falls at F′; if from the vertical plane, at F″. A similar construction would determine the position of the point (C,C′) should the plane be revolved about its vertical trace to coincide with the vertical plane.

PROBLEM V.

To show how two lines which intersect in space are situated in projection; and secondly, to find the angle which they make with each other.

§ 44. Pl. 3. Fig. 1. Let A′B′ be the ground line, AC, BC the horizontal, and A′C′, B′C′ the vertical projections of the lines.

As the point of intersection is common to the two lines, its horizontal and vertical projections will be found in the horizontal and vertical projections of each of the lines. The point C, in which their horizontal projections intersect, is, consequently, the horizontal projection of the point in which the lines intersect, and the point C′, in which their vertical projections intersect, is the vertical projection of the same point. The points C and C′, being the projections of the same point, are contained in the same perpendicular to the ground line (13). If, therefore, two lines intersect in space, *the points in which their projections intersect will be contained in a perpendicular to the ground line.*

Secondly, to find the angle which the lines make with each other

Plate 2.

Fig. 1.

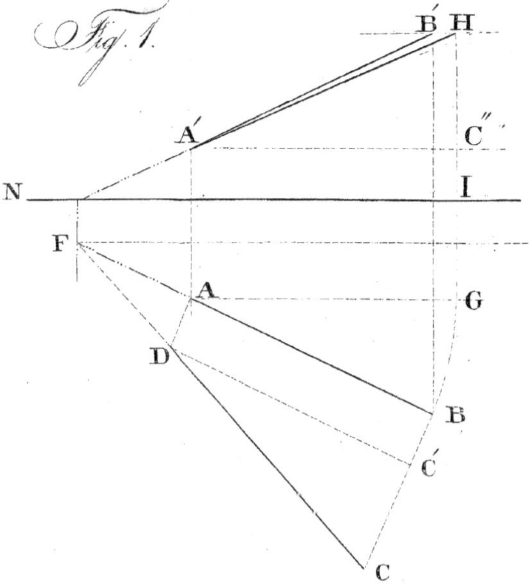

B′ H

A′ C″

N I

F

A G

D

B

C′

C

Fig. 3.

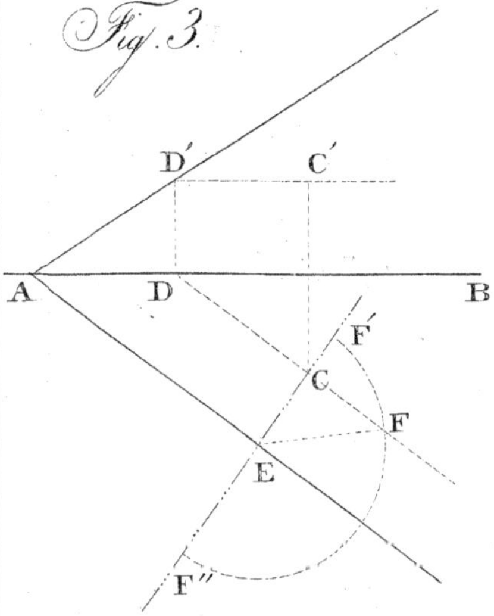

D′ C′

A D B

F′

C

F

E

F″

Fig. 2.

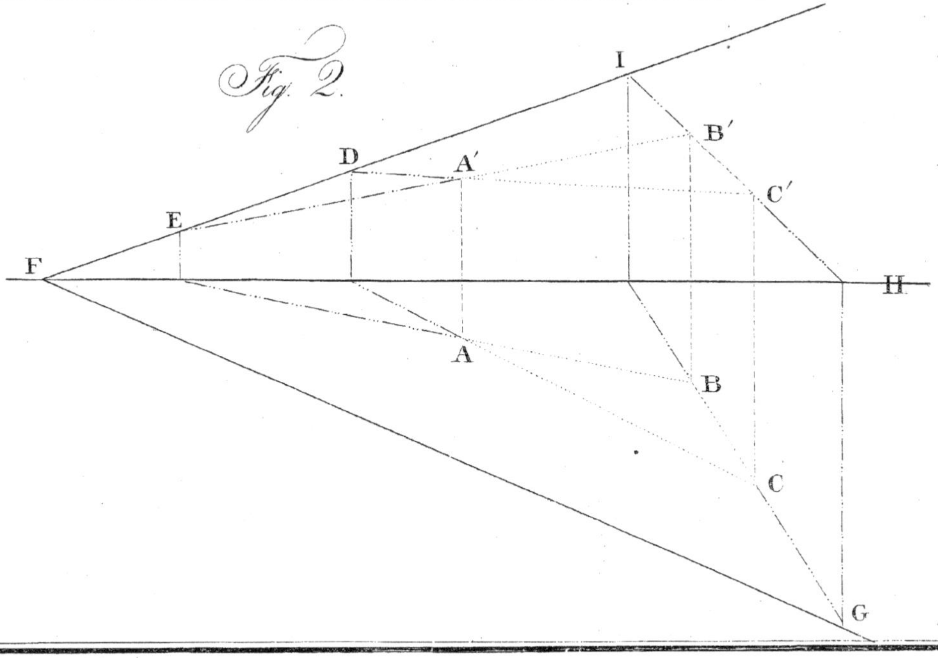

I

B′

D A′

C′

E

F H

A

B

C

G

The two lines intersecting, a plane can be drawn containing them. If this plane be revolved about its horizontal trace till it coincides with the horizontal plane, or about its vertical trace till it coincides with the vertical plane, in either of the revolutions the lines will not change their relative positions; hence, the *angle which they make in space* is equal to the *angle they will make after the revolution.*

The lines pierce the horizontal plane at A and B; hence, AB is the horizontal trace of their plane. Through the point C draw CD perpendicular to the trace AB. This line is the horizontal trace of a plane passing through the point (C,C′) and perpendicular to AB. When the plane of the two lines is revolved about its horizontal trace to coincide with the horizontal plane, their point of intersection falls at C″, a distance from D equal to C′G, the hypothenuse of a triangle whose perpendicular FC′ is equal to the height of the point (C,C′) above the horizontal plane, and whose base FG is equal to CD, the distance of its horizontal projection from the axis (11). But A and B, being in the axis, remain fixed; therefore, AC″ and BC″ are the lines in their revolved position, and AC″B is the angle included between them. A similar construction would determine the angle on the vertical plane; it would only be necessary to revolve the plane of the lines around its vertical trace till it coincided with that plane.

PROBLEM VI.

Two oblique planes being given by their traces, it is required to find the two projections of their line of intersection.

§ 45. Pl. 3. Fig. 2. Let AB be the ground line, and (AC AD), (BC, BD) the given planes.

Since the line of intersection is a line of the plane (AC, AD), it must pierce the horizontal plane in the trace AC, and the vertical plane in the trace AD. As the line of intersection is also a line of the plane (BC, BD), it will pierce the horizontal plane in the trace BC, and the vertical plane in the trace BD.

Hence, the intersection of the two planes pierces the horizontal plane at C, the point in which their horizontal traces intersect, and the vertical plane at D, the point in which their vertical traces intersect. We have, then, only to find the projections of this line. The point C is its own projection, on the horizontal plane (17), and the point D, being in the vertical plane, is horizontally projected in the ground line at D (17); therefore, CD′ is the horizontal projection of the intersection. Projecting C into the vertical plane at C′, determines C′D, the vertical projection of the intersection.

PROBLEM VII.

To find the angles included between an oblique plane and the planes of projection.

§ 46. Pl. 3. Fig. 3. Let AB be the ground line, and (AD, AC) the given plane.

If a plane be drawn perpendicular to the horizontal trace of the oblique plane at any point, it will be perpendicular to the horizontal plane, and to the oblique plane; and will consequently intersect these planes in lines perpendicular to their common intersection at the same point. The angle included between these lines is equal to the angle contained by the planes.

Let DC′, drawn perpendicular to AD, be the horizontal trace of such a plane. As this plane is perpendicular to the horizontal plane, its vertical trace C′C is perpendicular to the ground line at C′. Let this plane be revolved around DC′ till it coincides with the horizontal plane; the point C falls at C″, in a perpendicular to DC′, and at a distance from C′ equal to C′C, its height above the ground line. Draw DC″, and it will be the intersection of the oblique and perpendicular planes, in its revolved position, and the angle C′DC″ is equal to the angle which the oblique plane makes with the horizontal plane.

§ 47. If the perpendicular plane be revolved about its vertical trace CC′, till it coincides with the vertical plane, the point D will describe, in the horizontal plane, the arc DD′ about C′

as a centre, and will fall at D′; CD′ will be the revolved position of the line of intersection of the perpendicular and oblique planes, and C′D′ the revolved position of the intersection of the perpendicular and horizontal planes; hence, CD′C′ is equal to the angle which the oblique plane makes with the horizontal plane. This angle is evidently equal to the angle C′DC″. The angle which the plane makes with the vertical plane, is found by a construction similar to either of those just given.

PROBLEM VIII.

A plane being given by its traces, and a line not parallel to the plane by its projections, it is required to find the point in which the line pierces the plane.

§ 48. Pl. 3. Fig. 4. Let AB be the ground line, (AD, AD′) the given plane, and (EC, E′C′) the given line.

If *any* plane be drawn through the line, it will intersect the given plane in a right line; this line will contain the point in which the given line pierces the given plane. The point in which the given line meets this line of intersection is, therefore, the point sought. Let the plane which projects the line on the horizontal plane be the one drawn through it. This plane intersects the oblique plane in a line which pierces the horizontal plane at a, and the vertical plane at D′ (45); and a'D′ is its vertical projection. But since this line of intersection, and the given line, intersect in space, the intersection p' of their vertical projections is the vertical projection of their intersection (44); p' is therefore the vertical projection of the point in which the line pierces the plane; and p is its horizontal projection, since the horizontal projection is in the horizontal projection of the line, and in a perpendicular to the ground line through p'.

The point p might be found without demitting the perpendicular to the ground line from p'. For the plane which projects the given line (EC, E′C′) on the vertical plane, intersects the oblique plane (AD, AD′) in a line of which Db' is the horizontal projection, and the point p, in which Db' intersects the horizontal projection of the given line, is the horizontal projection of the required point.

PROPOSITION IX. THEOREM.

If a line be perpendicular to an oblique plane, the projections of the line are respectively perpendicular to the traces of the plane; that is, the horizontal projection to the horizontal trace, and the vertical projection to the vertical trace.

§ 49. For, the plane which projects the line on the horizontal plane is perpendicular to the oblique plane, since it contains a line perpendicular to it: it is also perpendicular to the horizontal plane, and is therefore perpendicular to their intersection, that is, to the horizontal trace of the oblique plane. Since the horizontal trace of the oblique plane is perpendicular to the projecting plane of the given line, it will be perpendicular to its horizontal trace, that is, to the horizontal projection of the given line (24). It may be shown, in a similar manner, that the vertical projection of the line is perpendicular to the vertical trace of the oblique plane.

§ 50. The converse of this proposition is also true, that is, *if the projections of a line are respectively perpendicular to the traces of a plane, the line in space is perpendicular to the plane.* For, the projecting planes of the line will be respectively perpendicular to the traces of the oblique plane, and therefore perpendicular to the oblique plane; hence, their intersection, which is the line, will be perpendicular to the oblique plane.

§ 51. If two lines are perpendicular to each other, and are projected on a plane to which one of them is parallel, *their projections will also be at right angles.* For, through the line which is parallel to the plane on which the projection is made, conceive a plane to be drawn perpendicular to the other line; its trace will be parallel to the line through which the plane is drawn, since the line is parallel to the plane of projection. But the projection of the line through which the plane is passed will be parallel to the trace of the plane, since they are parallel in space; and as the projection of the other line is perpen dicular to the trace (49), it will be perpendicular to any line parallel to the trace, and consequently to the projection of the line through which the plane is drawn.

PROBLEM X.

To draw from a given point a line perpendicular to a given plane; to find the point in which it pierces the plane, and the length of the perpendicular.

§ 52. Pl. 4. Fig. 1. Let AB be the ground line, (D, D′) the given point, and (AC, AC′) the given plane.

The horizontal projection of the line must pass through D, and be perpendicular to AC, since the line is perpendicular to the plane (AC, AC′) (49). The vertical projection must pass through D′ and be perpendicular to AC′. The lines DF and D′F′ drawn through D and D′, respectively perpendicular to the traces AC, AC′, are the projections of the perpendicular sought. Having determined the projections of the line, the point (F,F′) in which it pierces the plane (AC, AC′) is found as in Prob. 8. The length D″F″ of the perpendicular is found as in Prob. 2. To find the shortest distance between a point and plane, we have only to draw a perpendicular to the plane and find its length.

PROBLEM XI.

To draw through a given point a plane perpendicular to a given line.

§ 53. Pl. 4. Fig. 2. Let A′R be the ground line, (AD, A′D′) the given line, and (E,E′) the given point.

As the required plane is to be perpendicular to the line, the races of the plane must be respectively perpendicular to its projections (49); we know then the *directions* of the traces of the required plane. But the plane is to pass through the point (E,E). Therefore, through the point (E,E′) conceive a line to be drawn parallel to the horizontal trace of the required plane. This line will be horizontal, and also a line of the required plane. Its horizontal projection passes through E, and is perpendicular to AD, for the line in space being parallel to the horizontal trace of the required plane, its horizontal projection is parallel to this trace (30); that is, perpendicular to AD. The line, therefore, drawn through E, perpendicular to AD, is the horizontal projection of the line through (E,E′), the vertical projection of which passes through E′ and is parallel to the ground line. This line pierces the vertical plane at F, which is a point of the vertical trace of the required plane. Through this point draw C′FR perpendicular to A′D′, and it will be the vertical trace of the required plane. Through the point R, in which this trace intersects the ground line, draw RC perpendicular to AD, and it will be the horizontal trace of the required plane. If through the point (E,E′) a line were drawn parallel to the vertical trace of the required plane, it would pierce the horizontal plane at G, which is a point of the horizontal trace of the required plane: this point will fall in the line RC as before drawn, if the construction be correct.

PROBLEM XII.

To find the shortest distance between a point and line given by their projections.

§ 54. The length of the perpendicular from the point to the line is the distance sought. This perpendicular is contained in a plane passing through the point and perpendicular to the line. If, then, a plane be drawn through the point and perpendicular to the line (53), and the point in which it cuts the line be determined (52), the distance between this point and the given point is the distance required.

§ 55. The problem can be solved otherwise, thus. Draw

a plane through the right line and point. Let this plane be revolved about its horizontal trace till it coincides with the horizontal plane, or about its vertical trace till it coincides with the vertical plane. Find the position of the point and line after either of these revolutions, and draw through the point thus revolved a perpendicular to the revolved line. This will be the true length of the perpendicular sought, since the point and line do not change their relative position in the revolution of their plane.

Pl. 4. Fig. 3. Let A′B be the ground line, (AC, A′C′) the given line, and (D,D′) the given point.

First, to draw a plane through the point and line. Through the point (D,D′) draw a line parallel to (AC, A′C′), its two projections are respectively parallel to AC, A′C′, and it pierces the horizontal plane at F. The given line pierces the horizontal plane at A, therefore AFO is the horizontal trace of a plane passing through the two parallels, which plane contains the given point and line. Let this plane be revolved about its horizontal trace AO till it coincides with the horizontal plane. The point (D,D′) falls at D″, in a perpendicular drawn through D to the trace AO (11), and at a distance from the point O equal to D′B, the hypothenuse of a triangle whose perpendicular D′P is equal to the height of the point above the horizontal plane, and base PB equal to DO, the distance of the horizontal projection of the point from the axis. As F remains fixed, being in the axis, FD″ is the revolved position of the parallel line. But lines in the same plane, which are parallel before revolution, are parallel after (10). Draw, therefore, through A the line AM″ parallel to FD″, and we have AM″ for the position of the given line revolved on the horizontal plane. Through D″ draw D″M″ perpendicular to AM″, and it will be the perpendicular required. Making a counter revolution, or bringing the plane back to its first position, the point D″ will be horizontally projected at D, and the point M″ at M, since the point M″ revolves in a plane perpendicular to AO, and must, after the counter revolution is completed, be horizontally projected in the line AC. The vertical projection of the point of which M is the horizontal, is in a perpendicular to the ground line through M, and also in the line A′C′; hence it is at M′ their point of intersection. The line DM is then the horizontal, and D′M′ the vertical projection of the perpendicular, and M″D″ is its true length. The plane might have been drawn through the point and line by joining the given point and any point of the line, and drawing a plane through this and the given line.

PROBLEM XIII.

To measure the angle between two oblique planes.

§ 56. The angle between two planes is measured by the angle included between two lines, one in each plane, and both perpendicular to the common intersection at the same point. If a plane be drawn perpendicular to the common intersection of the two planes, at any point, it will intersect the planes in lines perpendicular to the common intersection, and when the angle between these two lines is determined, the angle between the planes will be known.

Pl. 4. Fig. 4. Let HP be the ground line, and (HC, HC′) (AC, AC′) the given planes.

The intersection of these planes pierces the horizontal plane at C, and the vertical plane at C′, and CD is its horizontal projection. If we suppose a plane drawn perpendicular to this intersection, its horizontal trace will be perpendicular to CD, the horizontal projection of the intersection (49). Let FG, perpendicular to CD, be the horizontal trace of such a plane. The lines in which this plane intersects the oblique planes, pierce the horizontal plane at F and G; and these two lines, together with FG, form a triangle of which FG is the base. The vertical angle of this triangle is equal to the angle included between the planes, and the vertex of this angle lies in their line of intersection. It is, then, only necessary to find this angle. The line joining the point N, and the vertex of the vertical angle of the triangle, is perpendicular to the common intersection of the oblique planes, since it is contained in a plane perpendicular to this intersection; it is also perpendicular to FG, since FG is perpendicular to the projecting plane of the intersection of the oblique planes, and this projecting plane contains the line drawn from N. The length of this line is, therefore, the shortest distance from the angular point to the line FG, and if this length were known, by revolving the plane of the triangle about FG as an axis, till it coincides with the horizontal plane, we could determine the position of the angular point, and consequently, the magnitude of the angle.

To find the length of this line, let the plane which projects the intersection of the oblique planes on the horizontal plane, be revolved around its horizontal trace CD, till it coincides with the horizontal plane. The point C′ falls at C″, and as C remains fixed, CC″ is the revolved position of the intersection. But the required line from N was perpendicular to the intersection before, and consequently will be perpendicular to it after the revolution. If, therefore, NI″ be drawn perpendicular to CC″, it will be equal to the distance of the vertex of the vertical angle of the triangle from the base FG. Let now the plane of the triangle be revolved about its base FG, till it coincides with the horizontal plane. The vertex of the vertical angle falls in DC (11), and at a distance from N, equal to NI′ (11); it falls therefore at I′. But since F and G remain fixed, being in the axis, draw FI′ and GI′, and FI′G is equal to the angle included between the oblique planes.

If from I″ we draw I″O perpendicular to CD, the point O is the horizontal projection of the angular point; and by joining it with F and G, we obtain the horizontal projection of the angle FI′G.

The line NI″ can be found by another construction. Let the plane which projects the intersection of the oblique planes on the horizontal plane, be revolved about its vertical trace DC′, till it coincides with the vertical plane. The points C and N describe arcs of circles in the horizontal plane, around D as a centre, and fall at P and N′; hence, C′P is the revolved position of the intersection of the oblique planes. From N', let N'I be drawn perpendicular to C'P; it is evidently equal to the line drawn from N, perpendicular to the intersection of the oblique planes. With N' as a centre, and radius N'I, let the arc IB be described; then, with D as a centre, and radius DB, let the arc BI' be described; the point I', in which this arc intersects DC, is the position of the angular point of the triangle, when its plane is revolved into the horizontal plane. The radius N'I is evidently equal to NI', and also to NI''.

PROBLEM XIV.

To find the angle which a line makes with a plane.

§ 57. The angle which a line makes with a plane, is the angle which the line makes with its projection on the plane. If from any point of the line, a perpendicular be drawn to the plane, the foot of the perpendicular is one point of the projection of the line on the plane. If the given line be produced till it meets the plane, the point of meeting will be another point of the projection of the line. Conceive the projection to be drawn. The given line, the perpendicular to the plane, and the projection of the line on the plane, form a right-angled triangle, and calling the projection of the line the base, the angle at the base is the angle sought; this angle is readily found when the vertical angle is known.

Pl. 5. Fig. 1. Let AB' be the ground line, (AC, AC') the given plane, and (BD, B'D') the given line.

From any point of the given line, as (D,D'), let a line be drawn perpendicular to the given plane; its projections will pass through the points D, and D', and be respectively perpendicular to the traces AC, AC' (49)—DE is the horizontal, and D'E' the vertical projection of this perpendicular. We will now find the angle between this perpendicular and the given line, and then between the given line and the plane. The perpendicular pierces the horizontal plane at E, and the given line pierces it at B: therefore, BEG is the horizontal trace of their plane.

Plate 4.

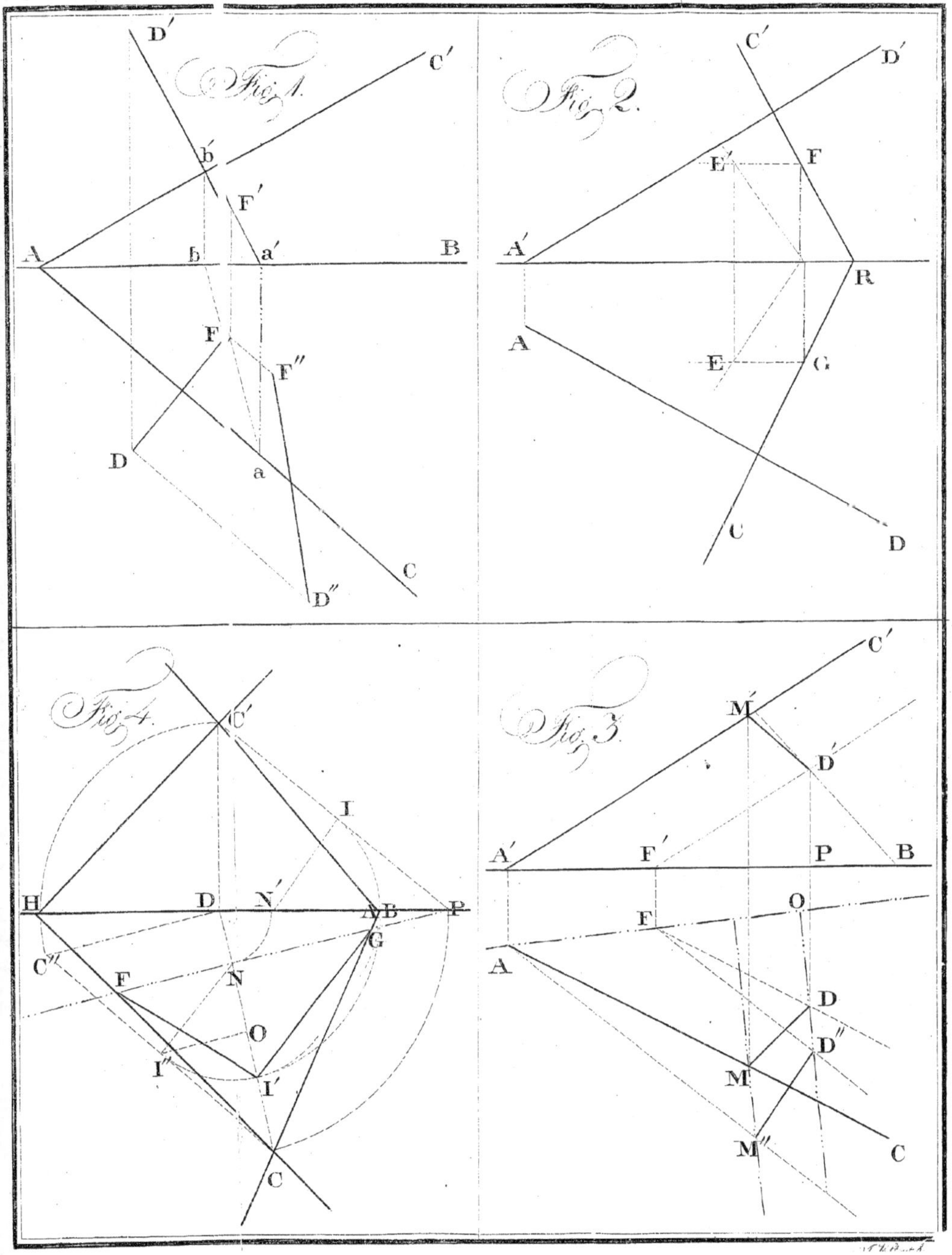
Fig. 1.
D′
C′
b′
F′
A
b
a′
B
F
F″
D
a
C
D″
Fig. 2.
C′
D′
E′
F
A′
R
A
E
G
C
D
Fig. 4.
C′
I
H
D
N′
A
B
P
G
C″
F
N
O
I″
I′
C
Fig. 3.
C′
M′
D′
A′
F′
P
B
O
F
A
D
D″
M
M″
C

Let this plane be revolved about BG till it coincides with the horizontal plane. The point (D,D′) falls at D″, and the points E and B remain fixed; therefore, BD″E is equal to the angle included between the lines. From E, draw EF perpendicular to ED″, and EFD″ will be equal to the angle which the line (DB, D′B′) makes with the plane (AC, AC′).

PROBLEM XV.

To pass a plane through a given line, and parallel to another given line.

§ 58. If through any point of the line, through which the plane is to be passed, a line be drawn parallel to the other line, the plane drawn through these two lines will be the plane required.

Pl. 5. Fig. 2. Let AB be the ground line, (DE, D′E′) the line through which the plane is to be drawn, and (NC, N′C′) the line to which it is to be parallel.

From any point, as (D,D′), of the line through which the plane is to be drawn, conceive a parallel to be drawn to (NC, N′C′); its projections DI, D′I′ are respectively parallel to CN, C′N′, and the point I′, in which this parallel pierces the vertical plane, is a point of the vertical trace of the required plane. The point E′ is a second point of this trace; hence E′I′A is the vertical trace, and AD the horizontal trace of the plane containing (DE, D′E′), and parallel to (NC, N′C′).

§ 59. If the point A, in which the vertical trace meets the ground line, were not on the paper, a point of the horizontal trace might be found thus: through any point of the line (DE, D′E′), as (F,F′), conceive a line to be drawn parallel to the vertical trace E′I′—its vertical projection will be parallel to this trace, and its horizontal projection FQ parallel to the ground line (27). This line will pierce the horizontal plane at Q, which is therefore a point of the horizontal trace: the trace can then be drawn through D and Q.

PROBLEM XVI.

It is required to find the shortest distance between two lines, not in the same plane; or, to draw a ine that shall be perpendicular to them both.

§ 60. If a plane be drawn through one line, and parallel to the other, the shortest distance between this plane and the line to which it is parallel, will be equal to the distance sought.

If the line, to which the plane is drawn parallel, be projected on the parallel plane, the projecting perpendiculars of its different points will be equal to each other, and equal, also, to the shortest distance between the two lines. But since the line is parallel to the plane, its projection on the plane is parallel to itself; and as the given lines are not parallel, this projection will intersect the line through which the parallel plane is drawn. *The projecting perpendicular which passes through this point of intersection, is perpendicular to the two given lines, and is, therefore, the line sought.*

Pl. 5. Fig. 3. Let AB′ be the ground line, (DG, D′G′) one of the given lines, and (CB, C′B′) the other.

Through the line (DG, D′G′) let a plane be drawn parallel to (BC, B′C′); AD and AG′ are its traces.

It is now required to project the line (CB, C′B′) on this plane. From any point of the line, as (C,C′), draw a perpendicular to the plane (52); this perpendicular pierces the plane in the point (F,F′); and this is one point of the projection of the line on the parallel plane (AD, AG′). But since the trace of the projecting plane on the parallel plane and the line (CB, C′B′) are parallel, their projections are parallel (30); therefore FO, drawn parallel to CB, is the horizontal projection of this trace. But, as this trace and the line (DG, D′G′) intersect, the point O, in which their horizontal projections intersect, is the horizontal projection of their point of intersection, and O′ is the vertical projection of the same point. If at the point (O,O′)

a perpendicular be drawn to the parallel plane (AD, AG′), it will be contained in the plane which projects the line (CB, C′B′) on the plane, and will consequently intersect the line (CB, C′B′) This perpendicular to the oblique plane at (O,O′) is perpendicular to, and intersects, both of the given lines; and its projections OP, O′P′ are respectively perpendicular to the traces of the oblique plane (AD, AG′). The length of the line (OP, O′P′) can be found as in Prob. 2.

§ 61. The solutions of the foregoing problems may be varied, by changing the positions of the given parts; and in some cases, the constructions will be quite different from those which have been given.

All the principles necessary to solve any problem involving the right line and plane, have, however, been developed, and the student who would be skilful in the application of these principles, must apply them to a great variety of cases. A few examples are given, to show how the data of the problems may be varied, and to lead the student to propose cases to himself.

1°. In Problem III. let the points be so situated that a line joining two of them shall be parallel to the ground line.

2°. In Problem IV. let the oblique plane be parallel to the ground line.

3°. In Problem V. suppose one of the lines to be parallel to the ground line.

4°. In Problem VI. let the planes be parallel to the ground line.

5°. In Problem VIII. suppose the line parallel to the ground line.

6°. In Problem X. let the plane be taken parallel to the ground line.

7°. In Problem XII. suppose the line parallel to the horizontal plane.

8°. In Problem XIII. let the planes be parallel to the ground line.

9°. In Problem XIV. suppose the plane to be parallel to the ground line.

10°. In Problem XV. let the line through which the plane is drawn be parallel to the ground line.

11°. In Problem XVI. suppose one of the lines to be parallel to the ground line.

12°. Let it be required to draw a plane through a given point, and parallel to a given plane.

CHAPTER III.

OF LINES AND THEIR TANGENTS.

§ 62. For the purposes of Descriptive Geometry, lines may be divided into three classes.

1°. The right line, which does not change its direction between any of its points.

2°. Curved lines whose points are in the same plane, which are called *curves of single curvature.*

3°. Curved lines whose points are not in the same plane, which are called *curves of double curvature.*

§ 63. Lines may be generated by the motion of points: the conditions which govern this motion fix their different positions, and determine the class to which the lines generated belong.

Pl. 6. Fig. 1. Suppose, for example, that a point should move from C, with the conditions of continuing in the plane of the paper, and at the same distance from the line AB; it would evidently generate a right line, passing through C, and parallel to AB.

Pl. 6. Fig. 2. If a point move from B, with the conditions that it shall not depart from the plane of the paper, and be constantly at the same distance from a fixed point A, it will generate the circumference of a circle, a curve of single curvature. If the point were subjected to the first condition only it would still generate a curve of single curvature, unless the point were to move in a right line. If the point B were sub

Plate 5.

Fig. 1.
D′
C′
A
E′
B′
G
E
B
F
D
C
D″
Fig. 2.
E′
N′
I′
F′
A
N
C′
I
D′
B
E
Q
F
C
D
Fig. 3.
G′
F′
O′
C′
P′
D′
C
A
G
B
F
P
O
D
B

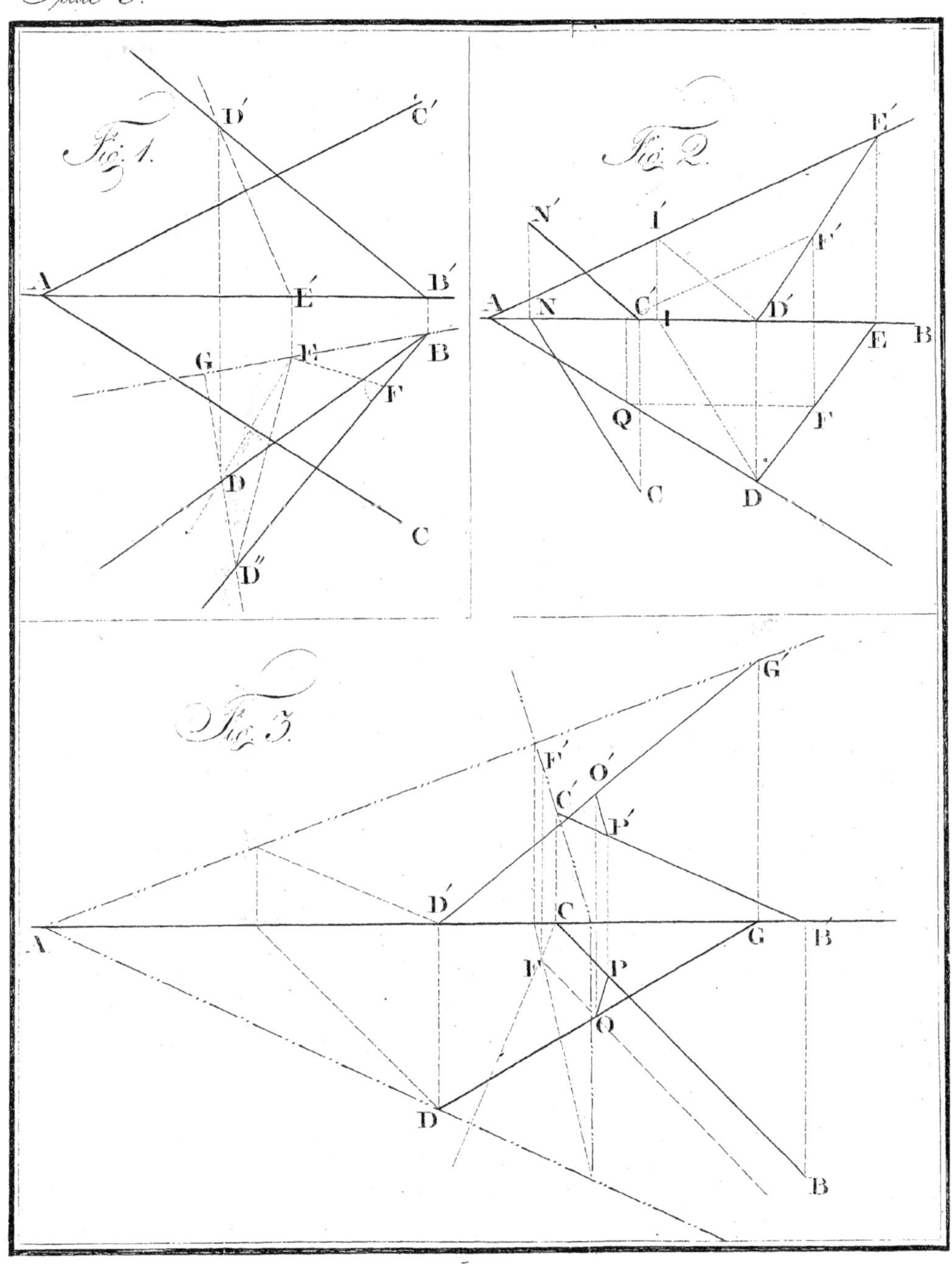

jected to the second condition, to the exclusion of the first, it would generate a curve of double curvature, which would lie on the surface of a sphere whose centre is A, and radius AB. Other curves, both of single and double curvature, may be generated, by changing the conditions which fix the different positions of the generating point. The generating point is called the *generatrix of the line.**

* NOTE.—If two points A and B (Pl. 6. Fig. 5) be taken in the plane of the paper, and a point H be moved around them, with the conditions that it shall not depart from the plane of the paper, and that AH+BH be equal to a constant quantity, the point H will describe a curve called an *ellipse*. The fixed points A and B are called *foci*. The line DABE, passing through the foci, is called the *transverse axis*, and its extremities D and E the vertices of the axis. The point C, the middle of DE, is called the *centre* of the ellipse, and CO perpendicular to DE at the point C, the *semi-conjugate* or *semi-lesser axis*.

To describe the curve mechanically, fix the two extremities of a thread, whose length is greater than AB, at the points A and B. Bear a pin close against the thread, and carry it round, its point will describe the ellipse. If the transverse axis DE, and the foci A and B, be given, points of the curve may be found thus: take any portion of the transverse axis, as DP; with this distance as a radius, and the point A as a centre, describe the arcs *t* and *o*; with the remaining part EP of the transverse axis, as a radius, and the point B as a centre, describe the arcs *q* and *s*; the points in which these arcs intersect those before described are points of the curve. After the arcs *t* and *o* are described from the centre A, it is most convenient to place the dividers at B, and describe with the same radius the arcs *m* and *n*; and after having described the arcs *s* and *q*, from the centre B, let the dividers be placed at A, and the arcs *r* and *p* be described; their intersections with the arcs *m* and *n* are points of the curve.

When the point H comes into the position of the point O, the lines AH and BH are equal to each other; and since their sum is equal to the transverse axis DE, either of them is equal to the semi-transverse axis CD. If, therefore, the two axes be given, the foci are easily found. For, take either vertex, as O, of the conjugate axis as a centre, and the semi-transverse axis DC as a radius, and describe the arc of a circle, the points A and B, in which it cuts the transverse axis, are the foci of the ellipse.

Pl. 6. Fig. 6. If a right line EF, and a point D, be taken in the plane of the paper, and a point, as G, be so moved in this plane that its distance from D be constantly equal to its distance from EF, that is, GD equal to GI′, and ID equal to IE, the point G will describe a curve, called *a parabola*. The line EF is called the *directrix* of the parabola, the point D the *focus*, the line AD, perpendicular to the directrix, *the axis*, and the point B, in which the axis intersects the curve, *the vertex of the axis*. Points of the curve may be found thus: take any point of the directrix, as E and draw ED to the focus. Draw also EI, per-

§ 64. Pl. 6. Fig. 3. Let EDD′ be any curve concave towards AC. Through any point, as B, let a right line BD′ be drawn, cutting the curve in the points B and D′. The generatrix of the curve, in its different positions, occupies all the points between B and D′. Let the point D be moved towards the point B. The chord BD′ approaches the tangent to the curve at B, and becomes the tangent when the point D′ occupies the first position which the generatrix assumes on departing from B, towards D′; because, in this position of the point D′, no point of the curve lies between it and B, consequently BD′ does not *intersect* the curve, and is therefore tangent to it. In this last position of the point D′, which is denoted by D, the points B and D are called *consecutive points.*

§ 65. *If a point be taken in a curve of double curvature, the right line joining this and its consecutive point will be tangent to the curve.*

For, the right line is determined in position, since it passes through two given points, and does not cut the curve, since no part of a curve lies between consecutive points. *A right line is therefore tangent to any line, when it passes through two consecutive points of the line.*

§ 66. If a line be tangent to a right line, it coincides with it throughout, and is the same line.

§ 67. If a line be tangent to a curve of single curvature, it is

---

pendicular to the directrix, and at the point D make the angle EDI equal to the angle DEI, the point I, at which the lines EI and DI intersect, is a point of the curve. In the same manner any number of points may be found.

Pl. 6. Fig. 7. If two points A and D be taken in the plane of the paper, and a point C be moved, with the conditions that it continue in the plane of the paper, and that the difference between the distances AC and DC be a constant quantity, the point C will describe a curve p'GC, called an *hyperbola.* A curve identical with p'GC can be described around the point A, by drawing lines DC′ and AC′, and making their difference equal to the same constant quantity. These two curves are called *opposite hyperbolas.* The points A and D are called foci; the line FB is named the transverse axis; and the points F and B, in which it intersects the curves, are the vertices of the axis, or vertices of the hyperbolas; the point E, the middle of FB, is the *centre*; and the line EO, perpendicular to FB, is called the *semi-conjugate axis* contained in the plane of the curve, since the consecutive points through which it passes are in the plane of the curve.

§ 68. If a right line be tangent to a curve of double curvature, it makes the same angle with a line, or plane, drawn through the point of contact, as the curve makes with the same line, or plane.

§ 69. Two curves are tangent to each other, when a line tangent to one, at a common point, is tangent also to the other.

§ 70. As no part of a curve lies between two consecutive points, the distance between them, *measured on the curve*, is equal to nothing. Considered then with respect to their distance apart, *measured on the curve*, they are regarded as the same point. The line AB, Fig. 3, is then to be considered as tangent to the curve BD′, at the point B.

CHAPTER IV.

Of surfaces—Their generation—How they are represented on the planes of projection—Of the projections of curved lines and their tangents.

§ 71. Surfaces are generated by lines moving according to some mathematical law. A line which by its motion generates a surface, is called the *generatrix;* and the lines of the surface which are determined by the different positions of the generatrix, are called *elements* of the surface.

When the generatrix of a surface begins to move from any position, the *first* position which it takes determines an element *consecutive* with the first position of the generatrix, and the two, that is, the first and second positions of the generatrix, are called consecutive elements.

§ 72. Although there is an infinite number of surfaces having different properties, yet, for the purposes of Descriptive Geometry, they may be divided into four classes.

1°. The plane surface, or plane, which is generated by a right line moving along another right line and continuing parallel to itself.

2°. Surfaces which may be generated by a right line, having its consecutive positions in the same plane; such are called *single-curved surfaces.*

3°. Surfaces which can only be generated by curves; such are called *double-curved surfaces.*

4°. Surfaces which may be generated by a right line, when the consecutive positions are not in the same plane; such are called warped surfaces.

§ 73. If any curve be taken in space, and an indefinite right line be drawn through any point of it, and then be moved around the curve, constantly touching the curve and parallel to its first position; the surface generated is called a cylindrical surface, the moving line the generatrix of the surface, and the curve around which it moves the *directrix.*

If the directrix of the cylinder were to move along the generatrix, parallel to itself, all its points would continue in the surface; hence, a cylindrical surface can be generated by a curve, *moving parallel to itself.* The cylindrical surface can therefore be generated in two ways, and has two generatrices, *a right line and a curve;* the directrix of the first generation is the generatrix of the second, and reciprocally. If the curve have a centre, the right line drawn through it, parallel to the right-lined elements, is called the *axis of the cylinder.*

§ 74. If through a point, not in the plane of a curve, a right line be drawn touching the curve, and be produced indefinitely in both directions, if the right line be then moved around the curve, continuing to pass through the point, the surface generated is called a conic surface, the fixed point the vertex of the cone, and the curved line the *directrix.*

That part of the surface which lies below the vertex is called the lower nappe, and the part of the surface which lies above the vertex the upper nappe of the cone. If the directrix were to move towards the vertex, decreasing according to a certain law, or from the vertex, increasing according to a certain law, its points would continue in the surface of the cone. The surface of the cone can then be generated by a curve; it has therefore two generatrices, a right line and curve. If the curve have a centre, the line drawn through the centre and vertex is called the axis of the surface. The cylinder and cone are surfaces of the second class, that is, single-curved surfaces.

§ 75. As the rectilinear generatrices of these surfaces are indefinite, the surfaces are also indefinite. When it is necessary to consider any finite portions of them, they are intersected by planes. The curves formed by the intersection of such planes with the surfaces, are called *bases;* the upper plane is named the plane of the superior base, and the lower plane the plane of the inferior base.

§ 76. A cylinder, whose rectilinear elements are perpendicular to the plane of its inferior base, is called *a right cylinder;* and if this base be a circle, *a right cylinder with a circular base.* Such a cylinder has all its rectilinear elements at the same distance from the axis, is the kind of cylinder treated of in geometry, and may be generated by the revolution of a rectangle about one of its sides. Cylinders are generally named from their inferior bases. If the inferior base be a circle, ellipse, hyperbola, or parabola, the cylinder takes the name of a cylinder with a circular, elliptical, hyperbolic, or parabolic base, and is either right or oblique according as its rectilinear elements are perpendicular, or oblique, to the plane of the base.

§ 77. A right cone is one whose axis is perpendicular to its base. If the base be a circle; such cone is a right cone with a circular base; it can be generated by the revolution of a right-angled triangle about one of its legs, and its rectilinear elements make equal angles with the axis. This is the kind of cone treated of in geometry. The cone, like the cylinder, takes particular names from its inferior base; that is, it is a cone with a circular, elliptical, parabolic, or hyperbolic base, according as its inferior base is a circle, ellipse, parabola, or hyperbola.

§ 78. We shall consider, at present, those surfaces of the third class which can be generated by the revolution of a curve of single curvature about an axis in its own plane. Such surfaces are called *surfaces of revolution.**

§ 79. Any plane passing through the axis of a surface of revolution is called a *meridian plane*, and its intersection with the surface a *meridian curve.* Every plane perpendicular to the axis intersects the surface in a circle, since every point of the revolving generatrix describes a circle around the axis. Let the curve EBDD′ (Pl. 6. Fig. 3) be revolved about AC, it will generate a surface of revolution.

If a circle of an indefinitely small radius were moved from the point E, its radius increasing according to a certain law its centre continuing in, and its plane perpendicular to AC, this circle will also generate the surface of revolution. A surface of revolution, therefore, has two generatrices, *a meridian curve, and a circle whose plane is perpendicular to the axis of the surface.*

§ 80. The surfaces generated by the revolution of the circle the ellipse, the parabola, and the hyperbola about their axes, are called respectively the surface of the sphere, of the ellipsoid of the paraboloid, and hyperboloid. The fourth class of surfaces is discussed in the Complement.

§ 81. *The projection of a curve on either plane of projection is the base of a cylindrical surface passing through the curve and perpendicular to the plane on which the projection is made.* This cylinder is called the *projecting cylinder of the curve.*

§ 82. A curve of single curvature, whose plane is perpendicular to either plane of projection, *is projected on that plane in a right line,* since the projecting cylinder becomes the plane of the curve. Both projections of a curve of double curvature are always curved lines.

§ 83. *Two projections of a curve determine its form and position.* For, the projections of a curve are made up of the pro-

---

* A surface of revolution is a surface generated by a line moving around a right line as an axis; the points of the moving line describing circles whose centres are in the axis, and whose planes are perpendicular to it. It is therefore proposed to discuss only one variety of this class of surfaces.

jections of all its points; the points are fixed in position when their projections are known; and a curve is known in form and given in position when all its points are determined. It is plain that this reasoning does not apply to the case in which the curve is of single curvature and its plane perpendicular to the ground line.

Pl. 6. Fig. 4. Let AB, A′B′ be the projections of a curve. If a cylinder perpendicular to the horizontal plane be drawn through AB, it will pass through the curve in space of which AB is the horizontal projection. If the cylinder which projects the curve on the vertical plane were drawn, its intersection with the cylinder that projects the curve on the horizontal plane is the curve in space; but this intersection is given in position, since the cylinders are given; hence *the two projections of a curve determine it in form and position.*

§ 84. *A plane is tangent to a surface when there is at least one point common to the plane and surface, through which, if any number of planes be drawn, the sections made in the plane will be tangent to the sections made in the surface.*

§ 85. *Two surfaces are tangent to each other when all the sections of the one made by planes passing through a common point are respectively tangent to the sections of the other made by the same planes; or, when a plane which is tangent to the one, at a common point, is also tangent to the other.*

§ 86. *A plane which passes through the consecutive rectilinear elements of a cylindrical surface is tangent to the surface.* For, if the cylinder be intersected by any plane, the consecutive elements will pierce the plane in the curve in which the plane intersects the surface, and in consecutive points of that curve. The right line passing through these consecutive points is tangent to the curve (67); but this line is also the intersection of the plane of the consecutive elements and the cutting plane; and as the same may be shown for any intersecting plane, it follows that the plane of consecutive elements is tangent to the cylinder (84). In the same manner it may be shown, that a plane passing through the consecutive rectilinear elements of a conic surface is tangent to the surface.

§ 87. As no part of a surface *lies between* consecutive elements, the distance between them, *measured on the surface*, is equal to nothing. The consecutive elements, therefore, considered with respect to their distance apart, *measured on the surface*, are to be regarded as the same line. The plane of consecutive elements is then to be considered as tangent to the surface along one element only.

§ 88. It follows from the definition of a tangent plane (84), that all right lines passing through a point of contact, and tangent to lines of the surface, are contained in the tangent plane; hence this plane is the locus, or place, of the right lines tangent to all the curves which lie on the surface and pass through the point of contact. But two right lines, which intersect, determine the position of a plane. If, therefore, through any point of a surface two elements be drawn, and, at their point of intersection, a tangent to each, *the plane of these tangents* is tangent to the surface at their point of intersection.

§ 89. *A plane tangent to a surface which has rectilinear elements will contain that element which passes through the point of contact.* For, if a right line be drawn tangent to this element of the surface, it will be a line of the tangent plane (88); but this tangent is the element itself; hence *a tangent plane always contains the element of the surface passing through the point of contact.*

§ 90. *If a right line be tangent to a curve in space, the projections of the line are respectively tangent to the projections of the curve.* For, if through the two consecutive points of tangency two lines be drawn perpendicular to either plane, they will be common both to the plane which projects the right line and to the cylinder which projects the curve; therefore, the plane and cylinder will be tangent to each other (86). The lines in which they are intersected by either plane of projection are therefore tangent to each other (84); but these lines are respectively the projections of the curve and tangent; *the projections of tangent lines are therefore tangent to each other.*

§ 91. Surfaces are represented on the planes of projection by the projections of their elements. The horizontal projection of a single-curved surface is generally made by projecting on the horizontal plane its inferior base, and the elements of contact of two planes tangent to the surface and perpendicular to the horizontal plane. The vertical projection of the surface is generally determined by projecting on the vertical plane its inferior base, and the elements of contact of two planes tangent to the surface and perpendicular to the vertical plane.

§ 92. The horizontal projection of a surface of revolution is the intersection by the horizontal plane of a cylinder perpendicular to this plane and tangent to the surface. The vertical projection is the intersection, by the vertical plane, of a cylinder perpendicular to the plane and tangent to the surface. A surface of revolution, having its axis perpendicular to the horizontal plane, may also be projected by projecting on the horizontal plane some one of its horizontal sections, and on the vertical plane the meridian curve which is parallel to this plane.

CHAPTER V

OF TANGENT PLANES TO SINGLE-CURVED SURFACES.

PROBLEM XVII.

To draw a plane through a given point of a conical surface, tangent to the surface.

§ 93. Pl. 6. Fig. 8. Let the circle BFEG in the horizontal plane be the base of the cone, A the horizontal, and A′ the vertical projection of the vertex, AL″ and A′L‴ the projections of the axis. The lines AF and AE are the traces of two planes tangent to the cone and perpendicular to the horizontal plane; they are also the projections of the elements of contact of the planes and cone; and AEGF is the horizontal projection of the cone (91). The line G′*a* is the vertical projection of the base of the cone; A′G′, A′a′ are the vertical traces of the two planes tangent to the cone and perpendicular to the vertical plane; hence, A′G′a′ is the vertical projection of the cone. The part FDE of the circumference of the base of the cone is dotted; for, being under the surface, it cannot be seen. Let C be the horizontal projection of the point of the surface through which the plane is to be drawn. The vertical projection of this point cannot be assumed; for, it being a point of the surface of the cone, its projecting lines must intersect on the surface. If we suppose a line to be drawn perpendicular to the horizontal plane at C, it will pierce the surface of the cone in two points; and these are the only points of the surface which are horizontally projected at C.

Through this perpendicular and the vertex of the cone let a plane be drawn; ACB is its horizontal trace, and the two elements in which it intersects the surface of the cone pierce the horizontal plane at D and B. The projections of these elements on the vertical plane are A′B′ and A′D′; (and the points C′ and C″, in which these projections intersect the vertical projection of the perpendicular from C, are the only points of the surface which are horizontally projected at C.)

Let it then be required to draw a plane through the point (C,C′), and tangent to the surface: the plane will contain the element (AC, A′C′) passing through this point (89). This element pierces the horizontal plane at B, which is a point of the horizontal trace of the required plane. But the trace must be tangent to the base of the cone (84); therefore BK, drawn tangent to the base of the cone, is the horizontal trace of the tangent plane. The element of contact (AB, A′B′) pierces the vertical plane at L′; and since this is a line of the tangent plane, L′ is a point of its vertical trace: hence KL′ is the vertical trace of the tangent plane.

If the point K were not used, the vertical trace could be found thus: through any point of the element of contact, as (C,C′), let a line be drawn parallel to the horizontal trace of the tangent plane; this line pierces the vertical plane at I, which is therefore a point of the vertical trace of the tangent plane.

The point L′ being previously determined, the trace L′I can be drawn. Had it been required to draw the plane through (C,C″), its traces would have been constructed in a similar manner.

PROBLEM XVIII.

To draw a plane through a given point without the surface of a cone, and tangent to the surface.

§ 94. Pl. 7. Fig. 1. Let A*n*G*m* be the horizontal, and A′C′D be the vertical projection of the cone, (A,A′) its vertex, and (E,E′) the given point through which the plane is to be drawn.

As every plane tangent to a cone passes through the vertex, if the points (A,A′), (E,E′) be joined by a right line, this right line (EA, E′A′) will be a line of the required plane; and the point F, at which it pierces the horizontal plane, will be a point of the horizontal trace. Two lines can be drawn through the p int F, tangent to the base of the cone, either of which will be the horizontal trace of a plane passing through the point (E,E′), and tangent to the cone: hence there are two planes that can be drawn, either of which will answer the conditions of the problem.

Draw the tangent FG, and produce it to I: FI is the horizontal trace of one of the tangent planes. The vertical trace is determined by drawing through the vertex of the cone, or any other point of the element of contact, a line parallel to the horizontal trace: the point H, at which this line pierces the vertical plane, being joined with I, determines IH, the vertical trace. That part of it which is concealed by the vertical projection of the cone, is made broken (35) The line (AG, A′G′) is the element of contact.

PROBLEM XIX.

To draw a plane parallel to a given line and tangent to the surface, of a cone.

§ 95. Pl. 7. Fig. 2. Let AGC be the horizontal, A′C′D′ the vertical projection of the cone, and (IH, I′H′) the given line.

Through the vertex of the cone let the line (AE, A′E′) be drawn parallel to the given line. This parallel is a line of the required plane, since the plane must pass through the vertex (A,A′), and be parallel to the line (IH, I′H′). The point E, at which the line (AE, A′E′) pierces the horizontal plane, is a point of the horizontal trace of the tangent plane, and two tangent planes can be drawn answering the conditions of the problem, since two lines can be drawn through E tangent to the base of the cone.

Let either, as the tangent EG, be taken for the horizontal trace of the tangent plane; (AG, A′G′) is the element of contact; and the point N′, at which it pierces the vertical plane, is a point of the vertical trace. The line (AE, A′E′) being a line of the tangent plane, the point F′, at which it pierces the vertical plane, is a second point of the vertical trace: hence F′N′ is the vertical trace of a plane parallel to (IH, I′H′), and tangent to the surface of the cone. If we draw through E the tangent EP, it will be the horizontal trace of the second plane which is parallel to the given line (IH, I′H′), and tangent to the surface of the cone. The vertical trace of this plane is easily constructed.

§ 96. This problem becomes impossible when the line (AE, A′E′), which is drawn through the vertex of the cone and parallel to the given line, passes within the surface: in this case. it would pierce the base of the cone within the circle CDG. If the parallel should become an element of the cone, the problem would be possible, but would admit of one solution only.

§ 97. The last three problems would have been constructed

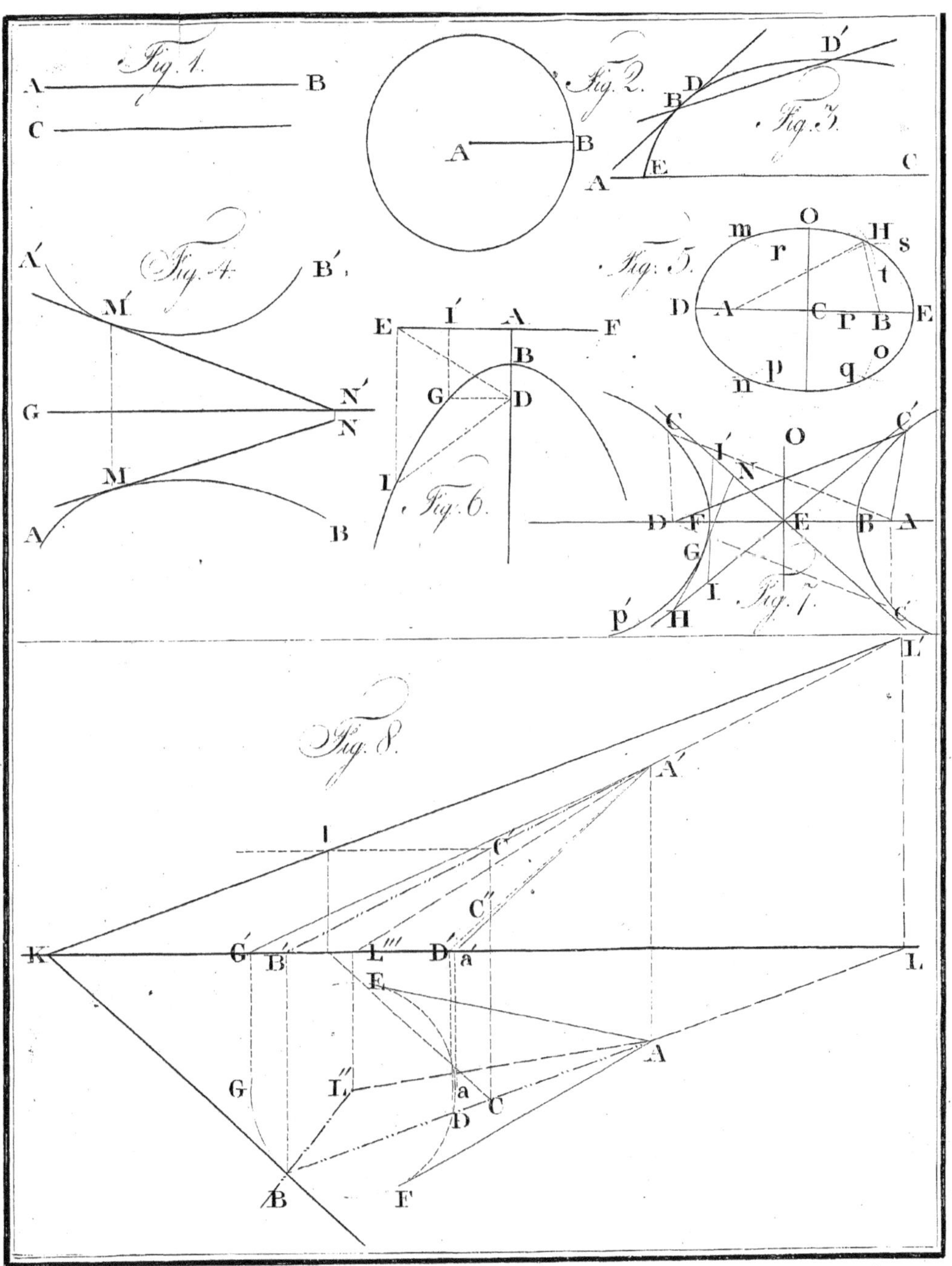
Fig. 1.
A B
C
Fig. 2.
A B
Fig. 3.
D′
B D
A E C
Fig. 4.
A′ B′
M′
G N′
N
M
A B
Fig. 5.
m O H s
r t
D A C P B E
p q o
n
Fig. 6.
E I′ A F
B
G D
L
Fig. 7.
C C′
I′ O
N
D F E B A
G
I
p′ H C′
Fig. 8.
L′
A′
I
C′
C″
K G′ B′ L‴ D′ a′ L
E
A
G L″ a C
D
B F

in nearly the same manner, had the surfaces been cylindrical instead of conical. Indeed, we may consider the cylinder as a cone whose vertex is at an infinite distance from the base; for, if the vertex of a cone be supposed to move from the base, the rectilinear elements will make a less and less angle with each other; and when the vertex is removed to an infinite distance, these elements become parallel, and the cone becomes a cylinder.

§ 98. In order to vary the constructions, and to apply the principles used in drawing tangent planes to single-curved surfaces, so as to embrace the greatest variety of cases, the positions of the cylinders to which tangent planes are to be drawn, will be so chosen as to require new applications of the principles which have already been developed.

PROBLEM XX.

To draw a plane through a given point of a cylindrical surface, tangent to the surface.

§ 99. Pl. 7. Fig. 3. Suppose the cylinder to be a right cylinder with a circular base, having its axis parallel to the ground line. Let AEFB be the horizontal, and CLGD the vertical projection of the cylinder, and I the horizontal projection of the point of the surface through which the tangent plane is to be drawn.

If a perpendicular be erected to the horizontal plane at I, it will pierce the surface of the cylinder in two points, both of which are horizontally projected at I. Through this perpendicular let a plane MHP be drawn perpendicular to the axis of the cylinder. This plane will intersect the surface of the cylinder in a circle, and H is the horizontal projection of its centre. The two points in which the perpendicular at I intersects this circle, are the two points in which it intersects the surface of the cylinder.

Let this plane be revolved about its horizontal trace MP, till it coincides with the horizontal plane. The centre of the circle, in which it intersects the surface of the cylinder, falls at H′: with this point as a centre, and a radius equal to the radius of the base of the cylinder, describe the circle ENFN′. But IN is the revolved position of the perpendicular to the horizontal plane at I; therefore N′ and N are the revolved positions of the two points in which this perpendicular pierces the surface of the cylinder.

Let it be required to draw the tangent plane through the upper point, which in its revolved position is at N. Through N draw the tangent ONM to the circle NEF; this tangent is the intersection, revolved, of the required tangent plane and the plane MP. Let now the plane of the circle ENF be revolved back into its primitive position, the point M remains fixed, being in the axis, and the point O describes the arc OO in the vertical plane; the tangent line will, therefore, pierce the planes of projection at M and O′, which are consequently points of the traces of the required plane. But, since the rectilinear elements of the cylinder are parallel to the ground line, and the plane must be tangent along an element, it follows that the plane will be parallel to the ground line. Therefore, the parallels to the ground line through M and O′ are the traces of the required plane. If the plane had been drawn through the point (I,I″) its traces would have been constructed in a similar manner.

PROBLEM XXI.

To draw a plane through a given point, without the surface of a cylinder, tangent to the surface.

§ 100. Pl. 7. Fig. 4. Let the axis of the cylinder be parallel to the ground line, and the projections of the cylinder as represented in the figure; and let (I,I′) be the given point through which the plane is to be drawn.

If through the point (I,I′) any plane be drawn intersecting the surface of the cylinder in a curve, and if through the same point two lines be drawn tangent to this curve, each line will

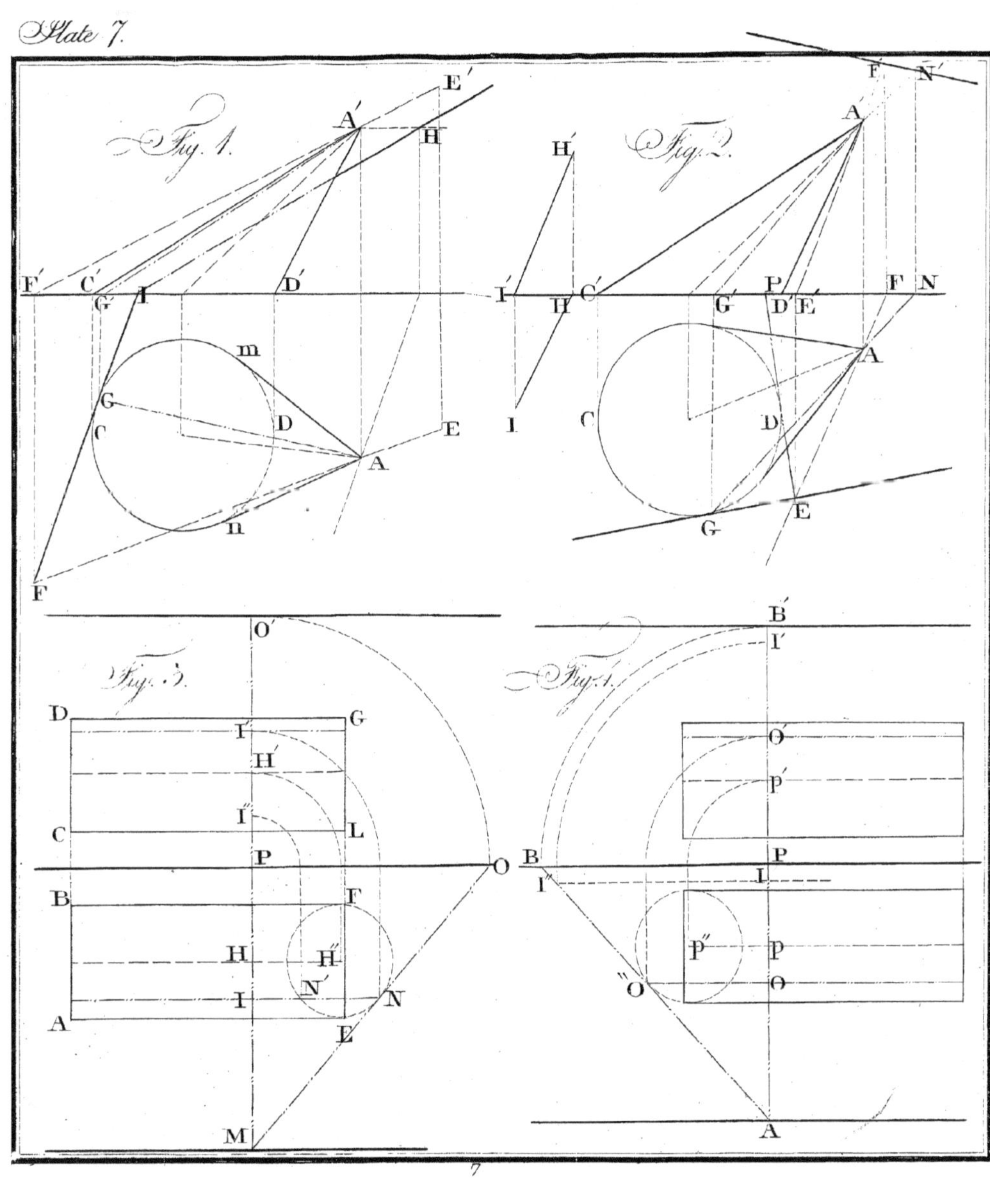
Plate 7.
Fig. 1.
Fig. 2.
Fig. 3.
Fig. 4.
7

be a line of a plane which can be drawn through the point (I,I'), and tangent to the cylinder.

Let AP be the horizontal trace of a plane passing through the point (I,I') and perpendicular to the axis of the cylinder; this plane will intersect the surface of the cylinder in a circle whose centre is horizontally projected at p, and vertically projected at p'. Let this plane be revolved around AP till it coincides with the horizontal plane; (p,p'), the centre of the circle, falls at p'', and the point (I,I') at I''. Describe the circle, and let the tangent I''O'' be drawn. Revolving this plane back into its primitive position, the point A remains fixed, being in the axis; and the point B describes the arc BB' in the vertical plane about the centre P: the tangent to the circle, therefore, pierces the planes of projection at A and B', which are points of the traces of the required tangent plane. But the traces are parallel to the ground line; therefore, the parallels to the ground line, drawn through the points A and B', are the traces of the required plane.

After the counter revolution of the plane, the point O'' is horizontally projected at O, and vertically at O': the lines drawn through these points, parallel to the ground line, are the projections of the element of contact.

Had a second tangent line been drawn through the point I'' to the circle whose centre is p'', it would have been a line of a second plane through the given point (I,I'), and tangent to the surface of the cylinder.

PROBLEM XXII.

To draw a plane parallel to a given line, and tangent to the surface of a cylinder.

§ 101. Pl. 8 Fig. 1. We shall again use a right cylinder with a circular base, and take its axis parallel to the ground line. Let ABGD and EFG'R be the projections of the cylinder, and (IH, I'H') the given line to which the plane is to be parallel.

Since a tangent plane to a cylinder is tangent along a rectilinear element, it is parallel to the axis. The required plane must then be parallel to the axis as well as to the line (IH, I'H'). A plane drawn through (IH, I'H'), and parallel to the axis of the cylinder, is, therefore, parallel to the required tangent plane.

But, since the axis of the cylinder is parallel to the ground line, the plane parallel to it is also parallel to the ground line: therefore, IT and H'Q', drawn through the points I and H', parallel to the ground line, are the traces of this plane. If, for a moment, we suppose the tangent plane to be drawn, and make an intersection by a plane perpendicular to the axis of the cylinder, this plane will intersect the cylinder in a circle, the tangent plane in a line tangent to the circle, and the parallel plane through (IH, I'H'), in a line parallel to that tangent.

Let MS be the horizontal trace of such a plane, and suppose it to be revolved around this trace to coincide with the horizontal plane. The centre of the circle, in which the cutting plane intersects the surface of the cylinder, falls at P, and the line of intersection with the parallel plane takes the position TQ: now, if the line MP'F be drawn parallel to TQ and tangent to the circle, it will represent, in its revolved position, the line which would have been cut from the tangent plane had that plane been drawn. The tangent MF is, therefore, a line of the required tangent plane; M is a point of its horizontal, and F' a point of its vertical trace; and as the traces are parallel to the ground line, the parallels drawn through these points are the traces of the required plane.

As two lines can be drawn parallel to TQ and tangent to the circle whose centre is P, it follows that two planes can be drawn parallel to the line (IH, I'H'), and tangent to the cylinder.

§ 102. We cannot, in general, draw a plane through a given line, and tangent to a single-curved surface; for, in the conic surface the tangent plane always passes through the vertex, and if a plane be drawn through the given line and the vertex of the cone, it will, in general, intersect the surface, though it may be tangent to it. If the given line contain the vertex and does not pass within the surface, a plane can *always be drawn through it tangent to the surface of the cone.*

As a tangent plane to a cylindrical surface contains an element of the surface, and as a plane can be drawn through two lines only when they intersect, or are parallel, it follows that *a plane cannot be drawn through a right line, and tangent to a cylindrical surface, unless the line touch the surface or be parallel to its rectilinear elements.*

§ 103. *The shortest distance between two lines in space, which are not in the same plane, is readily found by means of the cylinder and its tangent plane.*

Pl. 8. Fig. 2. Let (AB, A′B′) be one of the lines, and (CD, C′D′) the other.

Draw a plane through the line (AB, A′B′) parallel to the line (CD, C′D′). This is done by taking a point (B,B′) of the line (AB, A′B′), and drawing through it a line parallel to (CD, C′D′); B′C′ is its vertical and BF its horizontal projection, and AF is the horizontal trace of the parallel plane. If now we suppose (CD, C′D′) to be the axis of a right cylinder with a circular base, to which the plane just drawn shall be tangent, the radius of the base will be equal to the distance between the axis of the cylinder and tangent plane, which distance is equal to the distance between the given lines.

To find the radius of the base of this cylinder. Through the axis (CD, C′D′) let a plane be drawn perpendicular to the horizontal plane; its trace DCG intersects the trace of the parallel plane at G, and these planes intersect in a line parallel to (CD, C′D′). Let this plane be revolved around DG till it coincides with the horizontal plane. Any point of the axis of the cylinder, as (I,I′), falls in a perpendicular to, and at a distance from, the axis of revolution DG, equal to its height above the horizontal plane: making II″ equal to this distance, and drawing CI″, determines the revolved position of the axis. But the axis of the cylinder, and the line in which the vertical plane intersects the parallel plane are parallel; they are therefore parallel after revolution; hence GP, drawn parallel to CI″, is the revolved position of this line of intersection.

At the point C let a plane be drawn perpendicular to the axis of the cylinder; its trace CL is perpendicular to CD, the projection of the axis (49). This plane intersects the vertical plane through the axis of the cylinder in a line perpendicular to the axis at C. If then CH be drawn perpendicular to CI″, the revolved axis, it will represent this intersection revolved into the horizontal plane; and H is one point of the intersection of the tangent plane and the plane perpendicular to the axis of the cylinder. Let now the plane perpendicular to the axis of the cylinder be revolved about its horizontal trace LC till it coincides with the horizontal plane. The point L is one point of the intersection of this plane and the tangent plane, and remains fixed; the point H, which is another point, falls at H′ a distance from C equal to CH, its distance in space: LH′ is then the intersection of these planes revolved into the horizontal plane. Let CN be drawn perpendicular to LH′; it will be the revolved position of the perpendicular from C to the tangent plane, and is therefore the radius of the base of the cylinder. Making a counter revolution of the plane about LC, the point N returns in a perpendicular to the axis; and NE, drawn parallel to CD, is the horizontal projection of the element of contact.

Since (AB, A′B′) is a line of the tangent plane, and is not parallel to (CD, C′D′), it is consequently not parallel to the element of contact; it will, therefore, intersect this element; and E is the horizontal and E′ the vertical projection of their intersection. If from this point a line be drawn perpendicular to the tangent plane, it will intersect and be perpendicular to both the given lines: ED, E′D′ are its projections, and CN is its length.

Plate 8

Fig. 1.
F′
H′
Q′
R
G′
N
E
F
L′
H
S
N′
Q
F
D
G
P
L
P′
A
B
I
T
M
Fig. 2.
E′
B′
D′
I′
A′
C′
F
G
L
N
H′
A
C
H
I
B
E
I″
D
P

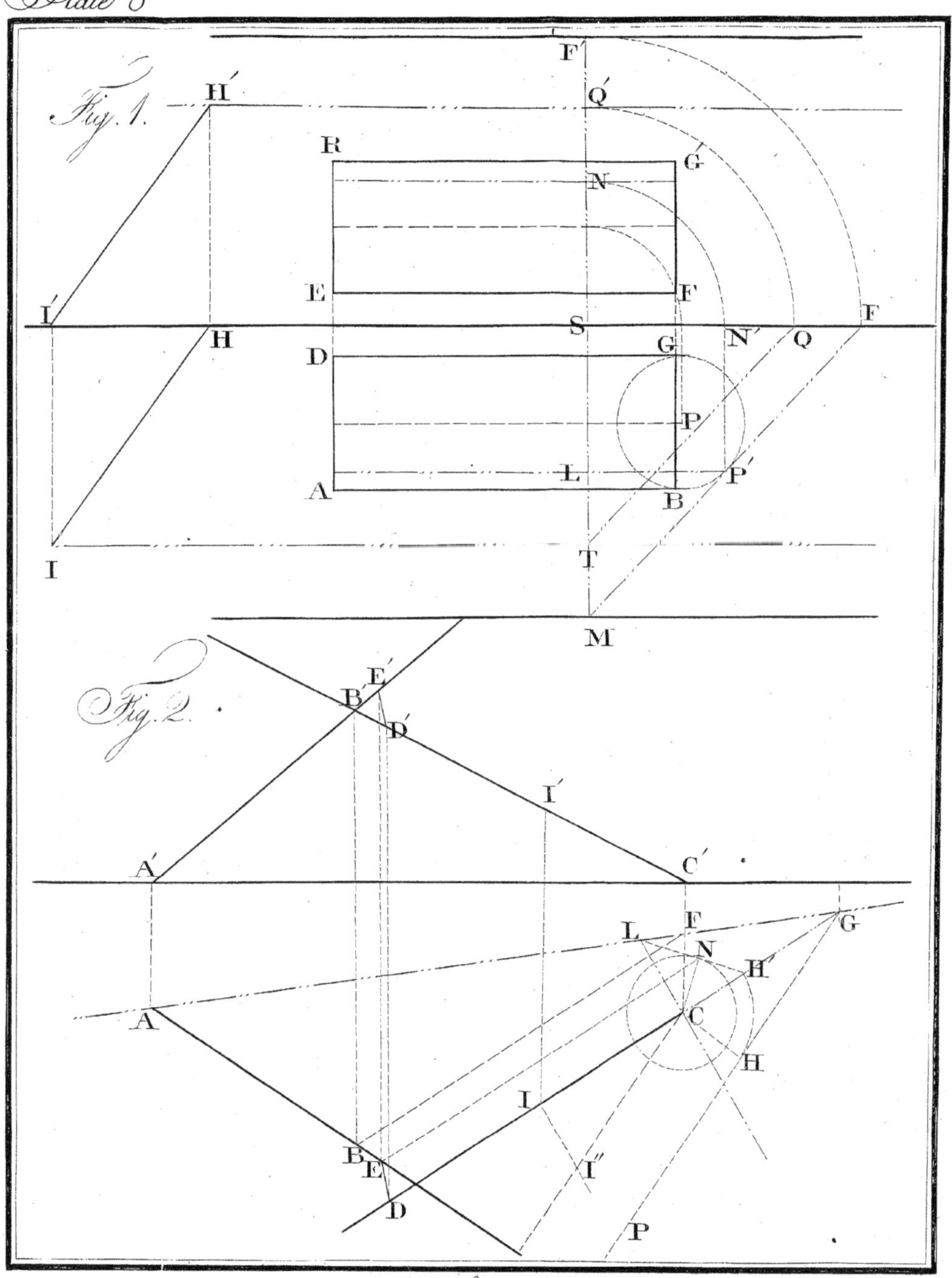

CHAPTER VI.

OF TANGENT PLANES TO SURFACES OF REVOLUTION.

PROBLEM XXIII.

To draw a plane tangent to a surface of revolution, at a given point of the surface.

§ 104. Let the surface of the paraboloid be the surface of revolution to which the tangent plane is to be drawn. As the planes of projection can be assumed at pleasure, let the horizontal plane be taken perpendicular to the axis of the surface; the vertical plane will then be parallel to it.

Pl. 9. Fig. 1. Let A be the horizontal and gg' the vertical projection of the axis; EHF the circle in which the surface is intersected by the horizontal plane; E′F′ the vertical projection of this circle; and E′gF′ the vertical projection of the meridian curve, whose plane is parallel to the vertical plane of projection.

Having made the projections of the surface, let the point C be assumed for the horizontal projection of the point at which the plane is to be drawn tangent. The vertical projection of this point cannot be assumed, for its projecting lines must intersect on the surface. To find it, erect at C a perpendicular to the horizontal plane; the vertical projection of the point in which this perpendicular meets the surface is the point required. Through this perpendicular draw the meridian plane IA, and let it be revolved about the axis of the surface till it becomes parallel to the vertical plane. In this revolution, C, the foot of the perpendicular, describes the arc CD on the horizontal plane, and D′D″ is the vertical projection of the perpendicular from its revolved position. The meridian curve having become parallel to the vertical plane, its vertical projection is the curve

E′gF′; and the point D′, in which it intersects the vertical projection of the perpendicular, is the revolved position of the point at which the perpendicular to the horizontal plane at C pierces the surface. Making the counter revolution, D returns in the arc of a horizontal circle, of which DC is the horizontal and D′C′ the vertical projection; C′ is, therefore, the vertical projection of the point of the surface of which C is the horizontal projection: hence, (C,C′) is the point at which the plane is to be tangent to the surface. If a line be drawn tangent to the meridian curve at the point (C,C′), and a second line be drawn tangent at the same point to the horizontal circle passing through (C,C′), the plane of these two tangents is tangent to the surface at the point (C,C′) (88).

If, when the meridian plane ICA is parallel to the vertical plane, the line A′D′L′ be drawn tangent to the meridian curve at the point D′, this line, being in the plane of the curve, revolves back with it, and continues tangent to the curve at the point D′. In this counter revolution the point A′, in which the tangent intersects the axis of the surface, remains fixed; and when the point (D,D′) comes into the position (C,C′), A′C′I′ is the vertical and ACI the horizontal projection of the tangent line. The line (AC, A′C′) being a line of the required plane, the point I, in which it pierces the horizontal plane, is a point of its horizontal trace. If at (C,C′) a right line be drawn tangent to the horizontal circle passing through this point, it will be a horizontal line, and perpendicular to the radius of the horizontal circle drawn through (C,C′); therefore its horizontal projection CM is perpendicular to AC, the horizontal projection of the radius; and its vertical projection C′M′ is parallel to the ground line (27). Since this line is horizontal, and a line of the tangent plane, the horizontal trace of the tangent plane is parallel to it, and, consequently, to its horizontal projection (30). The line IN, therefore, drawn through the point I, parallel to CM, is the horizontal trace of the required plane. The tangent to the horizontal circle at (C,C′) pierces the vertical plane at M′: hence, NM′ is the vertical trace of the tangent plane

§ 105. We may remark, that the tangent to the horizontal circle at (C,C′) is perpendicular both to the radius passing through (C,C′) and to the perpendicular demitted from this point to the horizontal plane: hence, it is perpendicular to the plane of these two lines; that is, to the meridian plane passing through the point (C,C′). But the tangent plane contains this tangent to the horizontal circle; therefore, it is perpendicular to the meridian plane: and as the same may be shown for any position of the point of contact, we conclude *that a tangent plane to a surface of revolution is perpendicular to the meridian plane passing through the point of contact.*

§ 106. The construction just made answers for all surfaces of revolution, with this slight difference, that the perpendicular to the horizontal plane at C may pierce the surface in several points. We find the vertical projections of these points by the methods already shown: assume either of them for the one at which the plane is to be tangent, and make the construction as in the last problem.

§ 107. Second Solution. Having determined the vertical projection of the point, as before, let the meridian plane passing through it be revolved about the axis of the surface till it becomes parallel to the vertical plane, and draw the tangent A′D′L′, which in this position pierces the horizontal plane at L. Let the meridian plane be revolved about the axis of the surface; the meridian curve generates the surface, and the tangent line the surface of a cone tangent to the surface of revolution. The point (A,A′) is the vertex of the cone, and LIQ is its base. The curve of contact of the cone and surface is the horizontal circle described by the point (D,D′); for, the point (D,D′), throughout the revolution, is common to both the surfaces.

Every plane tangent to this cone will be tangent to the surface of the paraboloid, and the plane which is tangent along the element passing through (C,C′) will be tangent to the surface at the point (C,C′). This element pierces the base of the cone at I; IN, tangent to the base of the cone, is the horizontal trace of the tangent plane; and NM′ is its vertical trace. This is the same plane as before determined.

§ 108. *If two surfaces of revolution, having a common axis, are tangent to each other, their curve of contact is the circumference of a circle whose plane is perpendicular to the axis.*

For, if a plane be drawn through the common axis, it will intersect each surface in a meridian curve (79), and these curves will be tangent to each other (85). If, then, the plane of these curves be revolved around their common axis, each will generate the surface to which it belongs; the point of contact will generate the circumference of the circle of contact of the surfaces; and the plane of the circle is perpendicular to the axis, since the axis is perpendicular to all the radii. If one of the surfaces of revolution be that of a cylinder or cone, similar reasoning would show, *that the curve of contact is the circumference of a circle whose plane is perpendicular to the common axis.*

§ 109. If through any point in the plane of a circle a line be drawn tangent to the circle, and through the same point a line be drawn to the centre; if the plane be then revolved about this latter line as an axis, the circumference of the circle will generate the surface of a sphere, and the tangent line the surface of a cone which will be tangent to the sphere. The elements of the cone, intercepted between the vertex and the points in which they touch the sphere, are equal to each other; and the line drawn to the centre of the sphere is the axis of the cone. Hence, *if any point be taken without the surface of a sphere, and through this point a system of lines be drawn tangent to the sphere, they form the surface of a right cone having a circular base; and the line drawn from the vertex to the centre of the sphere is the axis of the cone.*

§ 110. It has been shown, that a plane which is passed through a given point, without a single-curved surface, and tangent to the surface, is determined in position. Similar conditions do not determine the plane when the surface is of double curvature. For, through the point, conceive any number of planes to be passed intersecting the surface in curves. From the assumed point let lines be drawn tangent to the curves; these lines will form the surface of a cone tangent to the double-curved surface. There mav be an infinite number of planes drawn tangent to this cone, each of which will be tangent to the surface; therefore, *from any point without a double-curved surface, an infinite number of planes may be drawn tangent to the surface.*

§ 111. It has also been shown, in Chap. V., that a plane is determined in position when it is drawn parallel to a given line, and tangent to a single-curved surface. Similar conditions do not determine the plane when the surface is of double curvature. For, let the surface be intersected by any number of planes parallel to the given line, and let tangents be drawn to these curves also parallel to the given line; this system of parallels forms the surface of a cylinder whose right-lined elements are parallel to the given line, and this cylinder is tangent to the double-curved surface. Every plane tangent to this cylinder is also tangent to the double-curved surface and parallel to the given line; and as an infinite number of planes can be drawn tangent to the cylinder, it follows *that an infinite number of planes may be drawn parallel to a given line and tangent to a double-curved surface.*

§ 112. It has been shown, (102), that a plane cannot, in general, be drawn through a given line and tangent to a single-curved surface; but it is always possible to draw a plane through a given line which shall be tangent to a double-curved surface, provided the line does not meet the surface. For, suppose the surface to be circumscribed by a tangent cylinder, whose right-lined elements are parallel to the given line. A plane can be drawn through the line, and tangent to this cylinder (102). But this plane will also be tangent to the double-curved surface: hence, a plane can always be drawn through a given line and tangent to a double-curved surface

PROBLEM XXIV.

To draw a plane through a given line, and tangent to the surface of a sphere.

§ 113. Pl. 9. Fig. 2. Let the centre of the sphere be in the ground line at C, and (AB, A'B') the line through which the plane is to be drawn.

If any point of this line be made the vertex of a cone tangent to the sphere, and a plane be drawn through the line and tangent to the cone (102), the plane so drawn will be tangent to the sphere, and will consequently be the plane required.

Let (A,A′) be the point chosen for the vertex of the cone. Let the lines AI and AL be drawn tangent to the circle of intersection of the sphere and horizontal plane; join the points I and L and draw AC to the centre of the sphere. The line AC bisects the angle IAL, and is perpendicular to IL at the point P. If the horizontal plane be supposed to revolve about AC as an axis, the semicircle N′IN will generate the sphere, and the right-angled triangle IPA a cone tangent to it; and since the surfaces have a common axis, the plane of their circle of contact is perpendicular to that axis; that is, to the horizontal plane, since the axis AC is a line of that plane. The line HID′ is the horizontal trace of the plane of the circle of contact of the cone and sphere; and if this plane be revolved about its trace HL till it coincides with the horizontal plane, the circle of contact will be represented by the circle IG″L.

If we find the point in which the line (AB, A′B′) pierces this plane, and from that point draw a line tangent to the circle of contact of the cone and sphere, this tangent will be the trace, on that plane, of a plane which will contain the given line, and be tangent to the cone. To find this point, produce AB, the horizontal projection of the given line, till it meets the trace at D′, and erect the indefinite perpendicular D′F in the plane HID′: the line (AB,A′B′) will pierce the plane somewhere in this perpendicular (37), and therefore the point will be horizontally projected at D′. Through D′ draw the indefinite perpendicular DD′ to the ground line, and produce A′B′, the vertical projection of the line, till it meets the perpendicular at E. The point E is the vertical projection of the point of which D′ is the horizontal projection (13), and DE is the distance of the point above the horizontal plane (14). If, then, D′F be made equal to ED, F will be the point in which the line pierces the plane HID′. Through F draw the tangent FG″H to the circle IG″L; it will be the trace, on the plane of the cone's base, of a plane contain ing the given line and tangent to the cone. The tangent line pierces the horizontal plane at H; and since the tangent plane passes through the vertex A, AH is its horizontal trace. The vertical trace, on the vertical plane of projection, is found by drawing through any point, as (O,O′), of the line (AB, A′B′), a parallel to the horizontal trace; the point Q′, in which it pierces the vertical plane, is a point of the vertical trace; and since B′ is also a point, B′Q′ is the vertical trace of the tangent plane.

To find the projections of the point of contact. When the plane of the cone's base is revolved into the horizontal plane, the point of contact is at G″. In the counter revolution, G″ describes the circumference of a circle whose plane is perpendicular to the axis HL; and when the plane of the cone's base becomes perpendicular to the horizontal plane, G is the horizontal projection of the point of contact. The height of the point of contact above the horizontal plane is equal to GG″; drawing through G an indefinite perpendicular to the ground line, and making *g*G′ equal to GG″, gives G′ for the vertical projection of the point of contact.

As two lines can be drawn from the point F tangent to the circle IG″L, it follows that two planes can be drawn through the given line and tangent to the sphere. As it would confuse the figure to draw them both, only one is determined; the other is left to be constructed by the student.

§ 114. All lines drawn tangent to a sphere at any point of the surface are perpendicular to the radius passing through that point: hence, the tangent plane which contains these lines is perpendicular to the radius passing through the point of contact. The projections of the radius drawn through the point of contact pass through the projections of this point, and are respectively perpendicular to the traces of the tangent plane (49). We can verify the construction just made, by drawing CG, and examining whether or not it be perpendicular to AH; CG′ ought also to be perpendicular to the vertical trace Q′B.

PROBLEM XV.

To draw a plane through a given right line and tangent to the surface of a sphere, by means of two cones.

§ 115. Pl. 10. Fig. 1. Let (AB, A′B′) be the given line, C and C′ the projections of the centre of the sphere, and the circles described around these points as centres, the projections of the sphere.

If any two points of the given line be taken as the vertices of two cones which are drawn tangent to the sphere, a plane tangent to these cones will contain the given line and be tangent to the sphere.

First, through the centre of the sphere let the plane B′C′ be drawn parallel to the horizontal plane, and take the point (B,B′), in which the given line meets this plane, for the vertex of the first cone. Through the centre of the sphere let the plane DC be drawn parallel to the vertical plane, and take the point (D,D′), in which the given line pierces this plane, for the vertex of the second cone.

If from the point (B,B′) we conceive two lines to be drawn in the horizontal plane B′C′, and tangent to the great circle in which this plane intersects the sphere, they will be those right-lined elements of the tangent cone which lie in this plane, and will be horizontally projected in the tangent lines BE and BF (90). The axis of the cone is horizontal, and passes through the centre of the sphere (109); the plane of the circle of contact being perpendicular to the axis is perpendicular to the horizontal plane, and FE is its horizontal projection. The axis of the cone, whose vertex is (D,D′), is parallel to the vertical plane of projection; and the plane of the circle of contact, being perpendicular to the axis, is consequently perpendicular to the vertical plane.

We wish now to draw a tangent plane to these two cones. The planes of their bases intersect in a right line, of which EF is the horizontal projection and GH the vertical projection (24).

Plate 9.

Fig. 1.
A′
g
C
D′
M′
E′
g′
D″
I′
F′
L′
M
N
H
Q
E
A
D
F
L
C
I
Fig. 2.
E
F
D′
L
B′
G′
Q′
O′
N
A′
Q
B
D
P
C
O
N′
G″
G
A
I
H

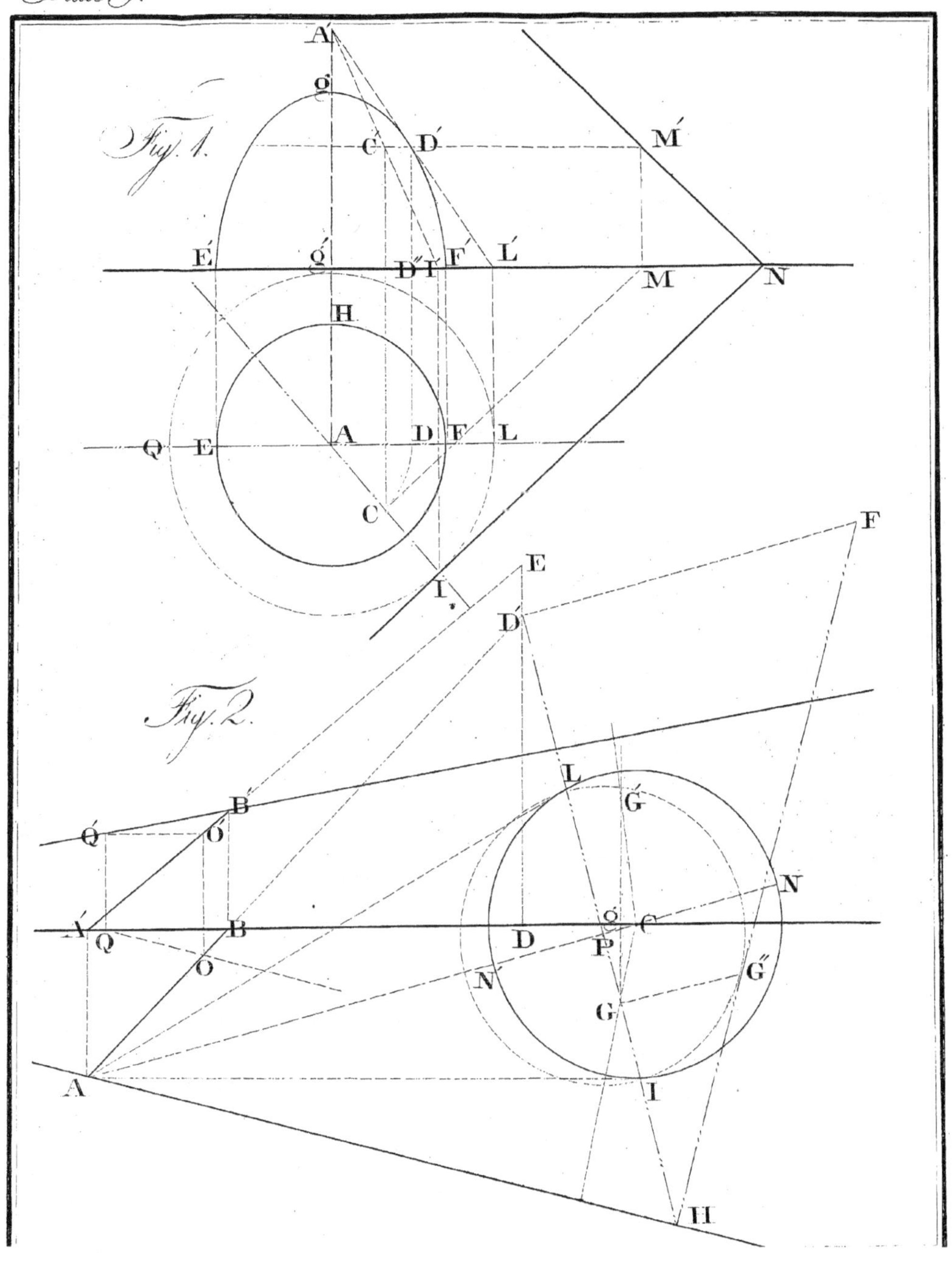

The points in which this right line pierces the surface of the sphere, are the points in which the circumferences of the circles of contact of the cones and sphere intersect, and are, therefore, common to the surface of the sphere and to the surfaces of both cones. If at either of these points a plane be drawn tangent to the sphere, it will be tangent to both cones, will contain the given line, and will therefore be the plane required.

To find the points in which this line of intersection pierces the surface of the sphere, it will first be necessary to find the point in which it pierces the horizontal plane B′C′, and secondly, the point in which it pierces the vertical plane DC. It pierces the horizontal plane B′C′ in the line in which this plane intersects the plane of the base of the cone whose vertex is (B,B′); that is, in the line of which EF is the horizontal projection. It also pierces the horizontal plane B′C′ in its intersection with the base of the cone whose vertex is (D,D′); that is, in a line perpendicular to the vertical plane at a'. The horizontal projection of this line is $n\,a$; therefore, the line in which the bases of the cones intersect, pierces the horizontal plane B′C′ at the point (a,a'). The base of the cone whose vertex is (D,D′) intersects the vertical plane DC in a line of which GH is the vertical projection; and the base of the cone whose vertex is (B,B′) intersects the same plane in a line of which f is the horizontal and $f'g'$ the vertical projection; therefore, the line of intersection of the cones' bases pierces the plane DC in the point (f,g').

Let the plane of the base of the cone whose vertex is (B,B′) be revolved about its intersection with the plane B′C′ till it becomes parallel to the horizontal plane. The point (a,a'), being in the axis, remains fixed; the point (f,g') falls in a perpendicular to EF, and at a distance from f equal to $f'g'$, its height above the plane B′C′. Making fg equal to $f'g'$, and drawing $a\,g$, $a\,g$ is the revolved position of the intersection of the bases of the cones. If a circle be described on EF as a diameter, it will be the base of the cone whose vertex is (B,B′) in its revolved position. The intersection of the cones' bases intersects this circle in the points d'' and c''; these are the revolved positions of the points in which it pierces the surface of the sphere. Making the counter revolution about EF, the points d'' and c'' describe arcs of vertical circles about the axis, and are horizontally projected at d and c. Since these points are in the base of the cone whose vertex is (D,D′), they are vertically projected at the points d' and c'. A plane drawn tangent to the sphere, through either of the points, will contain the given line; and conversely, a plane drawn through either of the points and the given line, will be tangent to the sphere. The lines Cc, C′c' are the projections of the radius of the sphere passing through the point (c,c').

But the horizontal trace of the tangent plane must pass through A, the point in which the given line pierces the horizontal plane, and be perpendicular to Cc; therefore AN, drawn perpendicular to Cc, is the horizontal trace of the plane tangent to the sphere at the point (c,c'). The point I, at which the given line pierces the vertical plane, is a point of the vertical trace; hence IP, drawn perpendicular to C′c', is the vertical trace of the plane which contains the given line, and touches the sphere at the point (c,c').

The second plane, which is tangent to the sphere at the point (d,d'), is determined in another way, thus: through the point (d,d') let a line be drawn parallel to the given line; its projections are parallel to the projections of the given line (30), and it pierces the horizontal plane of projection at the point Q; AQ is therefore the horizontal trace, and IMV the vertical trace of the second tangent plane to the sphere which contains the given line. The projections of the radius passing through the point (d,d') should be respectively perpendicular to these traces.

§ 116. If the centre of the sphere were placed in the ground line, and the points at which the given line pierces the planes of projection taken for the vertices of the tangent cones, the construction would not differ materially from the one already made. Let the construction be made when the sphere has this position.

§ 117. *Second method by which the points of contact may be determined.* If through the given line we conceive two planes to be passed tangent to the sphere, a plane drawn through the centre of the sphere and perpendicular to these tangent planes will be perpendicular to their intersection; that is, to the given line. The perpendicular plane will also contain the radii drawn through the points of contact, will intersect the sphere in a great circle, and the tangent planes in two lines tangent to this circle. The tangent lines will intersect at the point in which the perpendicular plane is pierced by the intersection of the tangent planes; that is, where it is pierced by the given line.

If, therefore, through the centre of the sphere a plane be passed perpendicular to the given line, and the point in which it cuts the given line determined, and through this point two lines be drawn tangent to the great circle in which the plane intersects the sphere, they will be lines of the required tangent planes; the points in which they touch the circle are the points at which the required planes will be tangent to the sphere.

Pl. 10. Fig. 2. Let C and C′ be the projections of the centre of a sphere; (AF, A′F′) the given line. First, to draw the plane through the centre of the sphere, and find the point at which it is pierced by the given line. Since the required plane through the centre of the sphere is to be perpendicular to the given line, it will be perpendicular to both the projecting planes of the line. Through the centre (C,C′) let two lines be drawn, one perpendicular to the plane which projects the given line on the horizontal plane, the other perpendicular to the plane which projects the given line on the vertical plane; these are lines of the required plane, and determine its position (20). The two points in which they pierce the plane that projects the given line on the horizontal plane, determine the intersection of this projecting plane with the plane through the centre of the sphere; and the point in which this intersection meets the given line, is the point in which the given line pierces the plane through the centre of the sphere.

The line CD, perpendicular to AD, is the horizontal projection of the line drawn through the centre (C,C′), and perpendicular to the plane which projects the given line (AF, A′F′) on the horizontal plane. The line C′D′ is the vertical projection of this line, and (D,D′) is the point at which it pierces the projecting plane.

The line drawn through (C,C′) perpendicular to the plane which projects the line (AF, A′F′) on the vertical plane, being parallel to the vertical plane, CE is its horizontal projection, and E is the horizontal projection of the point in which it pierces the plane which projects the given line (AF, A′F′) on the horizontal plane. The vertical projection of this line is found by drawing through C′ the line C′E′ perpendicular to A′F′; the point E′, in which this projection intersects the perpendicular to the ground line through E, is the vertical projection of the point in which the second line through (C,C′) pierces the plane which projects the line (AF, A′F′) on the horizontal plane. Therefore D′E′ is the vertical projection of the line in which the plane drawn through the centre of the sphere intersects the projecting plane of the line (AF, A′F′). This intersection meets (AF, A′F′) in the point (F,F′); hence (F,F′) is the point at which the plane through the centre of the sphere cuts the given line. Let the perpendicular plane be revolved about (CD, C′D′), its intersection with the horizontal plane passing through the centre of the sphere, till it coincides with this plane. The circle in which the plane intersects the sphere becoming parallel to the horizontal plane, is projected into the circle whose centre is C: the point (F,F′) falls at G; DG being made equal to F′g′, the hypothenuse of a triangle whose base Ig′ is equal to DF. From the point G draw the two tangents GNO″ and GL″: O″ and L″ are the revolved positions of the points of contact. In the counter revolution of the plane, the point N remains fixed, the point O″ describes the arc of a circle perpendicular to the axis, the point G returns to the point (F,F′), FNO is the horizontal projection of the tangent, and O is the horizontal projection of the point of contact. The point F is vertically projected at F′, and N at N′; hence, F′N′ is the vertical projection of the tangent line, and O′ the vertical projection of the point of contact.

To find the projections of the other point of contact. As the line GL″ does not intersect, on the paper, the axis DC about which the plane is revolved, a different construction from the one just made becomes necessary. In the line GL″ take any point, as h'', and draw the line Dh''; and note the point k'' in which Dh'' intersects the line GO″. In the counter revolution the point k'' describes the arc of a circle perpendicular to CD, and when the revolution is completed, is horizontally projected at k; and since D remains fixed, Dkh is the horizontal projection of the line which passed through h'' and k'' In the counter revolution the point h'' describes the arc of a circle of which $h''h$ is the horizontal projection. Hence h is the horizontal projection of h'' when it is revolved into its true place; FhL is then the horizontal projection of the tangent GL″, and L is the horizontal projection of the point of contact. The vertical projection of the point of which k is the horizontal, must be found in the line O′F′, and also in a perpendicular from k to the ground line; hence it is at k'. Since the point of which D is the horizontal projection is vertically projected at D′, D′$k'h'$ is the vertical projection of the line of which Dkh is the horizontal projection. Drawing from h a perpendicular to the ground line determines h', the vertical projection of the point of which h is the horizontal projection. The line F′h'L′ is therefore the vertical projection of the line of which FL is the horizontal projection, and L′ the vertical projection of the point of contact determined by the tangent (FL, F′L′).

The methods of constructing the tangent planes after the points of contact are found, have already been shown. If the centre of the sphere were taken in the ground line, the construction would be similar in every respect to the one already given.

§ 118. If we suppose a cylinder, having its axis parallel to the given line, to be drawn tangent to the sphere, the curve of contact will be a great circle whose plane is perpendicular to the axis of the cylinder or given line. If two planes be drawn through the given line and tangent to the cylinder (102), they will also be tangent to the sphere. The point at which the given line pierces the plane of the circle of contact of the cylinder and sphere, is the point from which the tangent lines to the base of the cylinder are drawn; for this point is common to the traces, on the base of the cylinder, of both the tangent planes. If the centre of the sphere be in the ground line, the construction is somewhat simplified, and the reader will find it an interesting problem to draw the tangent planes when the sphere has this position. The general problem, to draw a plane through a given line, and tangent to a surface of revolution, is solved in the Complement.

CHAPTER VII.

OF THE INTERSECTIONS OF CURVED SURFACES AND PLANES; OF TANGENT LINES TO THE CURVES OF INTERSECTION; AND OF THE DEVELOPMENT OF SURFACES ON PLANES.

§ 119. THE intersection of a curved surface by a plane is, in general, determined by intersecting the curved surface and plane by auxiliary planes, so chosen that the lines in which they intersect the surface and plane shall intersect each other; the points in which the right lines cut out of the plane intersect the curves cut out of the surface, will be points of the intersection of the surface and plane. The auxiliary planes should be so taken as to intersect the surface in its most simple elements, recollecting that the right line is a more simple element than the circle, and the circle than either of the conic sections.

§ 120. A tangent line to the curve of intersection of a plane and surface is contained in the plane of the curve (67); it is also contained in the tangent plane to the surface at the point (88): hence it is the intersection of these planes. If therefore, it be required to draw a line tangent to the curve of intersection of a plane and surface, we have only *to draw a plane tangent to the surface at the point, and determine its intersection with the cutting plane.*

§ 121. A plane being tangent to the surface of a cylinder along one of its rectilinear elements (87), if the cylinder be rolled on this plane, it will continue to be tangent to it, and the consecutive right-lined elements will successively come into contact with the plane. When it has rolled once over, every element, that is, the whole surface of the cylinder, will have been in contact with the plane. The portion of the plane touched during the revolution is equal to the surface of the cylinder, and is called *the development of that surface.*

§ 122. A plane is tangent to a cone along a right-lined element. If the vertex of the cone remain fixed, and the cone be rolled around on its tangent plane, its elements will successively coincide with the plane; and after they shall all have coincided, the part of the plane included between the extreme lines is called the development of the surface of the cone.

§ 123. If we suppose the cylinder and cone to be limited by planes, the curves in which these planes intersect the surfaces become lines on the developments of the surfaces.

§ 124. Double-curved surfaces cannot be developed. For, as a plane touches a double-curved surface in a point, if the surface be rolled around on its tangent plane, its successive contacts will form a line; hence, the surface will not develop itself on a plane. There exists, therefore, this striking difference between single-curved surfaces and double-curved surfaces: *the former can be developed on a plane; the latter cannot.* This difference has been made, by some authors, the basis of classification of curved surfaces; arranging into one class the developable surfaces, and those which are not developable into another.

PROBLEM XXVI.

To find the intersection of a plane with the surface of a right cylinder having a circular base; to draw a tangent line to this curve at any point; to find the curve and its tangent in their own plane; and to develop the cylindrical surface.

§ 125. Pl. 11. Fig. 1. Let the horizontal plane be taken perpendicular to the axis of the cylinder, and the vertical plane of projection at right angles to the cutting plane. The circle A*g*B*f* is the horizontal projection of the cylinder; E′A′B′*b*′ is its vertical projection, and (DE, DE′) is the intersecting plane.

Let the surface of the cylinder and the cutting plane be intersected by a system of auxiliary planes parallel to the axis of the cylinder and perpendicular to the vertical plane: FC, *a b*, *f g*, and *k h* are the horizontal traces of such planes. These planes intersect the plane (DE, DE′) in lines which are perpendicular to the vertical plane at the points D′, *d*′, &c.; the points in which these lines intersect the elements cut out of the surface of the cylinder are points of the curve of intersection. Since the cylinder is a right one, and the curve sought lies on its surface, the curve is horizontally projected into the circle A*g*B*f*; but, as FC is the horizontal projection of the line which is perpendicular to the vertical plane at D′, the points *n* and C are the horizontal projections of two points of the required curve, and D′ is their vertical projection. The points *a*, *b*, *f*, *g*, *k*, and *h* are the horizontal projections of other points of the curve determined in the same manner; their vertical projections are seen by inspecting the figure. Let the plane AB be drawn through the axis of the cylinder and perpendicular to the cutting plane: it intersects the cutting plane in a line which divides the curve symmetrically; this line, therefore, passes through the centre, and is, furthermore, the longest diameter of the curve: it is called the transverse axis, and the points (A,E′) and (B,G) in which it meets the curve, the vertices of the transverse axis.

Plate 10.

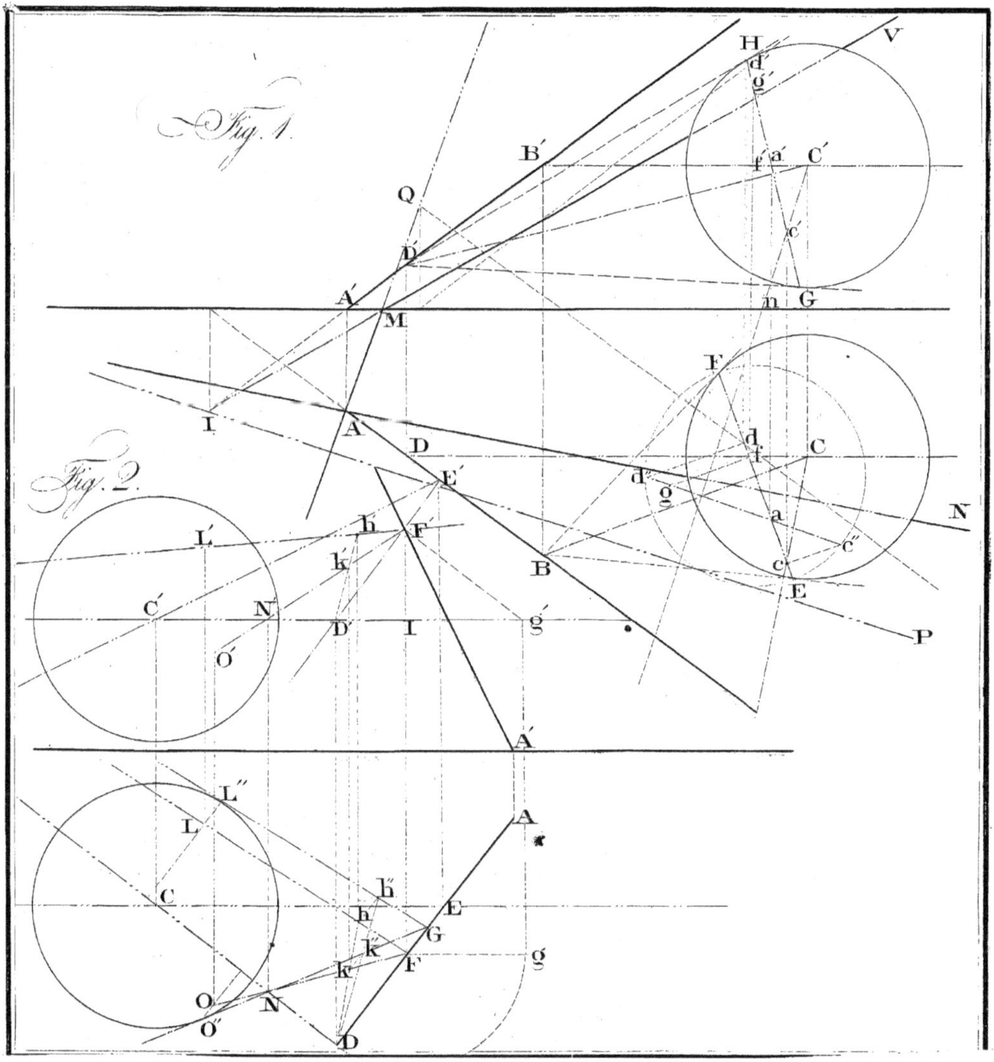

Fig. 1.

Fig. 2.

To draw a tangent line to this curve at any point, as (C,D′) Pass a plane tangent to the cylinder along the element containing the point (C,D′); the intersection of this tangent plane and the cutting plane is the tangent line required (120). The line NC is the horizontal trace of the tangent plane; it is also the horizontal projection of the tangent line, and N′D′ is its vertical projection.

To find the curve in its own plane. Let the plane of the curve be revolved around the transverse axis till it becomes parallel to the vertical plane; it will, from this position, be projected on the vertical plane in its true dimensions. The vertices (B,G) and (A,E′) remain fixed, being in the axis; the points (C,D′), (*n*,D′), (*b*,*d*′), (*a*,*d*′), &c., continue at their respective distances, DC, D*n*, *d b*, and *d a*, from the axis; therefore, making n the vertical plane the lines D′C′, D′*n*′, *d*′*b*′, and *d*′*a*′ respectvely equal to these lines determines points of the curve. Having found a sufficient number of points, let the curve be described through them; this curve is the curve of intersection of the cylinder and plane. The tangent line to the curve at the point (C,D′) intersects the transverse axis produced at (N,N′); and as this point remains fixed during the revolution, the tangent line assumes the position N′C′.

To develop the surface of the cylinder, suppose it to be so placed on the plane of the paper that the element (A, A′E′) shall have the position AE′ (Fig. 1. *n*); the plane of the paper will then be tangent to the cylinder along this element. Let the cylinder be divided into two equal parts, by a plane passing through the element of contact and perpendicular to the plane of the paper; and let one half of the cylinder be rolled out towards B′, the other towards B. The base of the cylinder being perpendicular to the plane of the paper, its circumference will be developed into the right line BAB′. From the point A lay off A*k* equal to the arc A*k* on the base of the cylinder, and at the point *k* erect a perpendicular to BB′ equal to the height above the horizontal plane of that point of the curve which is horizontally projected at *k*. Making *kf* equal to the arc *kf*, *fa* *fa*, *an*=*an*, *n*B′=*n*B, and laying off on the other side of the point A the distances A*h*, *h g*, &c., respectively equal to the corresponding arcs on the base of the cylinder, erecting at all these points perpendiculars to the line BB′, making these perpendiculars equal to their corresponding elements, and drawing a curve through their extremities, gives the curve of intersection on the development.

To find the position of the tangent line. When the point C comes into the line BB′, the element through C comes into the plane of the paper. But the plane of the paper being constantly tangent to the cylinder, the tangent plane through any element will coincide with the plane of the paper at the moment the element comes in contact with it. But the subtangent N″C, being perpendicular to the element through C, falls in the line BB′ when the element through C comes into the plane of the paper. But the tangent line pierces the plane of the base of the cylinder at N″; therefore, laying off CN equal to CN″ and drawing NC, determines the tangent line on the development.

§ 126. If a right line be tangent to a curve in space, and the curve be developed on a plane, the line will be tangent to the developed curve. For, suppose the surface of a cylinder to be passed through the given curve: the right line being tangent to the curve, passes through two consecutive points (65), and the elements of the cylinder passing through these points are also consecutive; when the surface of the cylinder is developed, these elements are consecutive lines, their extremities are consecutive points of the developed curve, and a right line passing through these points is tangent to the curve. But this line occupies the position which the tangent line in space assumes, since it passes through the two points which fix the position of the tangent in space.

§ 127. The surface of any right cylinder may be developed in the same way as we have developed the right cylinder with a circular base. For, the plane of the base being perpendicular to the tangent plane on which the development is made, the base of the surface will be developed into a right line; and by laying off on this right line parts of the base equal to the distances between the elements, we shall obtain the development of the surface.

§ 128. The finding a right line equal to the length of a given curve is called *the rectification of the curve.* In rectifying a curve we cannot, of course, take the exact lengths of the small arcs, but must use their chords instead of them. The smaller the arcs are taken, the nearer will the chords coincide with them, and, consequently the nearer will the right line, which is the sum of these small chords, be equal to the length of the curve which it is taken to represent.

PROBLEM XXVII.

To find the intersection of a plane with the surface of a right cone having a circular base; to draw a tangent line to the curve; to find the curve in its own plane; and to develop the surface of the cone.

§ 129. Pl. 11. Fig. 2. Let (C,C′) be the vertex of the cone; FPEI the horizontal projection of the cone; C′P′Q′ its vertical projection; and (AB, AB′) the cutting plane to which the vertical plane of projection is taken at right angles.

Let the cone and plane be intersected by a system of planes through the vertex and perpendicular to the vertical plane of projection: they will intersect the cone in right-lined elements, and the cutting plane in right lines; the intersections of these latter lines with the elements are points of the curve. Let C′D be assumed for the vertical trace of one of these planes; DF, perpendicular to the ground line, is its horizontal trace (31); this trace intersects the circumference of the cone's base in the points E and F; CF and CE are the horizontal projections of the elements in which the plane intersects the surface of the cone, and C′D is their vertical projection. The line in which the auxiliary plane intersects the cutting plane (AB, AB′) being perpendicular to the vertical plane, is vertically projected at f', and fg is its horizontal projection. The points g and f

in which the horizontal projection of this line intersects the horizontal projections of the elements before found, are the horizontal projections of two points of the required curve, and f' is their vertical projection. The points (n,m'), (m,m'), (G,G′), &c. are found in a similar manner. The plane PaCb, perpendicular to the cutting plane and containing the axis of the cone, determines the transverse axis of the curve (ab, $a'b'$); the points (a,a') and (b,b') are the vertices of the axis. Having determined as many points as are necessary, let the curve $a\,g\,b\,n$ be described through them: this is the horizontal projection of the required curve, and $a'b'$ is its vertical projection.

To draw a tangent line to the curve at any point, as (G,G′). Let a plane be drawn tangent to the cone along the right-lined element, passing through the point (G,G′). The line NI, drawn tangent to the base of the cone, is the horizontal trace of the tangent plane; N is one point in which the latter plane intersects the cutting plane, and (G,G′) is another point: hence NG is the horizontal projection of the tangent line, and its vertical projection is AB′, the vertical trace of the cutting plane.

To find the curve and tangent in their own plane. Let the plane of the curve be revolved about its vertical trace till it coincides with the vertical plane: the points of the curve will fall at their respective distances from the axis (10); that is, the distances of their horizontal projections from the ground line (13). Drawing through the points b' and a' perpendiculars to AB′, layingoff $b'b''$ and $a'a''$ respectively equal to the distances of the points b and a from the ground line, determines the positions of the vertices and of the transverse axis after the plane of the curve is revolved to coincide with the vertical plane. In the same manner the points n', f'', g' and m'' are determined; and through these points the curve is described. The position of the tangent is easily found; for the point N falls at N′, and joining this point with G″ determines the tangent line N′G″.

To develop the surface of the cone, and trace on the development the curve in which it is intersected by the plane (AB, AB′). Let the development be made on the plane which is tangent to the cone along the element (CP, C′P′). Suppose the cone to be placed on the plane of the paper, the vertex at C (Fig. 2. *n*), the point (P,P′) at P; the plane of the paper is then tangent to the cone along the element (CP, C′P′). Let us suppose the cone to be divided by a plane passing through this element of contact perpendicular to the plane of the paper, and let one half of it be developed from P towards Q′, the other from P towards Q. As all points of the circumference of the base are equidistant from the vertex, they will in the development be equidistant from the point C, and will consequently be found in the circumference of a circle described with the centre C and radius CP, equal to C′P′ the slant height of the cone. Let a part of this circle be described. From P lay off PE equal to the arc PE of the base of the cone; also Eh'=Eh', $h'k$=$h'k'$, kQ=k'Q; and on the other side of the point P lay off PF equal to the arc PF of the base of the cone, Fh=Fh, hI=hI, IQ′=IQ. Through C and the extremities of these arcs let lines be drawn; these lines are the several positions which the elements of the cone take on the development of its surface.

To trace the curve. If the distance of each point of the curve from the vertex of the cone be ascertained and laid off from the point C, the curve traced through these points will be the curve required. On the element CP lay off Ca=C′a'; on CF, Cf=C′r; on Ch, Cn=C′p; on CI, CG=C′q; on CQ′, Cb=C′b': lay off equal distances on the corresponding elements on the other side of CP; the curve bGnb, drawn through these points, is the curve sought.

To find the position of the tangent line. The line IN (Fig. 2) is perpendicular to the element of the cone passing through (G,G′); and when this element takes the position CGI (Fig. 2. *n*) on the development of the surface, the tangent plane becomes the plane of the paper, and the line IN (Fig. 2) preserving its position with CI, is tangent to the curve Q′PQ; hence, if we make NI=NI, and join N and G, GN will be the tangent line.

§ 130. The curves described in the note to Art. 63, and named conic sections, can be obtained by intersecting a right cone with a circular base by planes having different positions with its elements. If the cutting plane be oblique to the plane of the base, but intersect all the elements on the same nappe, as in the last example, the curve will be an ellipse. If the plane be parallel to one of the elements, the curve of intersection is a parabola. If it make a greater angle with the plane of the base than the elements of the cone make with the base, it will intersect both nappes of the surface, and the curves are opposite hyperbolas. To prove that these curves have the same properties as those described in the note to Art. 63 belongs rather to Conic Sections than to Descriptive Geometry.

PROBLEM XXVIII.

To find the intersection of a plane with the surface of a cylinder, the plane and cylinder having any position with each other and with the planes of projection; to draw a tangent line to the curve; and to find the curve in its own plane.

§ 131. Pl. 12. Fig. 1. Let the ellipse BGDC be the base of the cylinder. Let ABCDE be the horizontal projection of the cylinder, and A′C′B″E′ its vertical projection, and (DF, DF′) the cutting plane.

If the cylinder be intersected by a system of auxiliary planes parallel to the axis, they will intersect the surface of the cylinder in right-lined elements, and the cutting plane in right lines; the points in which these lines intersect are points of the required curve. To render the construction as simple as possible, let the auxiliary planes be taken perpendicular to the horizontal plane. Let F″*n*″ be the horizontal trace and F′F″ the vertical trace of one of these planes; F′*f*′ is the vertical projection of its intersection with the cutting plane (DF, DF′). But the right-lined elements in which this auxiliary plane intersects the surface of the cylinder pierce the horizontal plane at *h* and *g*; projecting these points on the vertical plane at *h*′ and *g*′, and drawing through *h*′ and *g*′ parallels to the vertical projection of the axis of the cylinder determines the vertical projections

Plate 11.

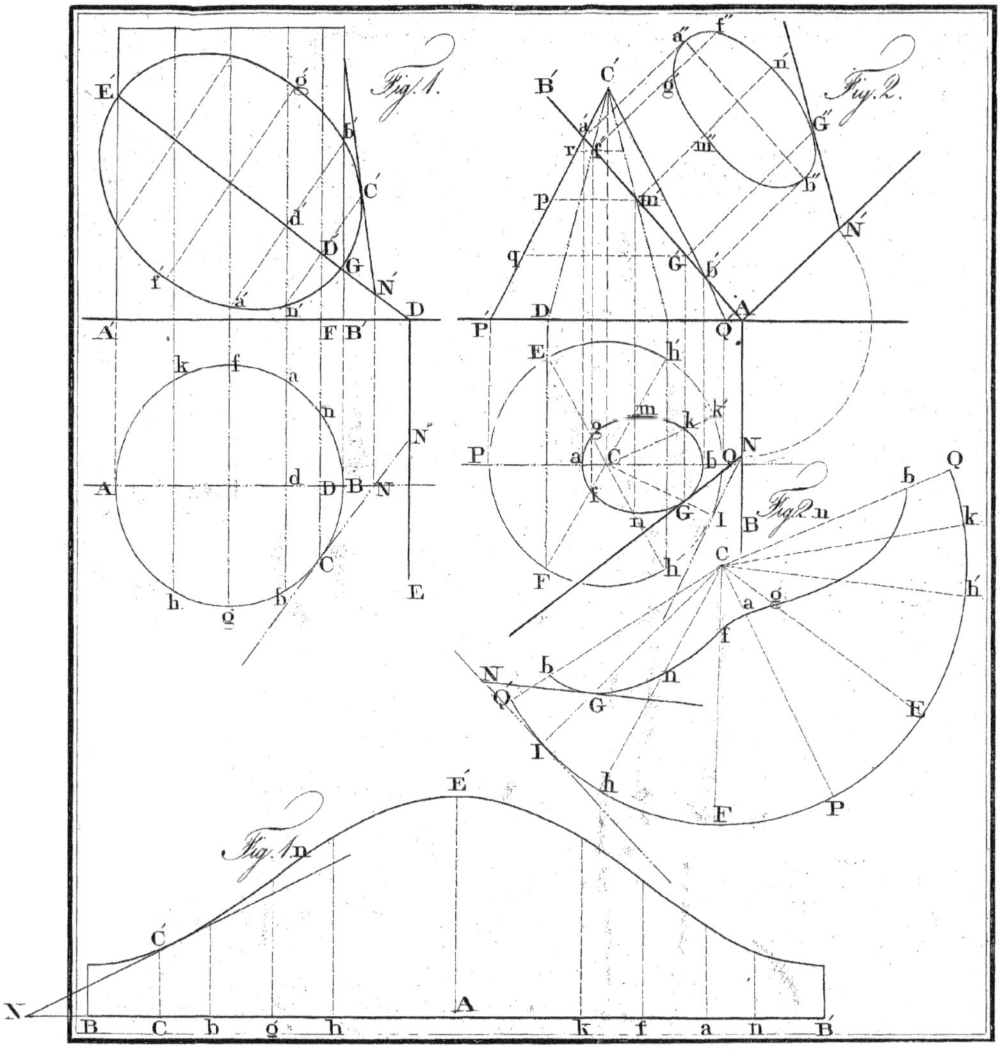

Fig. 1.

Fig. 2.

Fig. 2 n

Fig. 1 n

of these elements; the points n', k', in which they intersect the line $F'f'$, are the vertical projections, and n and k the horizontal projections of the two points of the required curve which are determined by the vertical auxiliary plane $F''n''$. If another auxiliary plane, as $o''C$, be passed, it will intersect the cutting plane (DF, DF') in a line parallel to ($F''f$, $F'f'$); the vertical projection of this intersection is, therefore, parallel to $F'f'$; and the same for all intersections determined by vertical auxiliary planes. The points (o,o'), (m,m') are determined by the plane $o''C$.

The part of the curve which is made full in horizontal projection, is the part which lies above the elements of contact of the tangent planes which are perpendicular to the horizontal plane; and the part of the curve which is made full in vertical projection, is the part which lies on the surface of the cylinder in front of the elements of contact of the tangent planes which are perpendicular to the vertical plane. The points at which the full part of the curve terminates and the dotted part begins, in either projection, are readily found by drawing auxiliary planes through the elements of the surface which contain these points. The points (o,o') and (p,p') are determined by drawing auxiliary planes through the elements (Co'', C'A') and (BA, B'I).

To draw a tangent line to the curve at any point, as (m,m'). Draw a tangent plane to the cylinder along the element passing through the point (m,m'); LG is its horizontal trace, and Hm the horizontal projection of its intersection with the cutting plane (DF, DF'), and consequently, the horizontal projection of the tangent line to the curve at the point (m,m') (120). The line $H'm'$ is the vertical projection of this tangent, and both its projections are respectively tangent to the projections of the curve.

To find the curve and its tangent in their own plane. Let the plane of the curve be revolved about its horizontal trace DF till it coincides with the horizontal plane; find where the different points of the curve fall, and the curve described through these points will be the curve in its own plane. In the example we are considering, the trace FD is perpendicular to the horizontal projection of the axis of the cylinder; so that, after the revolution of the cutting plane, the points of the curve will be found in the traces of the auxiliary planes. The point (n,n'), for example, is found at n'', a distance from the point f equal to the hypothenuse of a triangle whose base is fn, and whose perpendicular is equal to the altitude of the point above the horizontal plane. The point (k,k') is found at k'', the point (m,m') at m'', and so for other points. The point H of the tangent line remains fixed, being in the axis; Hm'' is the revolved position of the tangent line.

If the trace DF were not perpendicular to the horizontal projections of the elements of the cylinder, we could determine the curve in its own plane thus; find the position of the point (F'',F') after the cutting plane shall have been revolved to coincide with the horizontal plane, and join this point with the point f; this line would be the revolved position of the intersection of one of the auxiliary planes with the cutting plane; and since all such intersections are parallel, they will be parallel after they are revolved. Take any one of the points, as q, in which the trace of an auxiliary plane intersects the trace of the cutting plane; through this point draw a parallel to the revolved position of the intersection of the auxiliary and cutting plane which passes through the point f; from o and m let perpendiculars be drawn to the trace FD: the points in which they intersect the line through q are the points of the curve in its own plane.

If it were required to develop the surface of this cylinder it would be necessary, first, to intersect it by a plane perpendicular to the axis; a right cylinder would thus be formed the surface of which could be developed as in Art. 125; and any curve resulting from the intersection of a plane with the surface of the cylinder could be traced on the development, as in Prob. 26.

PROBLEM XXIX.

To find the intersection of a plane with the surface of a cone, the plane and cone having any position with each other and with the planes of projection; to draw a tangent line to the curve: and to find the curve in its own plane.

§ 132. Pl. 12. Fig. 2. Let V*b*CA be the horizontal and V′C′B′ the vertical projection of the cone, and (DI,DE) the cutting plane.

If the cone be intersected by a system of planes through its vertex, these planes will intersect the surface in right-lined elements, and the cutting plane in right lines; the points in which these lines intersect the elements are points of the required curve. We will take the system of planes through the vertex perpendicular to the horizontal plane; all the planes will then intersect each other in a line perpendicular to the horizontal plane; and the point in which this line pierces the cutting plane (DI, DE) is a point common to the traces of all the auxiliary planes on this intersecting plane. To find this point. The projecting line of the vertex (V,V′) pierces the cutting plane (DI, DE) in a point of which V is the horizontal projection; the vertical projection of the point is V″ (43): hence (V,V″) is the point through which the traces of the auxiliary planes pass. Take VF for the horizontal trace of one of the auxiliary planes; the elements in which it intersects the surface of the cone, as well as the line in which it intersects the plane (DI, DE), are horizontally projected into the trace VF; V′C′, V′*q*′ are the vertical projections of the elements, and V″F′ is the vertical projection of the intersection of the planes; hence *f*′ and *d*′ are the vertical projections, and *f* and *d* the horizontal projections of the points in which the intersection of the planes meets the elements of the cone: hence (*f*,*f*′) and (*d*,*d*′) are two points of the curve. By taking any other plane, the points of the curve which it would determine are found in the same manner The points

a and c, where the part of the curve which is made full in horizontal projection joins the part which is dotted, are constructed as in the cylinder, by taking auxiliary planes tangent to the surface. The part of the curve which is to be made full in the vertical projection is limited by the elements (VC, V′C′) and (VB,V′B′); the points f' and g' are determined by the auxiliary planes through these elements. The portion of the curve which lies on the front part of the cone is made full, the other dotted.

To draw a tangent line to any point of the curve, as (h,h'). Draw a tangent plane to the cone along the element passing through this point: Ik is its horizontal trace, and Ih is the horizontal projection of its intersection with the cutting plane; for, I is the point in which the traces of the planes intersect, and both the planes pass through the point (h,h'). The vertical projection of the tangent is found by projecting the point I into the vertical plane at I′ and drawing I′h'.

To find the curve in its own plane. Let the plane of the curve be revolved around its horizontal trace DI till it coincides with the horizontal plane. The point (V,V″) falls at v; and, as the intersections of the auxiliary planes and the plane (DI, DE) pass through the point (V,V″), they will, when revolved, pass through the point v. But the points in which the intersections meet the trace DI remain fixed; therefore, the revolved positions of these intersections are easily drawn. The line Fv is the revolved position of the intersection of the plane (DI, DE) and the auxiliary plane VF. But as the points of the curve revolve in planes perpendicular to the axis of revolution (11), the intersections f'' and d'', of the perpendiculars ff'' and $d\,d''$ with the line Fv, are points of the curve when its plane is revolved to coincide with the horizontal plane. The points h'', c'', g'', and a'' are determined in the same manner. The line Ih'' is the position of the tangent line when the plane of the curve is revolved to coincide with the horizontal plane.

§ 133. These points might also be determined by the general method of finding the hypothenuse of a triangle whose base is the distance from the horizontal projection of the point to the

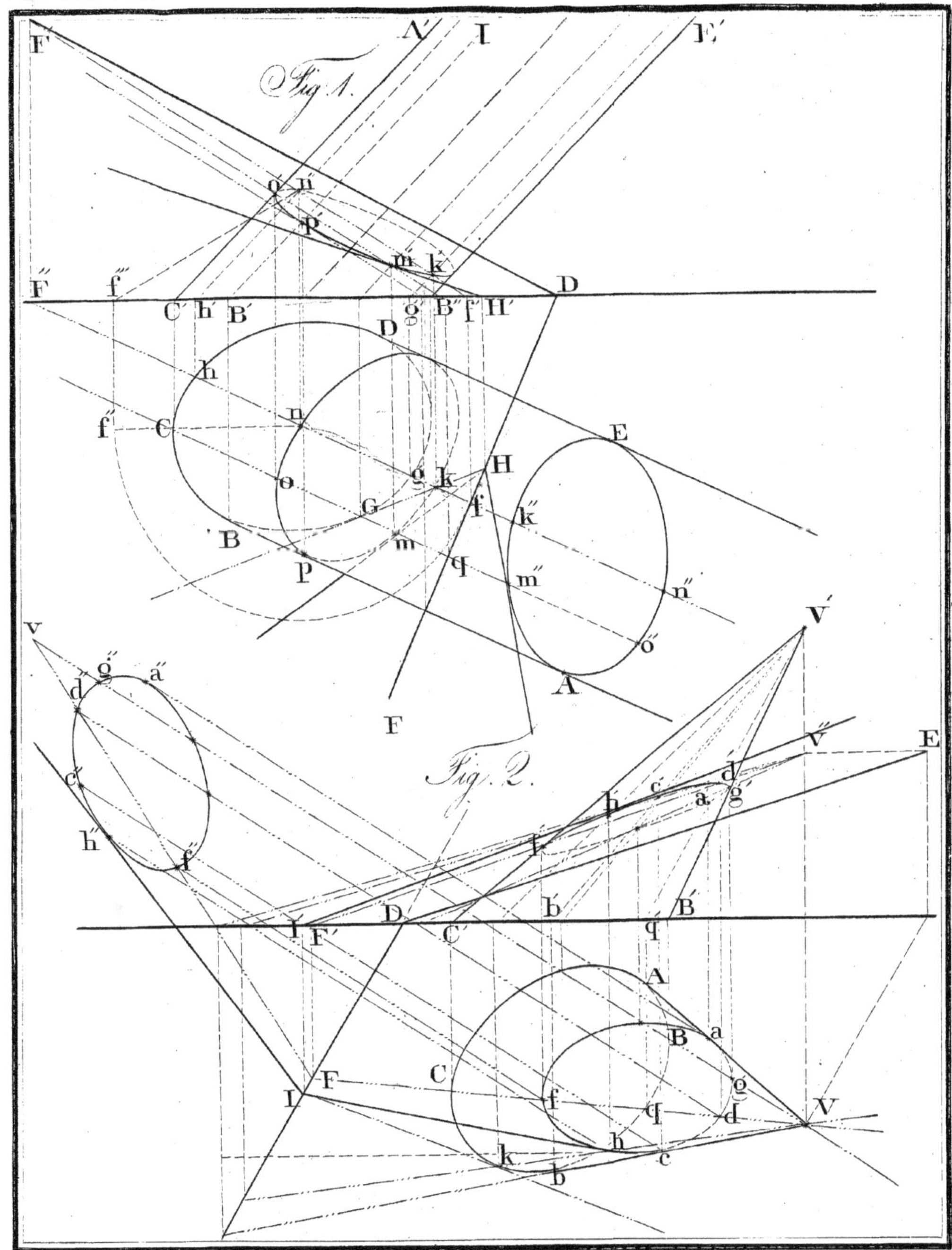
Fig. 1.
Fig. 2.

axis, and perpendicular, the altitude of the point above the horizontal plane, and then laying off these several distances from the axis on the perpendiculars drawn through the horizontal projections of the several points.

§ 134. The surface of this cone cannot be developed by the method used in Prob. 27 to develop the surface of a right cone with a circular base. For the lengths of the elements, measured from the vertex to the base, are unequal: hence, the curve of the base traced on the development will not be a circle; therefore, the positions of the different elements cannot be determined as in Prob. 27. The manner of making this development will be shown hereafter.

PROBLEM XXX.

To find the intersection of a plane and surface of revolution; to draw a tangent line to the curve; and to find the curve in its own plane.

§ 135. Pl. 13. Let the surface to be intersected be the surface of an ellipsoid. Let the horizontal plane of projection be taken perpendicular to the axis; let A be its horizontal and A′B its vertical projection. The circle whose centre is A and radius Ag is the horizontal projection of the surface, the ellipse A′F′BG is its vertical projection, and (CD, CD′) is the cutting plane.

If a system of horizontal planes be drawn, they will intersect the surface in horizontal circles; and the cutting plane (CD, CD′) in lines parallel to its horizontal trace; the points in which these lines and circles intersect are points of the required curve.

The transverse axis of any curve resulting from the intersection of a plane and surface of revolution is *the line of intersection of the cutting plane, and the meridian plane perpendicular to it;* the points in which this line pierces the surface are the vertices of the transverse axis, or vertices of the curve. First, to find the axis and vertices. The line AE, drawn at right angles to CD, is the horizontal trace of the meridian plane perpendicular to the cutting plane. The intersection of these two planes pierces the horizontal plane at E, and intersects the axis of the surface at the point in which the axis pierces the cutting plane (CD, CD′); that is, at the point of which A″ is the vertical projection (43): therefore, E′A″ is the vertica projection of the intersection of the planes; the horizontal projection is the trace AE. To find the points in which this line intersects the surface, let the meridian plane AE be revolved about the axis of the surface till it becomes parallel to the vertical plane. The meridian section of the surface is, from this position, projected on the vertical plane into the ellipse A′F′BG, and the line of intersection of the planes into the line E″A″; for, the point (A,A″), being in the axis, remains fixed, and the point E describes in the horizontal plane the arc EE′, and E″ is the vertical projection of E′. In this position the line of intersection pierces the meridian curve at f''' and d'''; in the counter revolution these points describe arcs of horizontal circles about the axis of the surface; and when the meridian plane takes its primitive position, are vertically projected at f' and d', and horizontally projected at f and d. Therefore (f,f') and (d,d') are the vertices of the curve, and $(fd, f'd')$ its transverse axis.

To find other points of the curve, intersect by horizontal planes, and let F′G be the vertical trace of one of them. Since the circle in which this plane intersects the surface is horizontal, its horizontal projection is an equal circle; and as its centre is in the axis of the surface, A is its horizontal projection. The point F′ is horizontally projected at F: hence AF is the horizontal projection of the radius, with which let the circle be described about the centre A. The line in which the plane F′G intersects the plane (CD, CD′) pierces the vertical plane at H′, and is parallel to the horizontal trace CD; therefore its horizontal projection Hm is parallel to the horizontal trace CD. But this horizontal projection intersects the horizontal projection of the circle in the points n and m; n and m are, therefore, two points of the horizontal projection of the curve; and n', m' are their vertical projections. In the same manner any number of points may be found. If it were required to find the points in which the curve intersects, on the surface of the ellipsoid, the circle whose plane passes through the centre, take the plane of this circle as an auxiliary plane; it determines the points (g,g') and (p,p'); the horizontal projection of the curve is tangent to the horizontal projection of the surface at the points g and p The part of the curve which lies above the horizontal plane through the centre of the ellipsoid is made full in horizontal projection; the part which lies below it is dotted. The points in which the curve determined by the plane (CD, CD′) intersects the meridian curve parallel to the vertical plane, are horizontally projected at i and h, and vertically at i' and h'; the vertical projection of the surface is tangent to the vertical projection of the curve at the points i' and h'. The part of the curve which lies in front of the meridian plane is made full in vertical projection; the part which lies behind it is dotted.

To draw a tangent line to the curve at any point, as (m,m'). Let the surface be circumscribed by a tangent cone whose vertex shall be in the axis of the surface, and whose contact with the surface shall be the horizontal circle containing the point (m,m'). The line F′G is the vertical projection of this circle. A plane tangent to the cone along the element passing through the point (m,m') will be tangent to the ellipsoid at this point, and its intersection with the cutting plane is the tangent required. The tangent line to the ellipse A′F′BG at the point F′ is the element of the cone which is parallel to the vertical plane; it pierces the horizontal plane at N; and a circle described with A as a centre, and radius AN, is the intersection of the cone and horizontal plane. The element of the cone passing through (m,m') pierces the horizontal plane at M, and PM is the horizontal trace of the tangent plane. This plane intersects the plane (CD, CD′) in the line (Pm, P′m'), which is therefore the tangent line sought.

To find the curve in its own plane. Let the plane be revolved about its vertical trace CD′ till it coincides with the vertical plane; the points will fall at their respective distances from the axis. To find the position of the horizontal trace of the plane of the curve, as also that of the tangent line, after the plane is revolved to coincide with the vertical plane, take any point of the horizontal trace, as P, and project it into the ground line at P′. Through the point P′ draw a perpendicular to D′C produced; with C as a centre, and radius CP, describe the arc PP″; CP″ is the revolved position of the trace CD. For, the point (P,P′) revolves in a plane perpendicular to the axis D′C, and continues at the same distance from the point C; therefore it must be found, after the revolution, in the perpendicular P′P″, and also in the arc PP″, and consequently at P″. The line P″m″ is the position of the tangent line in the plane of the curve.

CHAPTER VIII.

OF THE INTERSECTIONS OF CURVED SURFACES.

§ 136. The general method of determining the lines in which surfaces intersect, is to intersect them by auxiliary surfaces: these auxiliary surfaces intersect the given surfaces in lines; the points in which these lines intersect are points of the intersections of the given surfaces. The auxiliary surfaces should be of that class, and so chosen in position, that the simplest lines of section may be determined on the given surfaces; else a plain and simple problem might be rendered complex and difficult.

§ 137. A line is, in general, drawn tangent to the intersection of two surfaces at any point, by drawing two planes through the point, respectively tangent to the surfaces; the intersection of these planes is the tangent line.

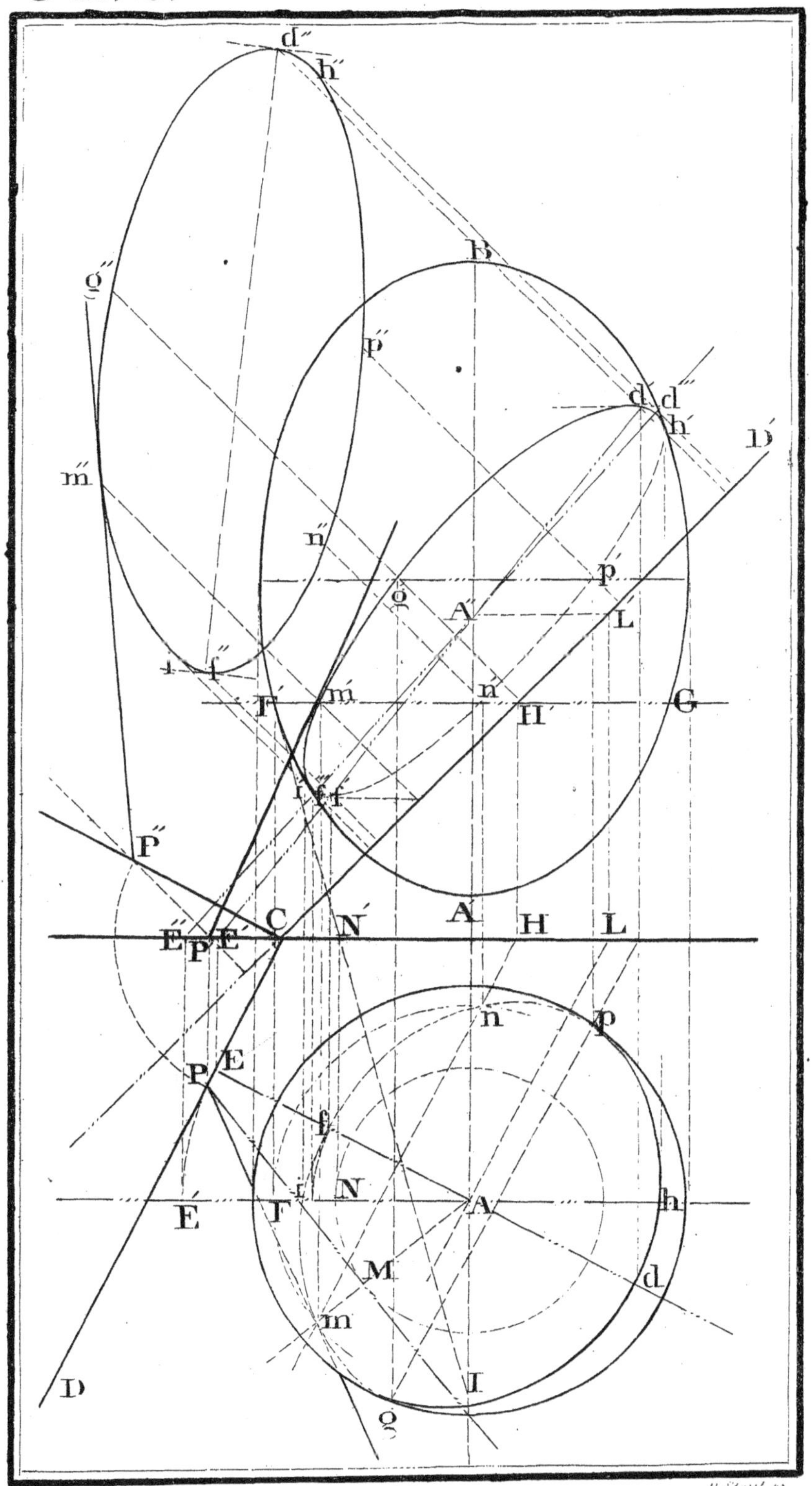

B. Stout sc

PROBLEM XXXI.

To find the intersection of the surfaces of two cylinders, and to draw a tangent line to the curve.

§ 138. Pl. 14. Let (CA′, C′D) be the axis of one cylinder, (AB, A′B′) the axis of the other. The manner of making their projections having already been explained, we will suppose them constructed as in the figure.

If through the axis of one cylinder a plane be passed parallel to the axis of the other, such plane will, if it cut the other cylinder, intersect the surfaces of both cylinders in right lines, since it is parallel to their rectilinear elements; and all planes parallel to it, if they intersect the surfaces of the cylinders, will also intersect them in right-lined elements.

Draw a plane through the axis (CA′, C′D) parallel to the axis (AB, A′B′) (58): CE is the horizontal trace of this plane; its vertical trace could be easily found, but is not used in the construction. As the system of auxiliary planes is to be parallel to this plane, their traces will be parallel to CE. The plane whose trace is ECX intersects the cylinder whose axis is (AB, A′B′) in two elements which pierce the horizontal plane at V and T; it intersects the cylinder whose axis is (CA′, C′D) in two elements which pierce the horizontal plane at M and X. Since these four elements are in the same plane, and are not parallel, they intersect each other; that is, each element of one cylinder intersects both elements of the other cylinder. The horizontal projections of these elements are respectively parallel to the horizontal projections of the axes of the cylinders, and the points *b*, *d*, *p*, and *q*, in which they intersect, are the horizontal projections of four points of the required curve. The vertical projections *b*′, *d*′, *p*′, and *q*′ are found either by projecting the elements of both cylinders on the vertical plane and determining their points of intersection, or by projecting the elements of one cylinder only and determining the points in which these projections intersect the perpendiculars to the ground line drawn through the points b, d, p, and q. By drawing lines parallel to CE, and considering them as the traces of auxiliary planes, any number of points of the curve are found in the same manner. Let the auxiliary plane RN be drawn tangent to the cylinder whose axis is (AB, A'B'); it determines two points of the curve (f,f') and (g,g'). Through the element $(fc,f'c')$ conceive a plane to be drawn tangent to the cylinder whose axis is (CA', C'D); this plane intersects the plane RN, tangent to the other cylinder, in the element $(fc.f'c')$: hence, this element is tangent to the curve of intersection of the two cylinders at the point (f,f') (137); and the projections of the element $(cf,c'f')$ are respectively tangent to the projections of the curve (90). In the same manner it may be shown, that the element $(Rg, R'g')$ is tangent to the curve of intersection of the cylinders, and that its projections Rg, $R'g'$ are tangent to the projections of the curve. If the auxiliary plane FGH be drawn tangent to the cylinder whose axis is (CA', C'D), it is easily proved that the elements $(Gz, G'z')$ and $(Ha, H'a')$ are tangent to the curve of intersection of the cylinders; and hence their projections Gz, Ha, $G'z'$, and $H'a'$ are tangent to the projections of the curve.

The surfaces of these cylinders intersect in one curve only, for, when they intersect in two curves the smaller cylinder will enter the larger in a curve returning into itself, and leave it in a curve also returning into itself. When this is the case, if two tangent planes be drawn to the lesser cylinder, parallel to the auxiliary secant planes, they will cut the larger cylinder; but if they be drawn to the larger cylinder, they will not intersect the smaller. *Hence, if two tangent planes be drawn to either cylinder, parallel to the auxiliary secant planes, and one of them cuts the other cylinder and one does not cut it, there will be but one curve of intersection. But when both the tangent planes intersect the other cylinder, or when neither of them intersects it, there will be two curves.*

As there is some difficulty in tracing this curve, and determining what part of its horizontal and what part of its vertical projection ought to be made full, and what part of each ought to be dotted, we shall examine it a little in detail. We will begin at the point (a,a'), and proceed around in the direction (q,q'), (h,h'), (f,f'), (b,b'), (z,z'), (t,x'), (d,d'), (g,g'), (p,p') and (n,n'). First, with respect to the horizontal projection. The point (a,a') is on the upper portion of the surfaces of both cylinders. At v the curve passes to the under part of the surface of the cylinder whose axis is (CA′, C′D), thence along through the points q, h, f, b, to u; at which point it returns to the upper part of the surface. From u it continues on the upper surfaces of the cylinders to t; at this point it passes to the under surface of the cylinder whose axis is (AB, A′B′), and continues on the under surface through d and g, to k'': at this point it returns to the upper surface, and passes through p, n, and a. The points v and u are determined by the auxiliary plane through S; the point t, by the plane through k; and the point k'', by the auxiliary plane passing through the element whose horizontal projection is tangent to the curve at this point. The part of the curve between u and t, as well as the part between k'' and v, is made full; the remaining portion is dotted (34). To trace the vertical projection of the curve. From b' to a point near d', the curve is made full, lying on the front portion of the surfaces of the two cylinders. At d' (determined by the auxiliary plane XE), it passes to the back surface of the cylinder whose axis is (CA′, C′D); at t' it comes to the front part of the surfaces of both cylinders, is made full to x, and dotted from x to b'.

To draw a tangent line to the curve at any point, as (h,h'). The elements of the cylinders which, by their intersection, determine this point, pierce the horizontal plane at P and s; PQ and sQ are the horizontal traces of the planes tangent to the cylinders along these elements: the intersection of these planes is the tangent line required (137); Qh is its horizontal and Q′h' its vertical projection.

PROBLEM XXXII.

To find the intersection of the surfaces of two cones, and to draw a tangent line to the curve.

§ 139. Pl. 15. Let (A,A′) and (V,V′) be the vertices of the cones; EG*a*D the base of one cone, and L*c*X*n* the base of the other.

If a system of cutting planes be drawn through the vertices of these cones, each plane will, in general, intersect each cone in two right-lined elements; the points in which these elements intersect are points common to the two surfaces. All these planes will pass through the line joining the vertices of the cones: hence, the point in which this line pierces the plane of the bases of the cones is a point common to the traces of all the auxiliary planes. Let it be remarked, that the cone whose vertex is (V,V′) intersects the upper and lower nappes of the cone whose vertex is (A,A′). The line joining the vertices of the cones pierces the horizontal plane at B; this point is common to the traces of all the auxiliary secant planes.

From B draw the two tangents B*b* and BC to the base of the cone whose vertex is (V,V′); they are the traces of two planes tangent to that cone, and V*b*, VC are the horizontal projections of the elements of contact. The plane whose trace is EB*b* intersects the cone whose vertex is (A,A′) in two elements of which A*ad* and EA*g* are the horizontal projections; and the points *d* and *g*, in which they intersect V*b*, are the horizontal projections of two points of the required curves; *d* belongs to the lower and *g* to the upper nappe of the cone whose vertex is (A,A′). The plane whose horizontal trace is *t*BC intersects the cone whose vertex is (A,A′) in two elements of which *t*A*h* and A*f*D are the horizontal projections; and the points *f* and *h*, in which they intersect VC, are the horizontal projections of two points of the required curves; the point *f* belongs to the lower and the point · to the upper nappe of the cone whose

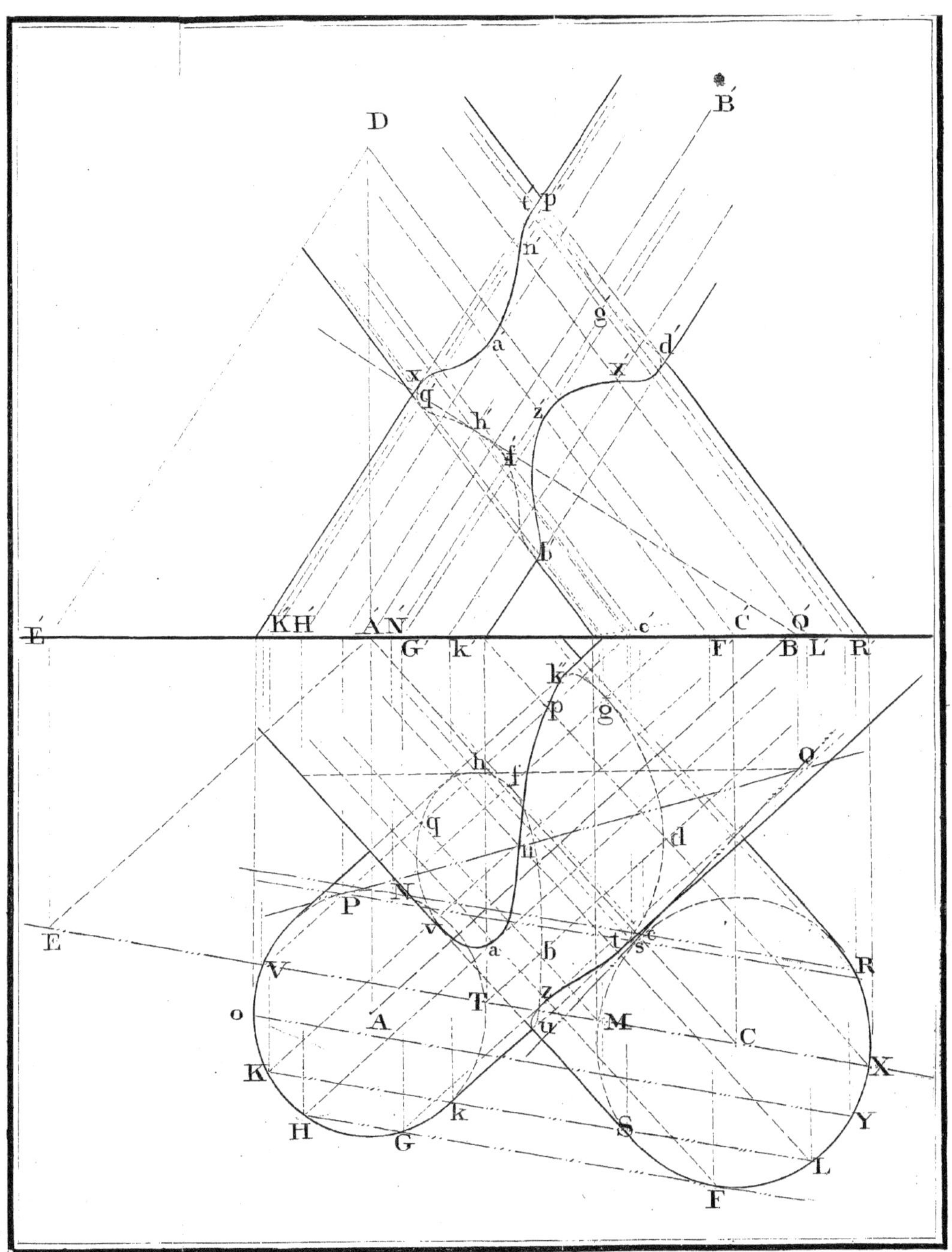
B′
D
t′ p′
n′
g′
a′
d′
x′
x′
q′
h′
z′
f′
b′
E′
K′ H′
A′ N′
G′
k′
c′
C′
Q′
F′
B′ L′
R′
k
p
g
h
f
Q
q
d
n
N
P
E
v
a
b
t s c
R
V
T
z
o
A
u
M
C
X
K
k
Y
H
G
S
L
F

vertex is (A,A′). The vertical projections of the elements in which the plane whose trace is E*Bb* intersects the cone whose vertex is (A,A′), are the lines E′A′*g*′ and A′*a*′*d*′; and *d*′ and *g*′ are the vertical projections of the points determined by this plane. Drawing perpendiculars to the ground line through the points *f* and *h*, and projecting on the vertical plane the elements which pierce the horizontal plane at D and *t*, determines the vertical projections of the two points of the curve contained in the plane whose trace is *t*BC. Thus, four points of the curves (*h*,*h*′), (*f*,*f*′), (*g*,*g*′), and (*d*,*d*′) are found.

The elements of the cone whose vertex is (A,A′) that pass through these points, are tangent to the intersections of the cones. For, through either of them, as the element (*h*A, *h*′A′), conceive a plane to be passed tangent to the cone whose vertex is (A,A′); this tangent plane intersects the plane tangent to the other cone along the element whose horizontal projection is VC, in the element (*h*A, *h*′A′): hence, this element is tangent to the curve of intersection of the cones (137); consequently, its projections are respectively tangent to the projections of the curve (90), and the same may be shown for each of the other elements.

The auxiliary plane xBL determines the points (*u*,*u*′) and (*s*,*s*′) in the lower curve, and the points (Q,Q′) and (M,M′) in the upper. Thus every auxiliary plane which intersects both cones determines two points of each curve. The lower curve intersects the horizontal plane at the points *c* and *n*. As we do not use the upper nappe of the cone whose vertex is (V,V′), we make the part of the curve which lies on the upper part of the surface of the lower nappe full. The horizontal projection of the lower curve is dotted, being entirely concealed by the upper nappe of the cone whose vertex is (A,A′). The portions of the curves which can be seen in vertical projection are made full on the vertical plane; the other parts are dotted. The bases of both cones are dotted, since they are concealed by the upper nappe of the cone whose vertex is (A,A′). Of the elements which show the vertical projections of the cones, the parts seen are made full, the parts concealed dotted.

To draw a tangent line to the upper curve at the point (O,O′), and to the lower curve at the point (*k*,*k*′). Let a plane be drawn tangent to the cone whose vertex is (V,V′) along the element passing through these points, NXH is its horizontal trace; this plane contains both the required tangents. Let a plane be drawn tangent to the other cone along the element (A*k*, A′*k*′); NI is its horizontal trace, and it intersects the tangent plane before drawn in the line (N*k*, N′*k*′), which is tangent to the lower curve at the point (*k*,*k*′) (137). The line N*k* is the horizontal and N′*k*′ the vertical projection of the tangent. Drawing a tangent plane along the element (OAG, O′A′G′), GH is its horizontal trace, and the line in which it intersects the tangent plane (of which NH is the trace) is tangent to the upper curve at the point (O,O′). The lines HO and H′O′ are the projections of this intersection, which are respectively tangent to the projections of the curve.

PROBLEM XXXIII.

To find the intersection of two surfaces of revolution whose axes are in the same plane, and to draw a tangent line to the curve.

§ 140. Pl. 16. If the axes are in the same plane, they will either intersect each other or be parallel. We shall first consider the case in which they intersect.

Let the horizontal plane be taken perpendicular to the axis of one surface, and the vertical plane parallel to the plane of the axes. Let one of the surfaces be an ellipsoid whose axis is (A,A′C), and the other a paraboloid whose axis is (AB, CB′); *d*B is the horizontal trace of the plane of the axes. The vertical projections of the curves in which this plane intersects the surfaces are the vertical projections of the surfaces. The large circle described around the centre A is the horizontal projection of the surface whose axis is (A,A′C); the horizontal pro-

Plate 15.

V′
M′
h′
o′
g′
O′
A′
s′
k′
H′
b′
c′
a′
u′
N′
B′
G′
H′
D′
E′
d′
t
G
x
E
u′
r
B
d
a
b
c
z
v
s
A
u
L
O
g
k
X
M
o
V
h
f
C
I
n
D
N
r

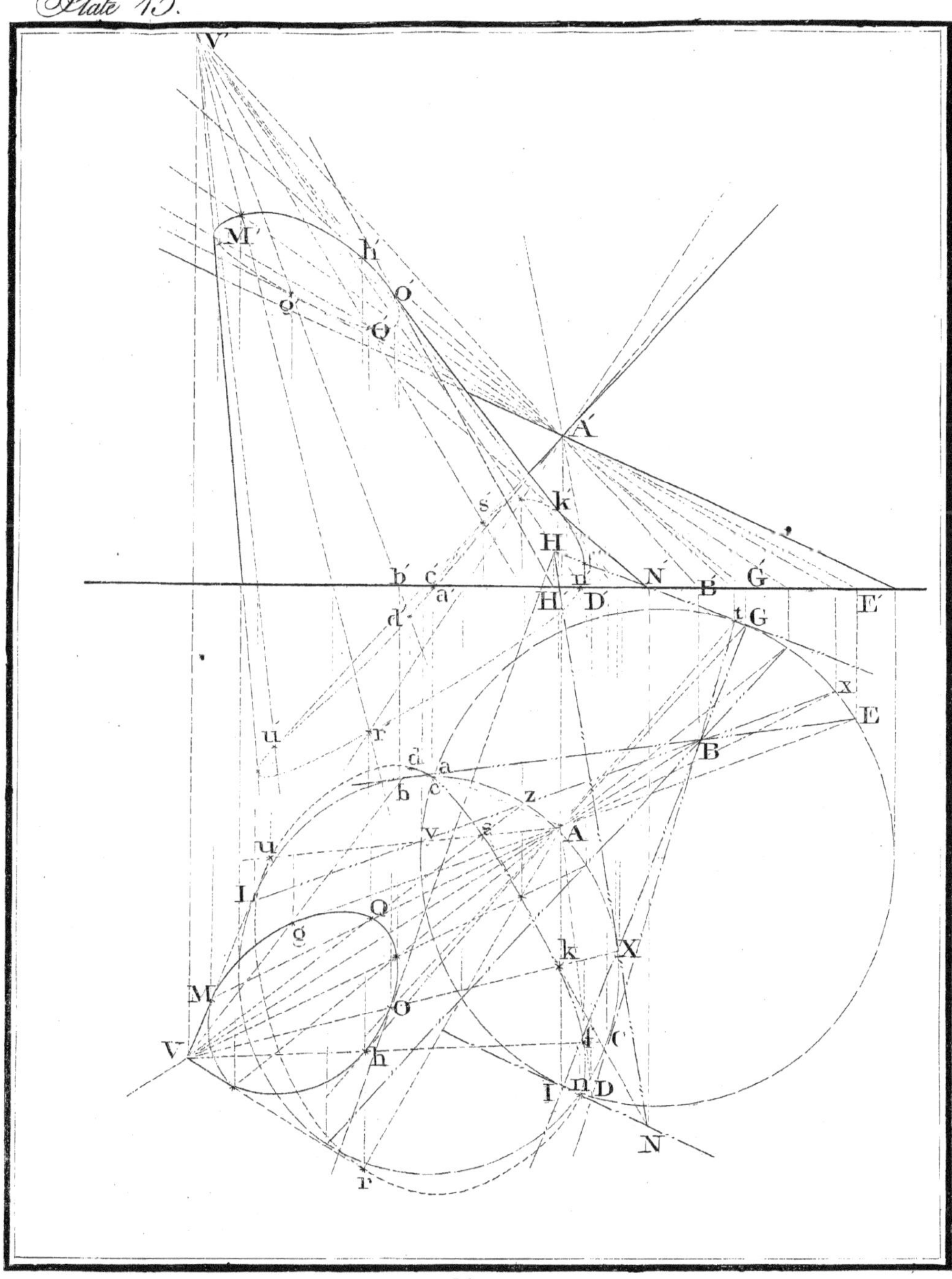

jection of the other surface, not being necessary in the solution of the problem, is not made.

Before constructing the intersection of the surfaces, we will remark, *that all surfaces of revolution having a common axis and intersecting each other, intersect in circles whose planes are perpendicular to the common axis.* For, let the surfaces be intersected by a plane through their common axis, this plane intersects each surface in a meridian curve; the points in which these curves intersect are points of the intersection of the surfaces. Let this plane be now revolved around the common axis; each meridian curve will generate the surface to which it belongs, and their points of intersection will describe the circumferences of circles whose planes are perpendicular to the axis; that is, to the common axis of the surfaces. But these circles are the intersections of the surfaces: hence, *two surfaces of revolution, having a common axis, intersect in circles whose planes are perpendicular to that axis.*

Let the point C, in which the axes of the surfaces intersect, be the common centre of a system of auxiliary spheres; every sphere will intersect each surface in a circle; the points in which the circumferences of these circles intersect are points of the required curve.

With C as a centre, and any radius, as CD, conceive a sphere to be described. This sphere intersects each of the surfaces in a circle; the planes of these circles are perpendicular to the vertical plane of projection, since the axes of the surfaces are parallel to this plane. The line DD′ is the vertical projection of one circle, and EE′ the vertical projection of the other. The point F, at which these lines intersect, is the vertical projection of the line in which the planes of the circles intersect; and the points in which this line of intersection pierces the surfaces are two points of the required curve. Let the circle of which DD′ is the vertical projection be projected on the horizontal plane; D is projected at d, and the circle described with A as a centre, and radius Ad, is the horizontal projection of the intersection of the sphere and ellipsoid. It is evident that $f'f$ is the horizontal projection of the line in which the planes of the two circles intersect; therefore f and f' are the horizontal projections, and F is the vertical projection, of two points of the curve. In the same manner any number of points may be found. To find the points in which the curve intersects the circle of the ellipsoid whose plane passes through the centre, describe a sphere which shall intersect the ellipsoid in its largest horizontal circle; this sphere will determine those points; they are (m,N) and (n,N). The points a' and b', in which the meridian curves parallel to the vertical plane of projection intersect, are horizontally projected at a and b.

To draw a tangent line to the curve at any point, as (f,F). This line could be determined by the general method of drawing two planes respectively tangent to the surfaces at the point, and constructing their line of intersection, which would be tangent to the curve. We shall, however, employ another method, which introduces new principles, and is, perhaps, more elegant. It is called the method by normals.

A line is perpendicular to a curve when it is perpendicular to the tangent drawn through the point in which it meets the curve. This perpendicular is called a normal. A line is perpendicular to a surface when it is perpendicular to the tangent plane at the point in which it meets the surface. This perpendicular is called a normal, and any plane passing through it a normal plane. If through the point (f,F), at which we wish to draw a tangent line, two lines be drawn, the one perpendicular to the surface of the ellipsoid, the other perpendicular to the surface of the paraboloid, the plane of these two lines is a normal plane to both the surfaces at the point (f,F). But as this plane contains the normal lines, it will be perpendicular to two planes drawn through the point (f,F), the one tangent to the ellipsoid, the other to the paraboloid; and, consequently, it will be perpendicular to their intersection. But, as this intersection is the tangent line to the curve at the point (f,F), we conclude that *the normal plane to both surfaces, at any point of their intersection, is perpendicular to a line tangent to their intersection at the same point.*

Let the point (f,F) be carried around on the surface of the ellipsoid, in a horizontal circle, till it comes into the meridian curve parallel to the vertical plane at (d,D); at this point draw the normal DH. It is evident that all normal lines which meet the surface in the circumference of the circle of which DD′ is the projection will intersect the axis at H. In like manner, by revolving the point (f,F) about the axis of the paraboloid till it comes into the meridian curve, parallel to the vertical plane, at E′, the normal E′H′ can be drawn: hence, FH, FH′ are the vertical projections, and fA, fH'' the horizontal projections of the two normal lines to the surfaces at the point (f,F); and HH′ is the trace of their plane on the plane of the axes. But since the plane of the axes is parallel to the vertical plane of projection, HH′ is parallel to the vertical trace of the normal plane. Since the tangent line passes through the point (f,F), and is perpendicular to the normal plane, its vertical projection passes through F and is perpendicular to HH′ (49). The normal plane intersects the plane of the horizontal circle of which DD′ is the vertical projection, in a line parallel to the horizontal trace of the normal plane. But as the diameter DD′ and the trace HH′ are both in the plane of the axes, the point (G,G′), in which they intersect, is one point of the intersection of the horizontal and normal planes; the point (f,F) is another point: hence, Gf is the horizontal projection of their line of intersection; which projection is parallel to the horizontal trace of the normal plane. Therefore the line drawn through F, perpendicular to HG′, is the vertical projection of the tangent line, and the line through f, perpendicular to fG, is its horizontal projection. Instead of determining the direction of the traces of the normal plane, by constructing its intersections with the plane of the axes and the horizontal plane DD′, we might construct its traces on the planes of projection, since we have two lines of the plane, viz. (fA, FH) and (fH'', FH'); the points in which these lines pierce the planes of projection are points of the traces of the normal plane.

§ 141. If the axes of the surfaces were parallel, their intersection could be obtained very easily by intersecting them by planes, since planes perpendicular to their axes would intersect both surfaces in circles, and the intersections of these circles would be points of the curve. The tangent line is drawn in the same manner as when the axes intersect. The construction is left for the student.

PROBLEM XXXIV.

To find the intersection of a cone and sphere, the vertex of the cone being at the centre of the sphere; and to draw a tangent line to the curve at any point.

§ 142. Pl. 17. Fig. 1. Let (C,C′) be the vertex of the cone and centre of the sphere, EGH the base of the cone, and the circle described with the centre C′, and radius C′A the vertical projection of the sphere. The horizontal projection of the sphere, not being required in the construction, is not made. Through the vertex of the cone let any number of planes be drawn perpendicular to the horizontal plane; they will intersect the sphere in great circles, and the cone in right-lined elements; the points in which the elements intersect the circles are points of the curve.

Let GCH be the horizontal trace of one of the auxiliary planes. Let this plane be revolved around the projecting line of the vertex of the cone till it becomes parallel to the vertical plane of projection. The points G and H describe the arcs GG′ and HH′, in the horizontal plane, around C as a centre; and the great circle in which the plane intersects the sphere becomes parallel to the vertical plane. From this position the great circle is vertically projected into the circle whose centre is C′, and the elements of the cone into the lines C′G″ and C′H″. These lines intersect the circumference of the circle at *b*″ and *h*″. In the counter revolution these points describe the arcs of horizontal circles; and when the plane has resumed its primitive position, they are vertically projected at *b*′ and *h*′, and horizontally projected at *b* and *h*. The points (*b*,*b*′) and (*h*,*h*′) are therefore two points of the required curve. In the same

Plate 10.

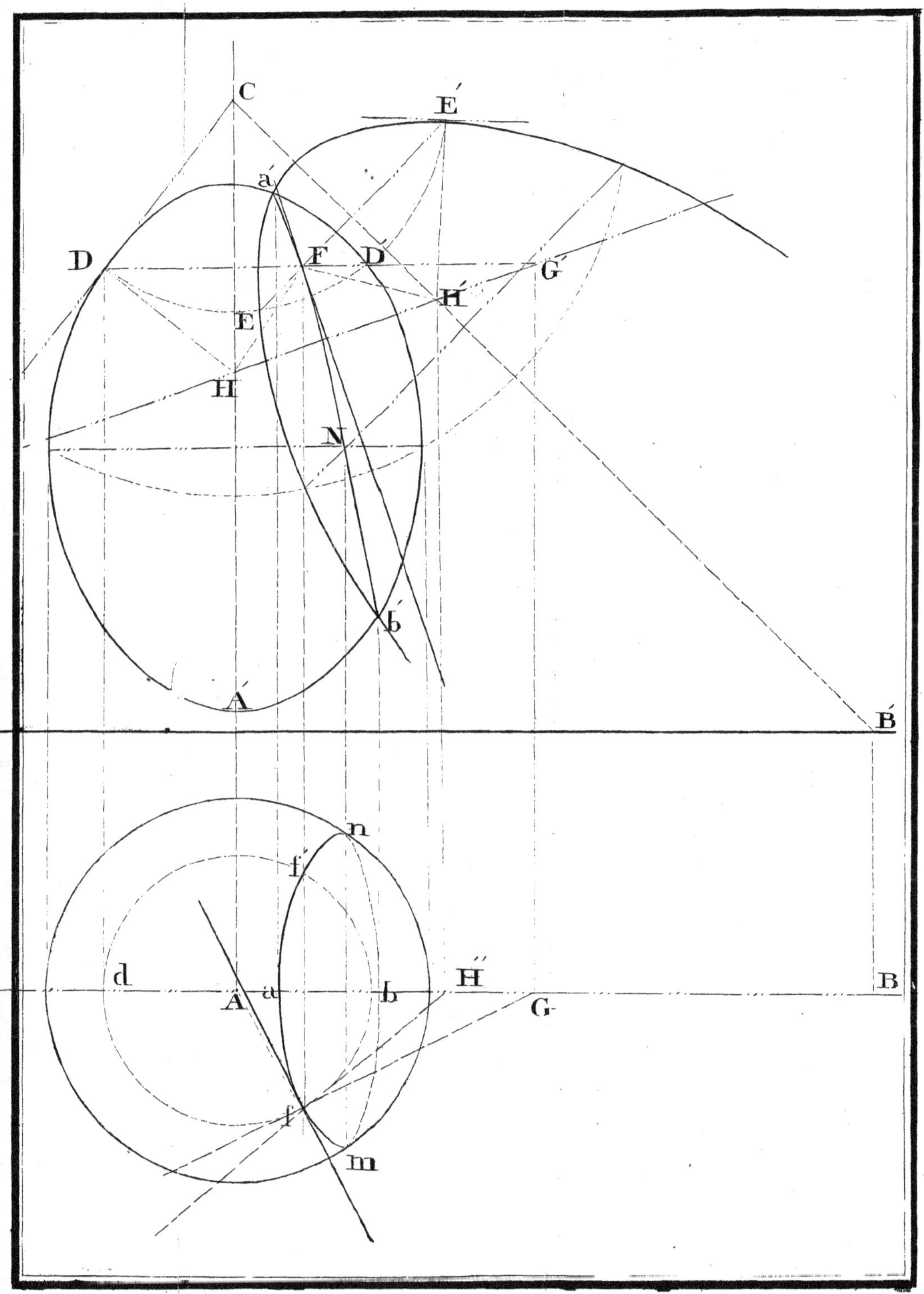

manner the points (a,a'), (n,n'), (m,m'), (l,l'), (g,g'), (f,f'), (e,e') and (c,c') are determined. The part $b'c'e'f'$, being seen, is made full in vertical projection; the remaining part is dotted. If we suppose the upper hemisphere, which is not used in the problem, to be removed, the horizontal projection of the curve should be made full.

To draw a tangent line to the curve at any point, as (c,c'). Let a cone be drawn tangent to the sphere whose circle of contact shall be horizontal, and also contain the point (c,c'). The line AI′V, drawn tangent to the vertical projection of the sphere, is one of the elements in which the plane G′CH′ intersects the cone. This element pierces the horizontal plane at I; and the circle described with the centre C and radius CI is the intersection of the cone and horizontal plane. The point (C,V) is the vertex of the cone. The element of this cone which passes through (c,c') pierces the horizontal plane at B; and BD is the horizontal trace of a plane tangent to the cone along this element. The element of the cone whose vertex is (C,C′), that passes through the point (c,c'), pierces the horizontal plane at E, and ED is the horizontal trace of a plane tangent along this element. The intersection of this plane with the plane whose trace is BD is the tangent line to the curve at the point (c,c'). The line Dc is the horizontal and D′c' the vertical projection of this tangent.

PROBLEM XXXV.

To develop the surface of a cone having any curve for its base, to trace on this development the intersection of the cone by a given plane; and to find, on the development, the position of a tangent line to the curve of intersection.

§ 143. If a cone be rolled around on any of its tangent planes, the vertex remaining fixed, all the elements will arrange themselves around the fixed point; and when the cone shall have been rolled once round, all the elements will have been in contact with the plane. If the elements of the cone, after coming in contact with the plane, remained in the plane, it is evident that the surface of the cone would gradually extend itself on the plane; that any line on the surface of the cone would develop into a line, and that the points of this line would be at the same distance from the common point around which the elements arrange themselves, as they were in space, from the vertex of the cone.

The curve in which a sphere, having its centre at the vertex, intersects the surface of a cone, will, when the surface of the cone is developed, become a circle; the centre of the circle being the point at which the vertex of the cone is placed, and the radius equal to the radius of the sphere. With the vertex of the cone as a centre, and any assumed radius, let a sphere be described, and the intersection of the sphere and cone determined. If, then, any two elements be chosen on the surface of the cone, and the length of that part of the intersection of the sphere and cone intercepted between them determined, this distance laid off on the circle into which the intersection develops, determines the position of the two elements on the development of the cone. It is then necessary to find the length of the curve of intersection of the cone and sphere. To do this, let us develop the right cylinder which projects this curve on the horizontal plane, and trace the curve on this development. Since the cylinder is a right cylinder, its base, which is the horizontal projection of the curve, will become a right line on the plane of development (127); the elements of the cylinder will become perpendicular to this right line, and the curve is traced through the upper extremities of these elements.

Let the curve in which the cone and sphere intersect each other be found, as in the last problem; and let the cylinder which projects the curve on the horizontal plane be developed on the plane which is tangent to it along the element that pierces the horizontal plane at e (Fig. 1). Draw the indefinite right line LED (Fig. 2); erect a perpendicular to it at E, and make Ee equal to the height of the point (e,e') (Fig. 1), above the horizontal plane; *e* is one point of the intersection of the cone and sphere on the plane of development. Laying off EC equal to the arc *ec*, CB equal to *cb*, BA equal to *ba*, AN equal to *an*, NM equal to *nm*, ML equal to *ml*; and on the other side of the point E make EF equal to *ef*, FG to *fg*, GH to *gh*, HL to *hl*; LEL will be the base of the cylinder rectified. Erect at L, H, G, F, &c., perpendiculars to the line LD, and make them respectively equal to the distances of the corresponding points in (Fig. 1) above the horizontal plane; the curve *lhg*, &c., tc *l*, traced through these points, is the curve of intersection of the sphere and cylinder on the plane of development. The tangent line to the curve at the point (*c*,*c*′) is determined on the plane of development, by laying off from C (Fig. 2) the distance CD equal to the subtangent *c*D (Fig. 1), and joining the points *c* and D (Fig. 2).

It is now required to develop the cone, and trace on the development the curve of intersection with the horizontal plane of projection. Let the cone be developed on the tangent plane passing through the point (*c*,*c*′), and let the vertex of the cone be placed at C (Fig. 3). With C as a centre, and a radius equal to the radius of the sphere, describe the arc of the circle *lmna*, &c., and draw a radius CE to represent the element (C*c*, C′*c*′). From the point *c* lay off the arc *cb* equal to *cb* (Fig. 2); and draw C*b*G; this is the position, on the plane of development, of the element of the cone that passes through the point (*b*,*b*′) (Fig. 1). By making, in like manner, *ba* equal to *ba* (Fig. 2), *an* equal to *an*, &c., and laying off on the other side of *c* the arcs *ce*, *ef*, *fg*, &c. respectively equal to their corresponding arcs in (Fig. 2), and drawing the lines C*a*, C*n*, C*e*, &c., we determine the positions of a series of elements of the cone on the plane of development. The tangent line being perpendicular to the radius of the sphere, or to the element of the cone passing through (*c*,*c*′), is perpendicular to this element on the plane of development, and therefore has the position *c*D (Fig. 3).

We will now trace on the plane of development the intersection of the cone with the horizontal plane Laying off from C the distance CE equal to the length of the element which passes through (c,c') (Fig. 1), determines one point. The length of the element is formed by revolving it about the axis of the cone till it becomes parallel to the vertical plane, its projection from this position will be equal to its true length: hence, C'E'' is the length of the element. Thus, the length of any element may be determined, which, being laid off from C, determines a point of the required curve. Making cD (Fig. 3) equal to cD (Fig. 2), and joining E and D, ED is the position which the tangent line ED (Fig. 1) assumes on the plane of development.

CHAPTER IX.

PRACTICAL PROBLEMS.

PROBLEM I.

Knowing the distance of a point from three given points, it is required to find its distance from the plane of these points, and its projection on the plane.

§ 144. As the line joining any two of these points is known, and as there are six such lines, the problem may be thus enunciated: *having given the six edges of a triangular pyramid, to construct the pyramid.*

Pl. 18. Fig. 1. Let the plane of the three points be assumed for the horizontal plane of projection, and let ABC be the triangle formed by joining the given points A, B, and C; and suppose the lines A, B, and C to be equal respectively to the distances of the fourth point from the angles A, B, and C. With the angular points A, B, and C as centres, and radii equal to the distances A, B, and C, let three spheres be described. As each condition, taken independently of the other two, fixes the required point on the surface of one of these spheres, the three conditions, taken together, fix it at their points of intersection. Since either two of the spheres intersect each other in a circle

Plate 17.

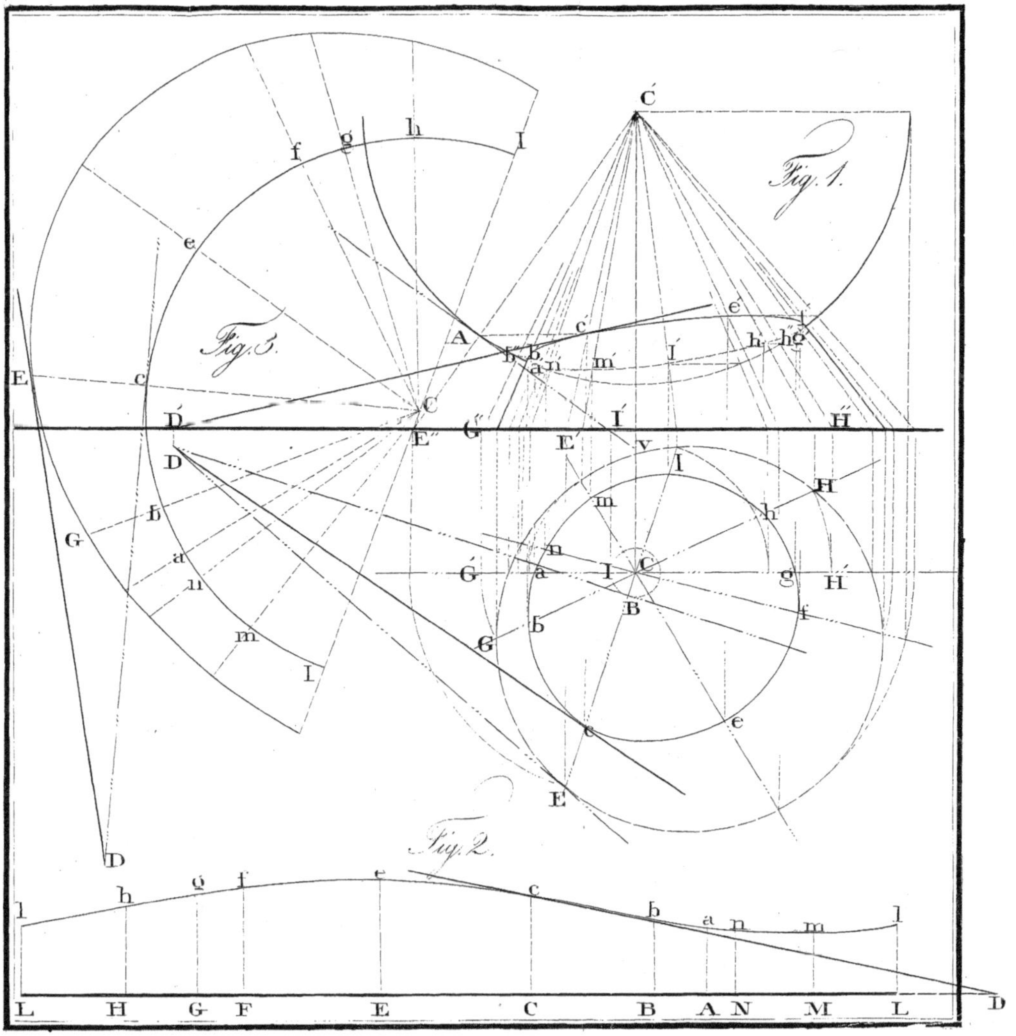

Fig. 1.

Fig. 3.

Fig. 2.

perpendicular to the line joining their centres (140), the spheres whose centres are B and C intersect in a circle perpendicular to CB, and of which ED is the horizontal projection. The spheres whose centres are A and C, intersect in a circle perpendicular to AC, and of which GZ is the horizontal projection. The line in which the planes of these circles intersect is perpendicular to the horizontal plane at I; the two points in which this line pierces the surface of either of the spheres are common to the surfaces of the three spheres: either of them, therefore, will answer all the conditions of the problem. Let the vertical plane of projection be taken perpendicular to CB, and project the circle of which ED is the diameter upon it. The line D′E′ is the vertical projection of the diameter; by describing the circle on this diameter, and projecting the perpendicular to the horizontal plane at I, the points I′ and I″, in which it intersects this circle, are determined. The fourth point is, therefore, horizontally projected at I, and is above or below the plane of the other three points a distance equal to NI″ or NI′. Either of these points will answer all the conditions of the problem, and may be regarded as the vertex of a triangular pyramid, three of whose edges lie in the horizontal plane, and whose three other edges are drawn from this point to the angles A, B, and C.

PROBLEM II.

To find the centre and radius of a sphere whose surface shall pass through four given points; or, by regarding the four points as the four angular points of a triangular pyramid, the problem may be enunciated, to circumscribe a sphere about a triangular pyramid.

§ 145. If any chord of a sphere be bisected by a plane perpendicular to it, the plane will pass through the centre of the sphere. Hence, if we bisect the line joining any two of the given points by a perpendicular plane, this plane will contain the centre of the required sphere. Bisecting a second line by a perpendicular plane, this plane will also contain the centre of the sphere. Bisecting in like manner a third line, not in the plane of the other two, the point in which this last plane cuts the common intersection of the other two planes is the centre of the required sphere, being a point equidistant from the four given points.

Pl. 18. Fig. 2. Take the plane of any three of the points for the horizontal plane of projection. Let A, B, and C be the three points situated in this plane, and (D,D′) the fourth point. Through L, the middle of BC, let the plane LI be drawn perpendicular to BC; through N, the middle of AB, let the perpendicular plane NI be drawn; these planes intersect in a line perpendicular to the horizontal plane at I; this line contains the centre of the sphere, and its vertical projection I″I′ contains the vertical projection of the centre. Through (E,E′), the middle of the edge of which DC is the horizontal projection, let a plane be drawn perpendicular to this edge (53); GH and GH′ are its traces; the point in which the plane cuts the line (I,I′I″) is the centre of the sphere.

To find this point, let a plane be drawn through the line (I,I″I′) parallel to the vertical plane; it intersects the plane (GH, GH′) in a line parallel to its vertical trace, and H″I′ is its vertical projection. The point (I,I′) is, therefore, the point in which the line (I,I″I′) pierces the plane (GH, GH′), and is, consequently, the centre of the sphere. A line drawn from (I,I′) to either of the four angular points, A, B, C, or (D,D′), is the radius of the sphere. Taking the radius passing through C, IC is its horizontal projection, and I′c its vertical projection. Revolving the plane which projects it on the horizontal plane about (I,I″I′) till it becomes parallel to the vertical plane, C describes the arc CC′, and the point (I,I′) remains fixed; I′C″ is, therefore, the length of the radius. With this radius, and about I and I′ as centres, let two circles be described; they are the projections of the required sphere.

If the vertical plane of projection had been taken parallel to (DC, D′c), the plane perpendicular to this line would have been perpendicular to the vertical plane, and the point (I,I′) would then have been vertically projected in the trace GH′.

PROBLEM III.

To find the radius of a sphere which shall be tangent to four given planes; or, to inscribe a sphere in a given triangular pyramid.

§ 146. If we bisect any three of the diedral angles of this pyramid by planes passing through three edges which do not meet in the same point, the point in which these three bisecting planes intersect, is the centre of the required sphere.*

It is, therefore, required to draw these planes, and determine their point of intersection.

Pl. 18. Fig. 3. Let OAB, in the horizontal plane, be the base of the pyramid, (D,D′) its vertex, DA, DB, and DO, the horizontal, and D′A′, D′O′,and D′B′, the vertical projections of its edges. The bisecting planes will be drawn through the lines AO, AB, and BO.

---

* For, let AC″B (Fig. 3, *n*) be the base, and (D,D′) the vertex of a triangular pyramid; suppose (C,C′) to be the point of intersection of the three bisecting planes passed through the edges AC″, AB and BC″; it is to be proved that this point is equidistant from the four faces of the pyramid.

Through the point (C,C′) let a plane be drawn perpendicular to either edge, as AC″. Now, as the bisecting plane through the edge AC″ divides equally the diedral angle included between the face DAC″ and the plane of the base, its intersection with the perpendicular plane bisects the angle contained by the line in which the perpendicular plane intersects the face DAC″ and the horizontal plane. Let this perpendicular plane be revolved around its horizontal trace GC till it coincides with the horizontal plane. The point (C,C′) falls at E; GF, GE, and GC, are the lines revolved, in which the perpendicular plane intersects the plane of the face ADC″, the bisecting plane, and the plane of the base: EF and EC are the perpendiculars let fall from the point (C,C′) on the face ADC″, and on the plane of the base. But, since the angles EGF and EGC are equal, the angles at F and C right angles, and the side EG common, the two triangles EFG and ECG are equal, and have the side EF equal to EC. In the same manner it may be proved, that the length of the perpendicular on either of the other faces is equal to the length of the perpendicular on the plane of the base of the pyramid: hence, the perpendiculars drawn from the point (C,C′) to the four planes are equal; (C,C′) is, therefore, the centre, and EC or EF the radius of a sphere to which the four planes will be tangent.

Through the vertex (D,D′) of the pyramid let three planes be drawn respectively perpendicular to the three edges AO, AB, and BO; and let these planes be revolved around their horizontal traces DE, DH, and DG, till they coincide with the horizontal plane. In revolving the plane ED to coincide with the horizontal plane, the point at which the vertex of the pyramid falls is determined by drawing DV perpendicular to ED, and making it equal to the height of the vertex above the horizontal plane. Let V and E be joined; EV is the revolved position of the intersection of the perpendicular plane ED with the face DOA; and EE′, bisecting the angle VED, is the revolved position of a line of the bisecting plane. By revolving the plane DH to coincide with the horizontal plane, the vertex of the pyramid falls at V″, and the line bisecting the angle DHV″ is the revolved position of a line of the bisecting plane passing through AB. In like manner, by revolving the plane GD to coincide with the horizontal plane, the vertex of the pyramid falls at V′; and Ga', bisecting the angle V′GD, is a line of the bisecting plane which passes through OB. We have, therefore, two lines of each bisecting plane, and may therefore conceive the planes to be drawn. These bisecting planes form a new pyramid, which the horizontal plane intersects in the triangle ABO; the edges of this pyramid pass through the points A, B, and O, and its vertex is the centre of the sphere.

Let this second pyramid be intersected by a plane parallel to the horizontal plane, and at the distance P′Q above it. This plane will intersect the faces of the new pyramid in lines respectively parallel to AO, AB, and OB, which lines will form a triangle similar to the triangle AOB; the angular points of this triangle are in the edges of the second pyramid. Recollecting that Ga', in its position in space, is directly above GD, we see, that if Ga'' be made equal to P′Q, and $a''a'$ drawn parallel to GD, a' will be the revolved position of one point of the intersection of the plane parallel to the horizontal plane, with the bisecting plane through OB. The point a', from its position in space, is horizontally projected at a; and as the plane parallel to the base of the pyramid intersects the bisecting plane in a line parallel to OB, it follows that *b*'P is the horizontal projection of this line. Making *sb*, in the angle VED, equal to P'Q, and drawing it parallel to OA, *bb*' will be the projection of the intersection of the plane parallel to the base of the pyramid with the bisecting plane through AO. In like manner, the parallel to AB is determined; and thus we have the horizontal projection of the triangle, in which the plane parallel to the base of the pyramid intersects the second pyramid. The horizontal projections of the edges of the second pyramid pass through the angular points of this triangle, and also through the points A, B, and O; drawing them, determines C, the horizontal projection of the vertex of the second pyramid, or centre of the sphere. The vertical projection of the centre of the sphere is in the perpendicular to the ground line through C, and also in the vertical projection of either of the edges of the second pyramid. The point B is vertically projected at B'; the point P, at P': hence, B'P'C' is the vertical projection of the edge which pierces the horizontal plane at B; and C' is the vertical projection of the centre of the sphere. The radius of the sphere is equal to C'S; with this radius let circles be described around C' and C as centres: these circles are the projections of the sphere. It is evident that this problem is the same as the problem *to find a point equidistant from four planes, neither two of which are parallel to each other.*

SPHERICAL TRIGONOMETRY.

CHAPTER X.

CONSTRUCTION OF SPHERICAL TRIANGLES.

§ 147. Descriptive Geometry can readily be applied to the graphic solutions of the several cases of Spherical Trigonometry.

Every spherical triangle being formed by the arcs of three great circles intersecting each other on the surfaces of a sphere, it follows that the planes of these circles must intersect each other at the centre. These three planes form what is called a spherical pyramid: the centre of the sphere is its vertex; the planes of the sides of the spherical triangle are its faces; and the lines in which these planes intersect are called its edges. The edges pass through the angular points of the spherical triangle, and through the centre of the sphere.

§ 148. If at either angle two lines be drawn respectively tangent to the sides of the spherical triangle, each line will lie in the plane of the side to which it is tangent (67); both the tangents will be perpendicular to the radius of the sphere passing through the angular point; and the angle contained by them will be the measure of the diedral angle of the two faces of the pyramid which intersect in the radius passing through the angular point. But since the lines are tangent to the arcs, the angle which they make with each other is the measure of the inclination of the arcs; therefore, the diedral angles of the pyramid are equal to the corresponding angles of the spherical tri-

Plate 18.

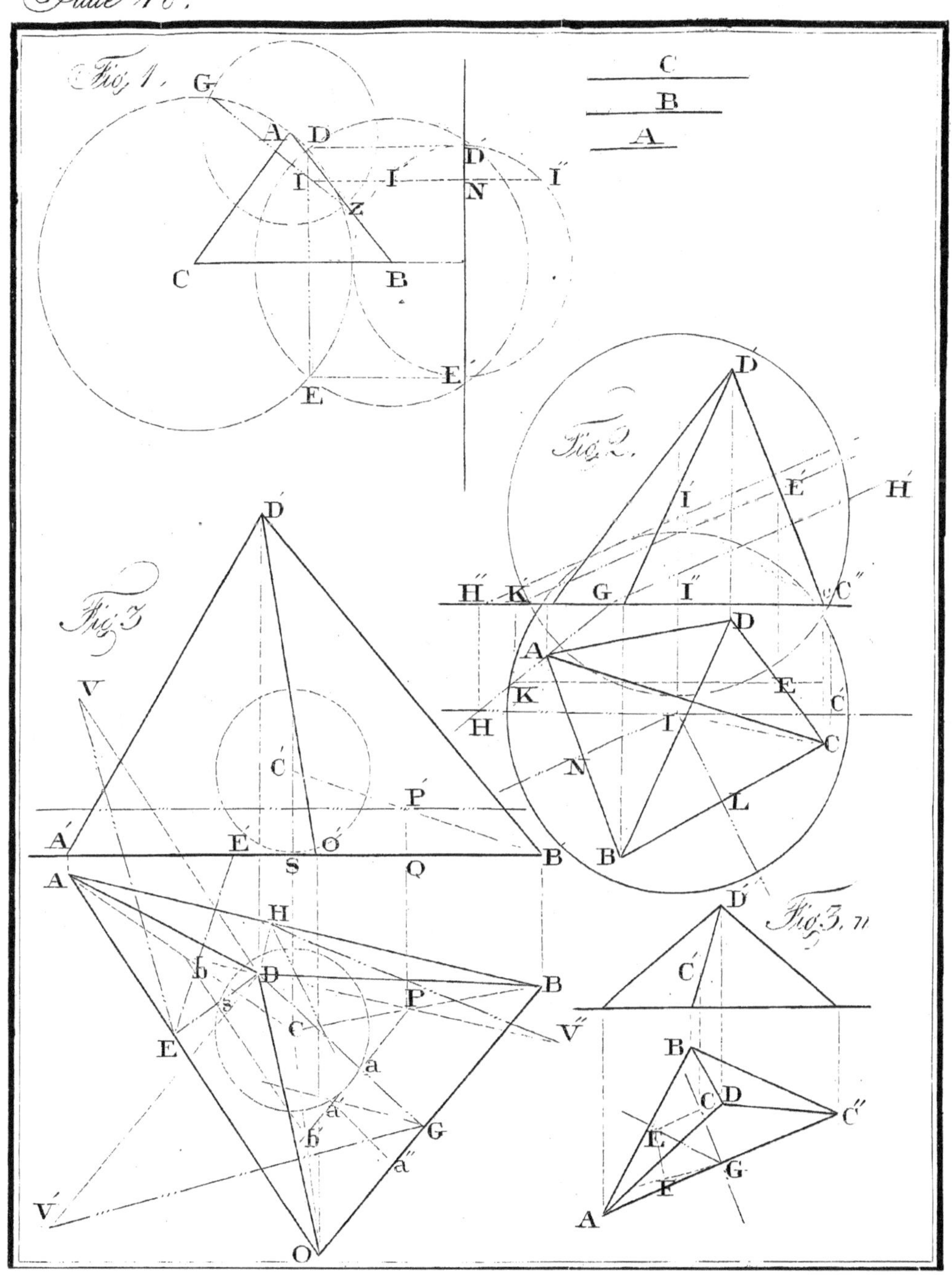

angle, and may be taken to represent them. The angle included between any two edges of the pyramid, being an angle at the centre of the sphere, is measured by the side of the spherical triangle contained in the plane of these two lines: hence, the sides of a spherical triangle measure the angles included between the edges of the pyramid; these angles may then be taken to represent the sides.

Seeing, therefore, that a pyramid can always be formed, having its diedral angles equal to the angles of a spherical triangle, and the angles formed by its edges equal to the sides of the triangle, it follows that all the cases which can arise in spherical trigonometry, will be comprised in the general problem, *to find the remaining parts of a spherical pyramid when any three parts of it are given.*

CASE I.

Having given the three sides of a spherical triangle, to find the angles: that is, having given the three angles included between the edges of a spherical pyramid, to find its diedral angles.

§ 149. Pl. 1. Fig. 1. Let ACB be the spherical triangle, having the sides a, b, and c given.

Make on the plane of the paper the angle DGH equal to the side c. If the pyramid were entirely constructed, and the two other faces revolved, the one around GD, the other around GH, to coincide with the plane of the paper, the third edge would, as it were, divide and fall into the two lines GC′ and GC″, making the angle DGC′ equal to the side a of the spherical triangle, and the angle HGC″ equal to the side b If, therefore, the angle DGC′ be made equal to the side a, and the angle HGC″ equal to the side b, they will represent these sides revolved into the plane of the paper.

It is now required to fold up this pyramid and determine its diedral angles. When the pyramid is folded up, every point of the line GC′ will unite with a point of the line GC″ at the same distance from the point G; the points F′ and F, at the same distance from G, will then become the same point. But, in turning the plane DGC′ around GD as an axis, the point F′ revolves in a vertical circle whose centre is B and radius BF′; and in revolving the plane HGC″ around GH, the point F describes a vertical circle whose centre is A and radius AF: the planes of these circles intersect in a line perpendicular to the face HGD at E, and GE is the projection of the intersection of the faces DGC′ and HGC″. Revolving the plane of the circle described by the point F′ about the trace F′E till it coincides with the plane of the paper, the point of which E is the projection will fall in a perpendicular to F′E at E′, a point of the arc of the circle described by the point F′: hence, BE′ is the intersection of the vertical plane F′BE with the plane of the face F′GB; and, consequently, E′BE is equal to the angle which this face makes with the face DGH. For the same reasons E″AE is equal to the angle which the face HGC″ makes with the face DGH.

It is now required to find the angle which the faces HGC′ and C′GD make with each other. Let a plane be drawn perpendicular to the edge of which GE is the horizontal projection, its trace DH is perpendicular to GE, and the lines in which it intersects the faces pass through the points H and D, and are both perpendicular to the edge at the same point. When the faces are revolved around GD and GH to coincide with the plane of the paper, this point will, as it were, divide and fall at C′ and C″, equidistant from G; the lines DC′ and HC′, perpendicular respectively to GC′ and GC″, are the lines in which the perpendicular plane intersects the planes of the faces. Let there be taken any two points in the lines GC′ and GC″ equidistant from G, as C′ and C″, and from these points let lines be drawn respectively perpendicular to GC′ and GC″: then construct a triangle with the lines HD, DC′, and HC″; the angle HCD will be equal to the angle C of the spherical triangle. It is plain that the angle EBE′ is equal to the angle B of the spherical triangle, and the angle EAE″ to the angle A.

CASE II.

Having given two sides and the included angle of a spherical triangle, to find the other parts.

§ 150. Pl. 1. Fig. 2. Let ABC be the triangle, c and b the given sides, and A the given angle.

Make, on the plane of the paper, the angle BHA equal to the side c, and the angle AHG′ equal to the side b: AHG′ is the face, revolved into the plane of the paper, which makes with the face AHB the angle A. Through any point, as A, of the edge HA, conceive a vertical plane G′AF to be drawn perpendicular to HA; the angle contained by the lines in which this plane intersects the faces is equal to the angle contained by the faces. These lines, however, can only be represented by revolving the vertical plane which contains them to coincide with the horizontal plane; when it is so revolved, let the line AF″ be drawn, making the angle FAF″ equal to the angle A of the spherical triangle; the line AF″ is a line of the face AHG′. With the centre A and radius AG′ let the arc of a circle be described; this arc meets AF″ at F″. Let the plane FAF″ be revolved back into its primitive position, the point F″ is horizontally projected at F. If now we suppose the face AHG′ to be revolved around AH till it shall make with the plane of the paper an angle equal to the angle A of the spherical triangle, the point G′ will describe a circle whose plane is perpendicular to HA; and when the face makes the required angle, the point G′ is horizontally projected at F: hence, HF is the projection of the intersection of the face AHG′ with the unknown face of the pyramid. Revolving this third face around HB till it coincides with the horizontal plane, the point of which F is the projection falls at G, in a perpendicular to HB, and at a distance from B equal to the hypothenuse of a triangle whose base is BF and altitude FF″ or FF′, the height of the point above the plane of the paper. The angle BHG is, therefore, equal to the side of the triangle opposite the angle A, and F′BF to the angle opposite the side *b*. The angle C, opposite the side *c*, can be found as in Case I.

CASE III.

Having given two angles and the included side of a spherical triangle, required the other parts.

§ 151. Pl. 2. Fig. 1. Let ABC be the triangle, A and B the given angles, and *c* the given side.

Draw, in the plane of the paper, the lines HA and HB, making the angle AHB equal to the given side *c*. At any point of HB, as B, let a perpendicular BI be drawn, and let the angle IBI′ be made equal to the angle B of the triangle. Conceive the line BI′ to be situated in the vertical plane whose trace is FBI, it will then be a line of the face which makes an angle equal to B with the plane of the paper; the lines BI′ and HB determine the position of this face. Drawing, in like manner, a perpendicular AE to the edge HA, and making the angle EAD equal to the angle A of the triangle, we determine AD, a line of the face which passes through HA, and makes an angle equal to A with the plane of the paper. The line AD, whose position in space is directly over AE, and the line HA, determine the position of this face. The pyramid is therefore determined, and the three parts which are unknown are the required parts of the triangle.

Let the unknown faces be intersected by a plane parallel to the plane of the paper; it will intersect the faces in lines respectively parallel to HA and HB. Suppose I″N to be the distance of this plane from the plane of the paper; PN is the projection of its intersection with the face passing through HA. From B lay off B*d* equal to I″N, and draw *dd′* parallel to BS; *d′*S is equal to B*d*, and, consequently, to NI″; therefore, S is one point of the projection of the line in which the parallel plane intersects the second unknown face. But the line of

Plate. 1. **Spherical Trigonometry.**

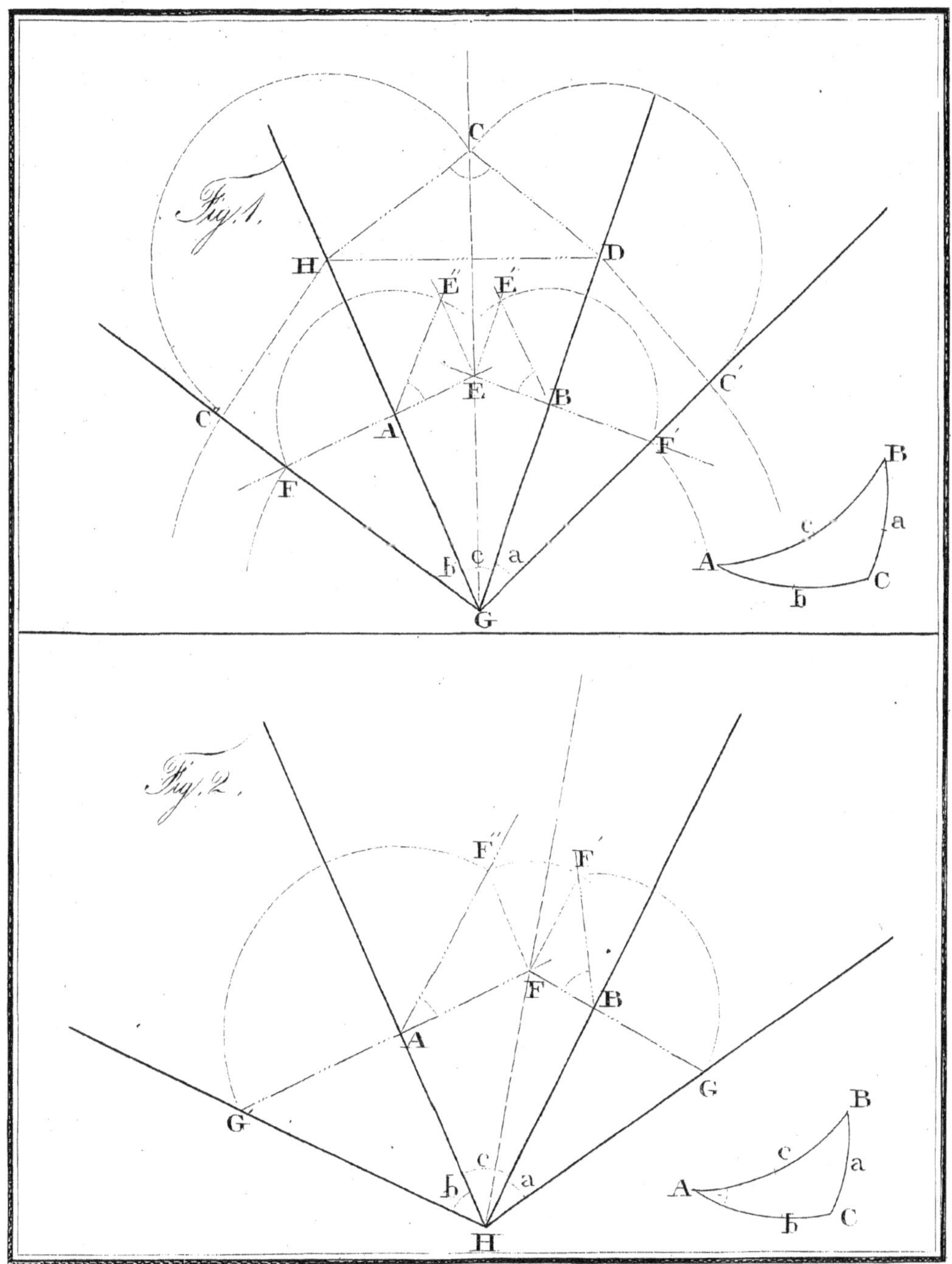

intersection is parallel to HB; therefore, its projection which passes through S must be parallel to HB. The point P is, therefore, the projection of a point common to both the unknown faces: hence, it is the projection of a point of their intersection, and HPE is the projection of the intersection. Produce AN to E, and draw the perpendicular ED. With A as a centre and radius AD describe the arc DG, and draw HG: AHG is equal to the side of the spherical triangle opposite the angle B. By producing BS to I, erecting the perpendicular II′, describing the arc I′F with the centre B, and drawing the line HF, we determine the angle BHF, equal to the side of the spherical triangle opposite the angle A. The unknown faces might have been found thus: from P draw a perpendicular POM to the edge HO, and make OM equal to AI″; M is a point in the edge of the unknown face revolved into the plane of the paper. The point M′ is found by making O′M′ equal to Bd'. The angle C opposite the side c, can be found as in Case I.

CASE IV.

Having given two angles and a side opposite one of them, required the other parts.

§ 152. Pl. 2. Fig. 2. Let ABC be the triangle, A and B the given angles, and b the given side.

Let HA be the intersection of the known face with the plane of the paper. Make the angle AHN equal to the side b; AHN is the known face revolved on the plane of the paper. At any point of HA, as A, draw the perpendicular NAI, and make the angle IAI′ equal to the angle A of the triangle: AI′ is the revolved position of the intersection of the known face with the plane NAI. With A as a centre and radius AN let the arc NI be described. From the point I′, in which it intersects the line AI′, demit the perpendicular I′I on the plane of the paper. In the vertical plane NAD let the line I′D be drawn, making the angle II′D equal to the complement of the angle B of the spherical triangle; the angle IDI′ is equal to the angle B. I et the right-angled triangle I′DI be revolved around its perpendicular I′I; it will generate a right cone whose elements make with the plane of the paper angles equal to the angle B. Let a tangent plane be drawn to this cone through the point H: this plane will make with the plane of the paper an angle equal to the angle B. Its trace is HB, drawn tangent to the circle DB, and BHA is equal to the side *c*.

The side *a* is found by revolving II′ till it becomes perpendicular to IB, joining I″ and B, and describing the arc I″N′ around the centre B. The angle C might be found as in Case I. If the angle B were obtuse, the tangent plane would be passed on the other side of the cone; if it were a right angle, I′D would coincide with I′I, and the cone would be reduced to a right line; in this case the trace of the tangent plane would pass through the point I.

CASE V.

Having given two sides and an opposite angle of a spherical triangle, to find the other parts.

§ 153. Pl. 3. Fig. 1. Let ABC be the triangle, *a* and *b* the given sides, and A the given angle.

Let the side *b* of the spherical triangle be placed on the horizontal plane, and the angle AHC be made equal to it. Make the angle CHF equal to the side *a*; CH is the intersection of the known faces of the spherical pyramid. At any point, as A, of the line HI, draw the perpendicular GAS, and make the angle DAD′ equal to the angle A of the triangle; AD′ is a line of the unknown face revolved into the horizontal plane around GS as an axis. At any point, as C, of the line HC, conceive a plane to be drawn perpendicular to HC. This plane and the plane of the lines AD and AD′ are perpendicular to the horizontal plane; their line of intersection is, therefore, perpendicular to it at D. This perpendicular, when revolved into the horizontal plane around GD, takes the position DD′; but when revolved around FI as an axis, it takes the position DD″. If a

Fig. 1.
D
I′
I″
d′
E
N
d
A
S
I
B
P
G
O
O
F
C
b
a
M
M
c
A
B
a
b
c
H
Fig. 2.
I′
I″
D
I
A
B
N
N′
c
b
a
C
b
a
A
B
c
H

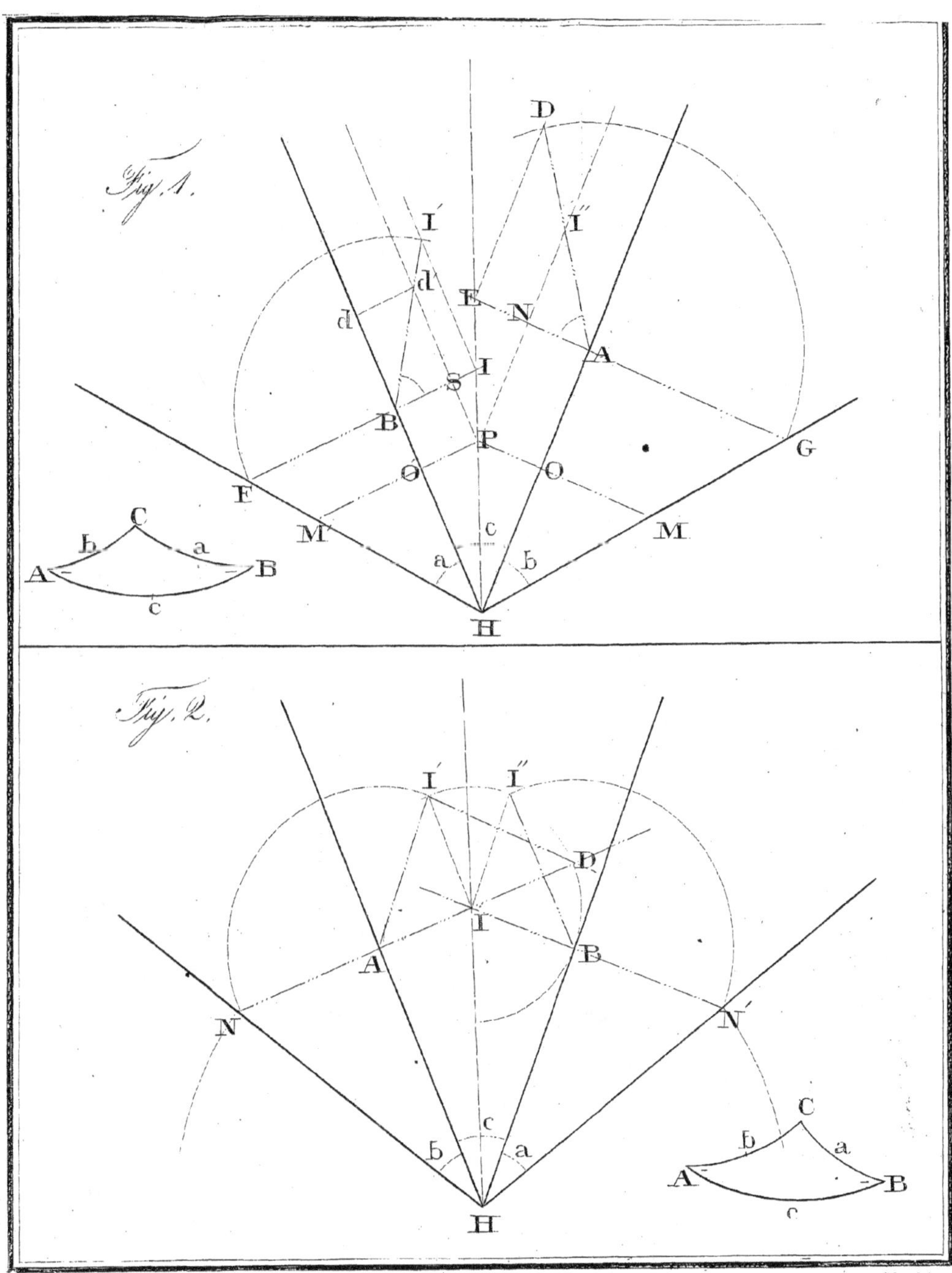

20

Steid sc

line be drawn from D″ to I, it will represent the revolved position of the intersection of the plane FCI with the unknown face of the pyramid. Let the face CHF be now revolved about HC; it will describe a cone which the plane of the unknown face will intersect, in general, in two elements; and when the face CHF has such a position that the line HF is either of these elements, all the conditions of the problem are evidently answered, and the remaining parts of the pyramid are easily determined. Were the cone described, the plane FCI would intersect it in a circle of which C is the centre and CF the radius; the points E and E″, in which this circle meets the line ID″, are the two points at which the elements in question pierce the plane FCI. As the remaining part of the construction is the same, whether we take the element that pierces at E or the one which pierces at E″, we can use either, and will take the one which pierces at E. The line drawn from H to the true position of the point E is, therefore, the intersection of the face CHF with the unknown face of the pyramid, and HE′ is the horizontal projection of this intersection. From the point S, in which the projection of the intersection meets GAD, draw SS′ perpendicular to AD; SS′ is the height, above the plane of the paper, of that point of the intersection which is projected at S. With the centre A and radius AS′ describe the arc S′G, and draw HG; AHG is equal to the side c of the spherical triangle.

To find the angle C: join the points C and E; ECE′ is equal to the angle C. The remaining angle can be found as in Case I. If ID″ were tangent to the circle FEE″, the unknown face IHG would be tangent to the cone; in this case there would be but one result, or one third side of the triangle, which would answer the conditions of the problem. If the line ID″ do not touch or cut the circle FEE″, the conditions of the problem are impossible, and then no triangle can be constructed with such data.

CASE VI.

The three angles of a spherical triangle being given, to find the sides.

§ 154. Pl. 3. Fig. 2. Let ABC be the triangle, and A, B, and C the given angles.

Let G′I be the intersection of two planes at right angles to each other. Draw a plane perpendicular to the vertical plane, and making one of the given angles, as A, for example, with the horizontal plane: *bo*, *bc* are its traces. If now a plane can be drawn, making with the plane (*bo*, *bc*), and with the horizontal plane, angles respectively equal to the angles C and B, these three planes will form a triangular pyramid whose diedral angles will be respectively equal to the angles of the triangle. To draw this plane, take any point within the angle which the plane (*bo*, *bc*) makes with the horizontal plane; and let this point be the common vertex of two right cones whose axes are respectively perpendicular to the planes, and whose elements make with them angles respectively equal to the angles C and B of the triangle. If a plane be then drawn tangent to these cones, it will make the same angles with the planes as the elements of the cones make; that is, angles equal to the angles C and B of the triangle: hence, this tangent plane is the plane sought.

Let V be taken for the common vertex of the two cones; it is assumed in the vertical plane in order to render the construction more easy. Draw V*o*′ perpendicular to the horizontal plane, and V*n* perpendicular to the plane (*bo*, *bc*). Make the angle *o*′V*d* equal to the complement of the angle B, and the angle *n*V*f* equal to the complement of the angle C. Let the right-angled triangles V*o*′*d* and V*nf* be revolved about their perpendiculars V*o*′ and V*n*; they will generate the two right cones whose elements make, respectively, with the horizontal and oblique planes, angles equal to the given angles B and C. It is now required to draw a tangent plane to these cones.

Inscribe a sphere in each cone, and draw a plane tangent to

these spheres through the point V; this plane will be tangent to both cones, and, consequently, the plane required. Let the spheres to be inscribed be equal. At *d* draw *dg* perpendicular to the element V*d*; the point *g*, in which it meets the axis of the cone, is the centre of a sphere inscribed in the cone whose axis is V*o*′; *gd* is the radius of the sphere, and *qd* is the vertical projection of its circle of contact with the cone. To inscribe an equal sphere in the other cone: at the vertex V, draw V*k* perpendicular to the element V*m*, and make it equal to *dg*; draw *km* parallel to V*n*, and from the point *m*, in which it cuts the element produced, draw *mu* parallel to V*k*, or perpendicular to V*m*: *u* is the centre and *um* the radius of the second sphere; *ms* is the vertical projection of its circle of contact with the cone. It is required to draw a tangent plane to these spheres through the point V.

Let the plane (*bo*, *bc*) be moved parallel to itself till it embraces the circle of contact of which *ms* is the projection; it then becomes the plane (FD, FG). Let the points *u* and *g* be joined; *ug* is a line of the vertical plane. Suppose a cylinder of which this line is the axis to be tangent to both spheres. A plane drawn through the point V, tangent to this cylinder, will be tangent to both the spheres and to both the cones, and will, consequently, be the plane required. But since this plane is tangent to all the surfaces, the element in which it touches the cylinder touches the cones and spheres, and therefore passes through the points in which the circles of contact of the cylinder and spheres intersect the circles of contact of the cones and spheres, for these are the only points common to all the surfaces. Through *g* let *gt* be drawn perpendicular to *gu*; it will represent the vertical projection of the circle of contact of the sphere whose centre is *g* with the cylinder. The plane of this circle intersects the plane of the circle of contact of the sphere and cone in a horizontal line, which is vertically projected at *t*; the points in which this line intersects the circle of contact, are common to the cone, sphere, and cylinder. The element of the cylinder passing through either of these points, is the element through which the tangent plane is to be drawn. The horizontal trace of this plane must be tangent to the base of the cone (84); the line Dt'I, drawn tangent to the base of the cone at the point t', is therefore the horizontal trace. As the tangent plane is to contain the point V, its vertical trace is IVG. The point D is the vertex of the pyramid, and the angles included between the edges are easily found. Revolve the plane (DF, FG) into the horizontal plane, around DF as an axis. The point G falls at G′, and DG′ is the revolved position of the edge of the pyramid of which DG″ is the horizontal projection: the angle FDG′ is equal to the side b of the triangle. We can verify this result by considering the circle of contact sm. In the revolution, its centre p describes the arc pp': with p as a centre, and $p's'$, equal to ps, as radius, describe a circle; the line DG′ should be tangent to this circle. The point which is common to the sphere, cone, and cylinder is vertically projected at h: this point, in the revolution, describes the arc hh': the ordinate $h'h''$ should pass through the point of contact. The side a is easily found, and may be constructed by the student.

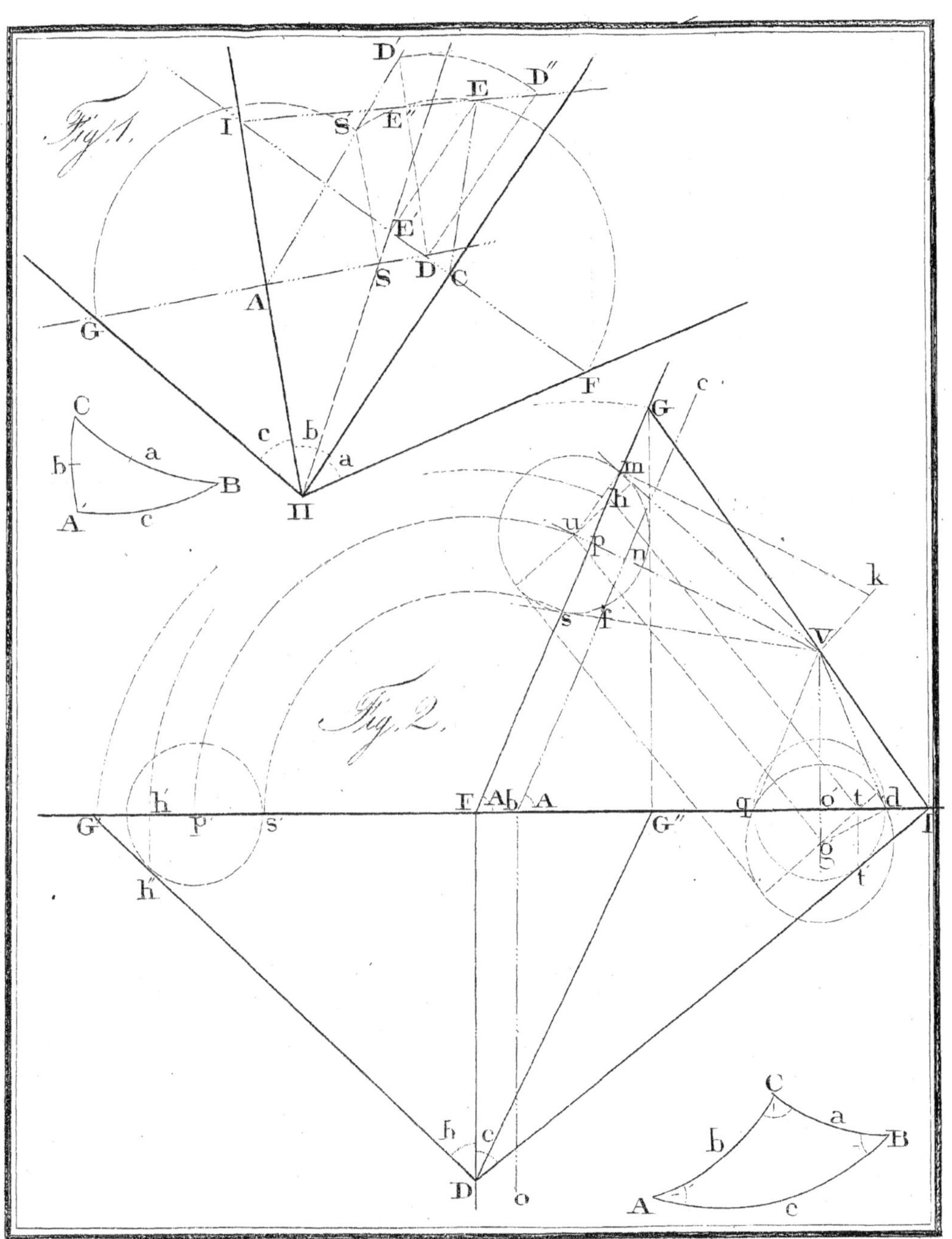
Fig. 1.
D′
D″
E
I
S
E″
E′
D
S
C
A
G
F
C
b
a
B
A
c
c
b
a
n
Fig. 2.
G
c
m
h
u
p
n
k
s
f
V
h′
G′
p′
s′
F
A
b
A
G″
q
o′
t
d
I
g
h″
t
h
c
D
o
C
a
b
B
A
c

SPHERICAL PROJECTIONS.

CHAPTER XI.

FUNDAMENTAL PRINCIPLES.

§ 155. To conceive of the whole surface of the earth, and the positions of objects situated on it, it is necessary to have recourse either to artificial globes or to drawings which represent the earth and the different points of its surface.

§ 156. As it is quite difficult to construct artificial globes, and indicate on them the different places upon the surface of the earth, as well as their relative positions, the method by drawings, or the representation on planes, has been generally adopted.

§ 157. Spherical Projections show the manner in which these drawings are to be made, so that they shall present to the eye, situated at a particular point, the same appearance as the sphere would present if the drawing were removed and the sphere placed in its stead.

§ 158. Three kinds of projections are generally used to make these representations, viz. the *Orthographic*, the *Stereographic*, and the *Globular*.

§ 159. The plane of that circle of the sphere on which the representation or projection is made, is called the *Primitive Plane;* and the intersection of this plane with the surface of the sphere, the *Primitive Circle.*

§ 160. In the Orthographic projection the eye is supposed to be situated in the axis* of the primitive circle, and at an infinite distance from its plane.

§ 161. In the Stereographic projection the eye is placed at the pole of the primitive circle, whose plane in this, as well as in the other projections, is supposed to offer no obstruction to seeing that part of the sphere which lies beyond it.

§ 162. In the Globular projection the eye is supposed to be situated in the axis of the primitive circle, without the surface of the sphere, and at a distance from it equal to the sine of 45°.

§ 163. It has sometimes been found convenient to draw a cylinder tangent to the earth in the circumference of some one of its great circles, or a cone tangent to it in the circumference of one of its small circles; to suppose the eye to be at the centre of the sphere, and to project from this point all the circles on the tangent cylinder, or cone: then, by developing the surface of such tangent cylinder, or cone, the surface of the sphere will be reduced to a plane, and we can easily conceive of the different positions of its points. The Orthographic and Stereographic methods are, however, the most common and the most useful. We shall treat of these projections only.

§ 164. Before examining in what manner the sphere is to be projected by these methods, we shall define those points and circles of the sphere to which particular names have been given, which are used by geographers in locating places on the surface of the earth, and which are generally delineated on maps.

§ 165. The line about which the earth revolves is called its

---

* The axis of a circle is a line passing through its centre, perpendicular to its plane: the points in which this line meets the surface of the sphere are called the poles of the circle. Either pole is at the same distance from every point of the circumference of the circle; since, if a line be perpendicular to a plane all points of the plane equidistant from the foot of the perpendicular are equidistant from any point of the line. The distance from the pole to any point of the circumference of a circle, measured on the sphere is called the polar distance of the circle.

axis; the points in which the axis pierces the surface are called the poles; one the north, the other the south pole.

§ 166. The circumference of the great circle whose plane is perpendicular to the axis, is called the equator; and this circumference is 90° from the poles.

§ 167. Circles whose planes pass through the axis of the earth, and which are consequently perpendicular to the equator, are called meridians. Twelve entire circles, or twenty-four semicircles, fifteen degrees distant from each other, are generally represented on the maps of the earth: the semicircles are called hour circles. Although every point on the surface of the earth has its meridian, yet, for the sake of convenience, we shall project the hour circles only.

§ 168. The distance of any point from the equator, measured on the meridian passing through it, is called the latitude of the point, and is north or south according as the place is north or south of the equator.

§ 169. Small circles parallel to the equator are called parallels of latitude.

§ 170. The ecliptic is a great circle making an angle of 23° 30′ nearly, with the equator; the points in which it intersects the equator are called the equinoctial points.

§ 171. The meridian passing through the equinoctial points is called the *equinoctial colure*, and the meridian which is perpendicular to this last is called the *solstitial colure*. The points in which the solstitial colure intersects the ecliptic are called solstitial points; the parallels of latitude passing through these points are called tropics; the one north of the equator the tropic of Cancer, the one on the south of it the tropic of Capricorn.

§ 172. The parallels of latitude which are 23° 30′ distant from the poles, measured on a meridian, are called polar circles; the one around the north pole the arctic circle, and the one around the south pole the antarctic circle.

§ 173 The horizon of any place is the circumference of a great circle whose plane is perpendicular to the radius passing through the place.

§ 174. *The elevation of the pole above the horizon of any place is equal to the latitude of that place.* For, let (Pl. 1. Fig. 1) HESP be the meridian passing through the place P on the surface of the sphere; HO perpendicular to PP′, the horizon, NS the axis, and EQ the equator. The arc NH measures the elevation of the pole above the horizon, and QP is the latitude of the place (168). But the arc PNH is equal to 90° (173), and QPN is also equal to 90° (166); taking away the common part PN, there remains NH equal to PQ; that is, the elevation of the pole above the horizon of any place is equal to the latitude of that place.

We may also remark, that the distance QO from the equator to the horizon is equal to NP, the complement of the latitude.

§ 175. The angle included between the planes of two circles is equal to the angle contained by their axes, since the axes are respectively perpendicular to the planes. This is shown in Fig. 1, where NS is the axis of the equator, and PP′ the axis of the horizon: it is evident that the angle NP′P, contained by the axes, is equal to the angle HP′E, contained by the planes.

§ 176. The line of measures of any circle is the line of intersection of the primitive plane, and a plane passed through the axis of the primitive circle and the axis of the given circle. This latter plane is perpendicular to the planes of both the circles, since it contains lines respectively perpendicular to them: hence, its trace on the primitive plane is perpendicular to the line in which the plane of the given circle intersects the primitive plane.

CHAPTER XII.

OF THE ORTHOGRAPHIC PROJECTION.

§ 177. In this projection, which is the same as we have used in Descriptive Geometry to represent geometrical magnitudes, the eye, or projecting point, being at an infinite distance from the plane of projection, the projecting lines through the different points to be projected are perpendicular to the plane of projection. The manner of making the projections of points and right lines has already been shown, and no further remarks on this part of the subject seem necessary.

§ 178. The projections of all circles whose planes are perpendicular to the primitive plane are right lines (82).

§ 179. Every circle which is parallel to the primitive plane is projected into a circle equal to itself; for the projecting lines through the different points of its circumference form the surface of a right cylinder; and the intersections of a right cylinder, by parallel planes, are equal.

THEOREM I.

The projections of all circles oblique to the primitive plane are ellipses.

§ 180. Pl. 1. Fig. 2. Let ADB be a circle in the plane of the paper, AB one of its diameters, and CD a radius perpendicular to AB.

Revolve the plane of this circle around AB till the point D shall be elevated above the plane of the paper any convenient distance, as D′D″; join C and D″; the plane of the triangle D″CD′, in its true position, is perpendicular to the plane of the paper, though it is now revolved into this plane around the axis CD. The angle D″CD′ is equal to the angle which the plane of the circle to be projected makes with the plane of the paper, and D′ is the projection of one point of its circumference. Now we have this proportion, CD″ : CD′ :: radius : co-sine of the inclination of the planes. At any point of AB, as N, conceive a plane to be drawn perpendicular to it, and let this plane be revolved around NI till it coincides with the plane of the paper; the point of which I′ is the projection falls at I″, making the distance NI″ equal to NI: the angle I″NI is equal to the inclination of the planes; that is, equal to the angle D″CD′. But in the triangle NI″I′ we have NI′ : NI′ :: radius : co-sine of the inclination of the planes. Comparing this with the previous proportion, we see that the third and fourth terms of each are the same; therefore, the first couplets are proportional; that is, CD″ : CD′ :: NI″ : NI′, or $CD''^2 : CD'^2 :: NI''^2 : NI'^2$. But CD''^2, or CD^2, is equal to AC.CB; and NI''^2, or NI^2, is equal to AN.NB: therefore, AC.CB : AN.NB :: $CD'^2 : NI'^2$; that is, the rectangles of the abscissas are to each other as the squares of their corresponding ordinates; and as this is a known property of an ellipse, we conclude that *the projections of all circles oblique to the plane on which they are projected are ellipses.* The semicircle which is above the plane of the paper is projected into the semi-ellipse AD′B; the semicircle below the plane of the paper, into the semi-ellipse AFB.

§ 181. We see that the transverse axis AB is equal to the diameter of the circle, and that the semi-conjugate axis CD′ is equal to the cosine of the inclination of the plane to the radius of the circle which is projected. If the plane on which the projection is made should not pass through the centre of the circle, its projection is still an ellipse: for, conceive a plane to be passed through its centre parallel to the primitive plane, the projections of the circle on these parallel planes are equal curves. The projection of that diameter which is parallel to the primitive plane, is the transverse axis of the ellipse; for this diameter is projected into its true length, and all the other diameters, being oblique to the primitive plane, are projected into lines less than themselves. That diameter of the circle which is perpendicular to the one that is parallel to the primitive plane, will, in projection, be the conjugate axis of the ellipse. For, the two lines being at right angles in space, and one of them parallel to the plane on which they are projected, their projections are also at right angles (51). The conjugate axis will evidently lie in the line of measures, since its projecting plane is perpendicular both to the primitive plane and to the plane of the projected circle. The length of the conjugate axis is the same, whether the primitive plane does or does not pass through the centre of the circle which is projected. The projections of all circles made by the orthographic method are either right lines, circles, or ellipses.

§ 182. If the whole surface of a sphere were projected on a plane passing through the centre, it is evident that each point within the circumference of the primitive circle would be the projection of two points of the surface of the sphere, since each projecting line meets the sphere in two points. In order to delineate the whole surface, so that each point of projection shall represent but one point of the surface, we generally project that hemisphere which is nearest the eye, and then revolve the other hemisphere 180°, around a line tangent to the primitive circle, thus bringing it between the eye and the primitive plane; and then project it from this position.

PROBLEM I.

To project the circles of the sphere on the plane of the equinoctial colure.

§ 183. Pl. 1. Fig. 3. Let SE′NE be the equinoctial colure, and suppose the eye to be situated above the plane of the paper.

Assume any point, as N, for the place of the north pole, and draw the line NIS; NIS is the projection of the solstitial colure, and S is the projection of the south pole. The equator, being a great circle perpendicular to the primitive plane, is projected into EE′ perpendicular to NS, and E and E′ are the equinoctial points. The ecliptic passes through E and E′; and as it makes with the equator an angle of $23\frac{1}{2}°$, it makes with the equinoctial colure an angle equal to $66\frac{1}{2}°$; its projection, therefore, is an ellipse whose transverse axis is EE′, and whose semi-conjugate axis is ID, the cosine of $66\frac{1}{2}°$, to the radius IE. Laying off from S, with a scale of chords, or protracter, SC equal to $66\frac{1}{2}°$, and drawing CD parallel to EE′, determines ID, the cosine of $66\frac{1}{2}°$, and the semi-conjugate axis of the ellipse EDE. The projections of all the meridians have the common transverse axis NS; and laying off from I, on their common line of measures EE′, the cosines of 15°, 30°, 45°, &c. determines the extremities of their conjugate axes, and having the axes, the ellipses are easily described. The half of the meridian which lies above the plane of the paper, and makes with it an angle of 60°, is projected into the semi-ellipse SFN; IF, the cosine of the inclination, is equal to half the radius IE′. The semi-meridians which lie between the solstitial colure and the semi-circle NES are projected by laying off the cosines of their inclinations from I towards E.

The parallels of latitude, being perpendicular to the primitive plane, are projected into right lines (82). To find the projection of the arctic circle, lay off from N to A′ $23\frac{1}{2}°$, and draw AA′ parallel to EE′; A′A is the projection of the arctic circle. The projection of the tropic of Cancer is found by laying off NB equal to $66\frac{1}{2}°$, and drawing through B a parallel to EE′. The antarctic circle and the tropic of Capricorn are found in a similar manner. The projection of the tropic of Capricorn passes through D, and is tangent to the ellipse EDE′; for D is the projection of the southern solstitial point, at which point the ecliptic touches the tropic in space.

Let the hemisphere which is behind the plane of projection be revolved 180° around a line through E′ parallel to NS; this brings the hemisphere in front of the primitive plane. It now has the same position with the primitive plane as the hemisphere which has been projected, and its projection is made in a similar manner. The line E′Q is the projection of the remaining half of the equator, and E′D′Q of the remaining half of the ecliptic. The line N′S′ is the projection of the half of the solstitial colure corresponding to NS, and N′GS′ the projection of the half of the meridian corresponding to SFN; the projections of the parallels of latitude are also drawn in the figure.

§ 184. If the projection of the sphere were made on the solstitial colure, it would be the same in every respect as the one just constructed on the equinoctial colure, excepting that the ecliptic would be projected into the right line CIB passing through the centre of the primitive circle: for, the solstitial colure is perpendicular both to the ecliptic and equator. Conceive the line EDE′D′Q to be removed, and the figure will represent the projection of the sphere on the plane of the solstitial colure.

PROBLEM II.

To project the sphere on the plane of the equator.

§ 185. Pl. 2. Fig 1. Let AEBD represent the equator, and suppose the eye to be placed on the north of it: under this supposition the northern hemisphere will be first projected.

The meridians are projected in right lines passing through the centre N: for the planes of the meridians are perpendicular to the primitive plane and pass through the axis of the sphere, and the axis is projected at N. The centre N is also the projection of the north pole. Let A and B be assumed for the equinoctial points; ANB is the projection of the equinoctial colure, and DNE of the solstitial colure. To project a meridian making any angle with the equinoctial colure: lay off from A an arc AF equal to this angle, and through the extremity F draw the diameter FNN′: this line is the projection required. Every diameter passing through N is the projection of a meridian. The ecliptic makes an angle of $23\frac{1}{2}°$ with the equator, and passes through the equinoctial points A and B: hence AB is the transverse axis, and NI the cosine of $23\frac{1}{2}°$, the semi-conjugate axis of the ellipse into which it is projected.

The parallels of latitude being parallel to the primitive plane, their projections are circles (179); N, the projection of the axis of the sphere, is their common centre, and the radii with which they are described are the sines of their polar distances; for the radius of any small circle of the sphere is equal to the sine of its polar distance. The projections of the tropic of Cancer and the arctic circle are described about N as a centre, and with radii respectively equal to the sine of 66½°, and the sine of 23½°. The projection of the tropic of Cancer passes through the point I. By revolving the southern hemisphere in front of the primitive plane, around a line tangent to the primitive circle at B, its projection can be made in the same manner. The remaining half of the ecliptic, the antarctic circle, whose radius is SQ′, equal to the sine of 23½°, the tropic of Capricorn, whose radius is SI′, and the meridians made in the figure, are easily recognised.

PROBLEM III.

To project the sphere on the horizon of any place; that place, for example, the latitude of which is 45° north.

§ 186. Pl. 3. Fig. 2. Let ADBC be the horizon, and A and B the equinoctial points. The elevation of the pole above the horizon is equal to 45°, the latitude of the place (174).

The equinoctial colure passes through the points A and B, and makes an angle with the horizon equal to the elevation of the pole above it; that is, equal to the latitude of the place. The line AB is the transverse axis of the ellipse into which it is projected; and ON, the cosine of 45°, is its semi-conjugate. The semi-ellipse ANB is the projection of that part of the colure which is above the horizon. The point N is the projection of the north pole, and CN is the versed-sine of the latitude. The equinoctial colure intersects the planes of the parallels of latitude in lines parallel to AB, its intersection with the equator; that is, in lines parallel to the primitive plane, since AB is a line of that plane. These lines are diameters of the parallels of lati tude, their projections are equal to the lines themselves, and

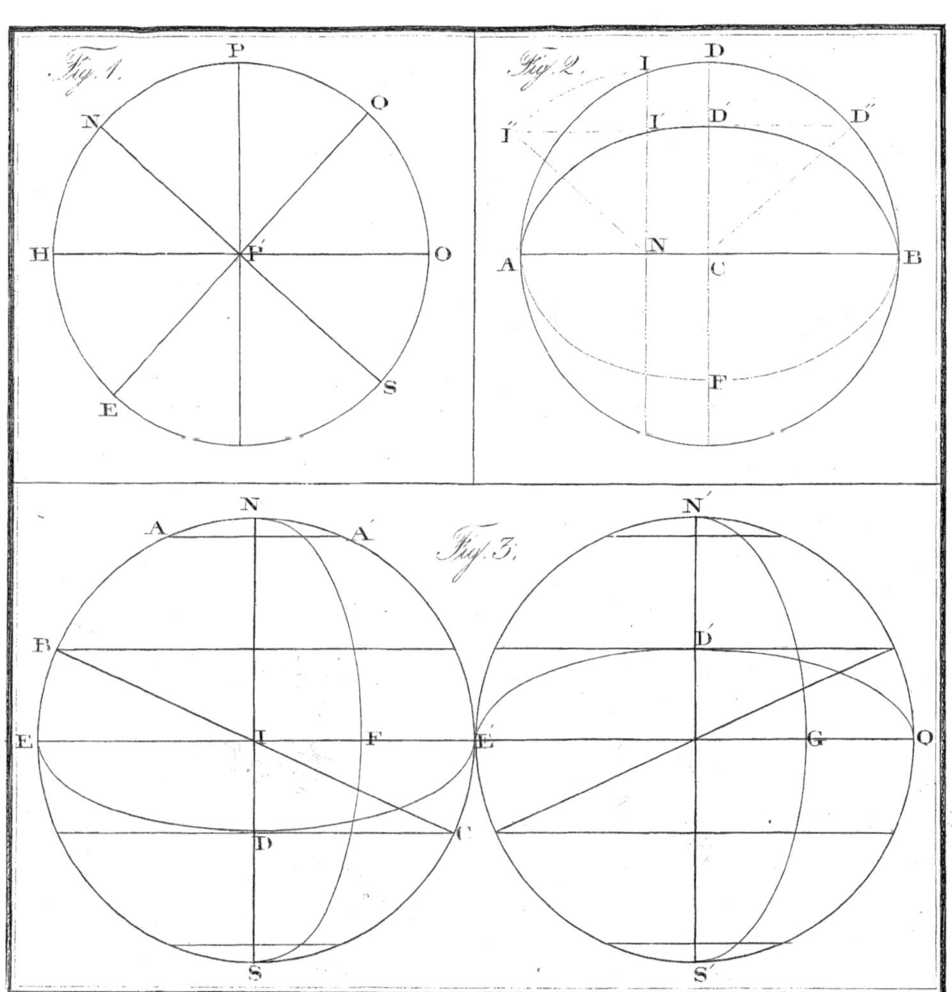
Fig. 1.
P
N
O
H
P′
O
E
S
Fig. 2.
I
D
I″
I′
D′
D″
A
N
C
B
F
N
A
A′
Fig. 3.
B
E
I
F
E′
D
C
S
N′
D′
G
O
S′

are the transverse axes of the ellipses into which the parallels are projected; and the vertices of these axes are all found in the projection of the equinoctial colure. Let the plane of the equinoctial colure be revolved around AB till it coincides with the primitive plane. The pole falls at C. From C lay off $23\frac{1}{2}°$ to E; the chord EG is the line of intersection, in its revolved position, of the plane of the equinoctial colure and the plane of the arctic circle. Let the plane be revolved back again; E′G′ is the projection of this diameter, and is the transverse axis of the ellipse into which the arctic circle is projected. In like manner, making CL equal to $66\frac{1}{2}°$, drawing LP parallel to AB, erecting the perpendiculars LL′ and PP′ to AB, determines L′P′, the transverse axis of the ellipse which is the projection of the tropic of Cancer. The transverse axes of the projections of any number of parallels of latitude may be found in the same manner.

To find the conjugate axes. The points in which the transverse axes intersect the line CD are the centres of the ellipses. The planes of the parallels of latitude, being parallel to the plane of the equator, make the same angle with the primitive plane; that is, an angle equal to the complement of the latitude, or 45°. Find then the cosine of 45° to the radius of the parallel; this cosine is the semi-conjugate axis of the ellipse into which the parallel of latitude is projected. The conjugate axis is determined by laying off this distance on both sides of the centre of the ellipse in the line CD (180). Those parallels of latitude whose northern polar distances are less than 45° will be entirely above the horizon, and will therefore be seen, while those whose polar distances are greater than 45° pass below the horizon, and therefore a part of them will not be seen. The tropic of Cancer passes below the horizon at the points *b* and *a*.

The equator and ecliptic will be next projected. The line AB is the transverse axis of the ellipse which is the projection of the equator. Laying off from O the distance OU equal to the cosine of 45°, OU is the semi-conjugate axis. The semi-ellipse AUB is the projection of that part of the equator which is above the primitive plane. If that half of the ecliptic which is on the upper hemisphere lie between the equator and north pole, it would make with the primitive plane an angle greater than the angle which the equator makes by $23\frac{1}{2}°$; but if it lie between the equator and south pole, it will make with the primitive plane an angle less than the angle which the equator makes by $23\frac{1}{2}°$. It is taken in the latter position. AB is the transverse axis of the ellipse into which it is projected, and OU′, equal to the cosine of $21\frac{1}{2}°$, is the semi-conjugate axis, and AU′B is the projection of that part of the ecliptic which is above the primitive plane.

To project the meridians. Let a tangent plane be drawn to the sphere at its north pole: this plane will be perpendicular to the axis, and will intersect the planes of the meridians in lines making angles of 15° with each other; the points in which these lines pierce the primitive plane are points of the traces of the meridian planes. To pass this plane. Suppose the plane of the solstitial colure to be revolved around CD till it coincides with the primitive plane; the solstitial colure then coincides with the primitive circle, and the pole falls at N′. Through N′ draw the tangent line N′S; the point S, in which it meets DC produced, is a point of the trace of the tangent plane. But, as the plane is to be perpendicular to the axis of the sphere, its trace must be perpendicular to the projection of the axis (49); therefore SH, drawn perpendicular to DS, is the trace of this plane. Let this tangent plane be revolved around its trace SH, from the sphere, till it coincides with the primitive plane; the pole falls at N″, SN″ being made equal to SN′. Drawing N″R, making the angle SN″R equal to 15°, determines R, a point of the trace of the meridian plane which makes an angle of 15° with the solstitial colure; for N″R is the revolved position of the intersection of this meridian plane with the tangent plane, and the point R, being in the trace, remains fixed. But the point O is another point of the trace of this meridian plane; the trace can therefore be drawn. Laying off the angle SN″R′ equal to 30° determines R′, a point in the trace of the meridian plane that makes an angle of 30° with the solstitial colure. Thus, laying off at N′ and from the line

N″D, an angle equal to the angle which any meridian plane makes with the solstitial colure, determines a point of its trace on the primitive plane. The line N″R″ makes an angle of 45° with N″D: hence, R″C′V is the trace of that meridian plane which makes an angle of 45° with the solstitial colure, and C′V is the transverse axis of the ellipse into which the meridian is projected. In a similar manner, the transverse axis of the ellipse into which any meridian is projected can be found. It only remains to find the conjugate axes, and then the ellipses can be described. To find the conjugate axis of the ellipse whose transverse axis is C′V. Through the pole let a plane be drawn perpendicular to C′V; NA′ is its horizontal trace. Let this plane be revolved to coincide with the primitive plane; the pole falls at P″; A′P″ is the intersection, revolved, of the perpendicular and meridian planes, and P″A′N is equal to the angle included between the meridian and primitive planes. Find the cosine of this angle to the radius of the primitive circle, and lay it off from O to S′, in the line of measures OS′; OS′ will be the semi-conjugate axis. Or, the semi-conjugate axis may be found by a better construction, thus: produce A′N and OS′ till they meet the circumference of the circle in the points N″ and S″. Draw the line S″N″, and produce it till it intersects VC′R″ at M. Draw a line through M and N; the point S′, in which it meets OS″, is the extremity of the semi-conjugate axis. The semi-ellipse VS′C′ is the projection of that part of the meridian which is above the primitive plane. In the same manner any number of meridians can be projected. The other hemisphere is revolved in front of the primitive plane, and its projection made in the same way. The figure shows the circles that are projected.

§ 187. By considering the principles of the orthographic projection, we see that if the primitive circle be a great circle of the sphere, all the points of the surface are projected within it, and that the projection of any point is at a distance from the centre of the primitive circle equal to the sine of the arc intercepted between the point on the surface of the sphere and either pole of the primitive circle.

The poles of any circle are projected in its line of measures at distances from the centre of the primitive circle equal to the sine of its inclination. They are projected in the line of measures, since they are projected in the trace of the plane passing through the poles and perpendicular to the primitive plane (176). They are projected at distances from the centre of the primitive circle equal to the sine of the inclination; since the arcs intercepted between the poles of the primitive circle and the poles to be projected, are equal to the inclination of the circles (175)

CHAPTER XIII.

OF THE STEREOGRAPHIC PROJECTION.

§ 188. In this projection, the eye, or projecting point, is supposed to be at the pole of the primitive circle (161).

§ 189. The projection of any point of the surface of a sphere, is the point in which the line drawn through it and the eye pierces the primitive plane.

§ 190. The tangent of half an arc is called the semi tangent of the arc: thus, if the arc be sixty degrees, its semi-tangent is the tangent of thirty degrees.

§ 191. The polar distance of a point is its distance from that pole of the primitive circle which is opposite the eye.

THEOREM I.

The projection of any point of the surface of a sphere is at a distance from the centre of the primitive circle equal to the semi-tangent of its polar distance.

§ 192. Pl. 2. Fig 2. Suppose a plane to be passed through the point to be projected and the axis of the primitive circle, and let the plane of the paper be this plane: ACPB is the circumference of the circle in which it intersects the sphere. Let A be the place of the eye, or projecting point, and BC the trace of the primitive plane; this trace is perpendicular to AP, since AP is the axis of the primitive circle. Let D be the point to be projected. Draw the line AD; the point D′, in which it pierces the primitive plane, is the projection of the point D. With A as a centre, and radius AP′, let the arc P′E be described. The angle DAP, being at the circumference, is measured by half the arc PD; but P′D′ is the tangent of the angle P′AD′ to the radius of the primitive circle; it is therefore the semi-tangent of the polar distance PD (190).

§ 193. It follows, from the preceding demonstration, that the projections of all points which have equal polar distances are equidistant from the centre of the primitive circle: hence, *all circles which are parallel to the primitive plane are projected into circles; the radii of the projections of such circles are the semi-tangents of their polar distances.*

§ 194. The tangent of 45° being equal to radius, it follows that when the primitive plane passes through the centre of the sphere, all points whose polar distances are less than 90° will be projected within the circumference of the primitive circle, and all points whose polar distances are greater than 90° without it. The polar distances of the points of the primitive circle being 90°, it follows that they are neither projected *without* nor *within* it, but *in* it: hence, the primitive circle is its own projection. The polar distance of the pole opposite the eye being nothing, this pole is projected at the centre of the primitive circle; and the eye, whose polar distance is 180°, is projected at an infinite distance from the centre of the primitive circle. It is easily shown from the figure, that all points of the semicircle BPC are projected within the primitive circle, and all points of the semicircle BAC without it. If through the eye, at A, and any point of the surface of the sphere, a line be drawn, and the point be then moved along the surface of the sphere towards A, the line will make a less and less angle with the primitive plane, and when the point unites with A the line becomes parallel to the primitive plane and tangent to the sphere. Hence the eye is projected on the primitive plane at an infinite distance from the centre of the primitive circle.

§ 195. *If the plane of a circle pass through the eye, the projection of the circle is a right line.* For, the lines which are drawn from the eye to the different points of the circumference are contained in the plane of the circle, and therefore pierce the primitive plane in the line in which it is intersected by the plane of the circle; that is, in a right line: hence, *the projections of all circles whose planes pass through the eye are right lines.* The projections of the great circles of the sphere pass through the centre of the primitive circle.

§ 196. The projections of right lines which pass through the eye are points. Right lines which do not pass through the eye are projected into right lines. For, if through the eye lines be drawn to the different points of the right line to be projected, they form a plane; the intersection of this plane with the primitive plane is the projection of the line.

THEOREM II.

The projections of all circles oblique to the primitive plane, and whose planes do not pass through the eye, are circles.

§ 197. Pl. 2. Fig. 3. Let the circle to be projected be a small circle.

Through the axis of the circle and the axis of the primitive circle suppose a plane to be passed: this plane may be taken for the plane of the paper. The circle ACOB is its intersection with the sphere. The primitive circle and the circle to be projected are perpendicular to this plane. Let A be the position of the eye, CB the trace of the primitive plane, and ED the orthographic projection of the circle to be projected. Conceive the circle to be circumscribed by a cone of which A is the vertex: the intersection of this cone by the primitive plane is the projection of the circle. It is then to be shown that this intersection is a circle.

The point D is projected at D', and the point E at E'. The

angle AED being at the circumference, is measured by half the arc ABD; the angle DD′B, formed by the intersection of two chords, is measured by half the sum of the arcs AC and BD, or half the arc ABD: hence, the angles AED and AD′E′ are equal. The triangles AED and AE′D′ have the angle EAD common; they are consequently equiangular, and have the angle ADE equal to the angle AE′D′: hence, the intersection of the cone by the primitive plane is a sub-contrary section, and therefore a circle.* But this intersection is the projection of the oblique circle: hence, the projection of every small circle oblique to the primitive plane is a circle. If the primitive plane be revolved around CB till it coincides with the plane of the paper, the projected circle will be represented by the circle described on the diameter E′D′.

§ 198. Had the line ED passed through the centre O′, the

---

* A cone whose axis is oblique to the plane of its base is called a *scalene cone;* and if it have a circular base, a scalene cone with a circular base. If the surface of such a cone be intersected by a plane parallel to its base, the section is a circle; a cutting plane may be oblique to the plane of the base, in a certain angle, and still intersect the surface in a circle. Let ABC (Pl. 2. Fig. 4) be the triangle in which a scalene cone with a circular base is intersected by a plane passing through its axis and perpendicular to the plane of its base. The line BC is the orthographic projection of the base on the plane of the paper. If any plane, as EF, be drawn perpendicular to the plane of the triangle ABC, and making the angle AEF equal to the angle ABC, or the angle AFE equal to the angle ACB, this plane EF will intersect the surface of the cone in a circle, and the section is called a *sub-contrary section.* Through any point of FE, as I, let the plane LIM be drawn parallel to the plane of the base BHC. The plane LIM intersects the plane FIE in a line perpendicular to the plane of the paper at the point I; this line is a common ordinate of the two curves in which the planes intersect the surface of the cone. Since the angle AEF is equal to the angle ABC, that is, to the equal angle ALI, and the opposite angles EIM and LIF are equal, it follows that the two triangles LIF and EIM are equiangular:

Therefore, LI : FI :: IE : IM;
Hence, LI.IM = FI.IE.

But, since the plane LIM intersects the surface of the cone in a circle, LI.IM is equal to the square of the ordinate at the point I: hence FI.IE is also equal to the square of the ordinate of the curve in which the plane FIE intersects the surface of the cone: consequently, that curve is a circle.

circle projected would have been a great circle. It can be shown, by similar reasoning, that the cone having such a circle for its base and A for its vertex, would be cut by the primitive plane in a sub-contrary section.

THEOREM III.

If at any point of the surface of a sphere a line be drawn tangent to the sphere, and produced till it meets the primitive plane, the part intercepted between the point of contact and the primitive plane is equal to its projection.

§ 199. Pl. 3. Fig. 1. At the point of contact conceive a plane to be drawn tangent to the sphere; this plane will contain the tangent line (88).

Let a plane be passed through the point of contact perpendicular to the tangent and primitive planes, and take this plane for the plane of the paper: ABDC is the circle in which it intersects the sphere, BCE is the trace of the primitive plane, A the place of the eye, and D the point of tangency. The plane of the paper intersects the tangent plane in a line tangent to the circle in which it intersects the sphere: hence, DE, drawn tangent to the circle at D, is the trace of the tangent plane. Since the tangent and primitive planes are perpendicular to the plane of the paper, their intersection is perpendicular to it; therefore, EF, drawn perpendicular to the plane of the paper at E, is the intersection of these planes. Every tangent line to the sphere at D pierces the primitive plane at some point of the line EF. Let the tangent which pierces it at E′ be first projected. The point D is projected at D′, and E′ is its own projection; therefore, D′E′ is the projection of the tangent, and it only remains to be proved that this projection is equal to the tangent DE′ in space. The angle ADE, being formed by a tangent and chord, is measured by half the arc ACD; the angle DD′C, being formed by two chords, is measured by half the sum of AB and CD, or half the sum of AC and CD, or half of ACD: hence, the triangle EDD′ is isosceles, and ED is

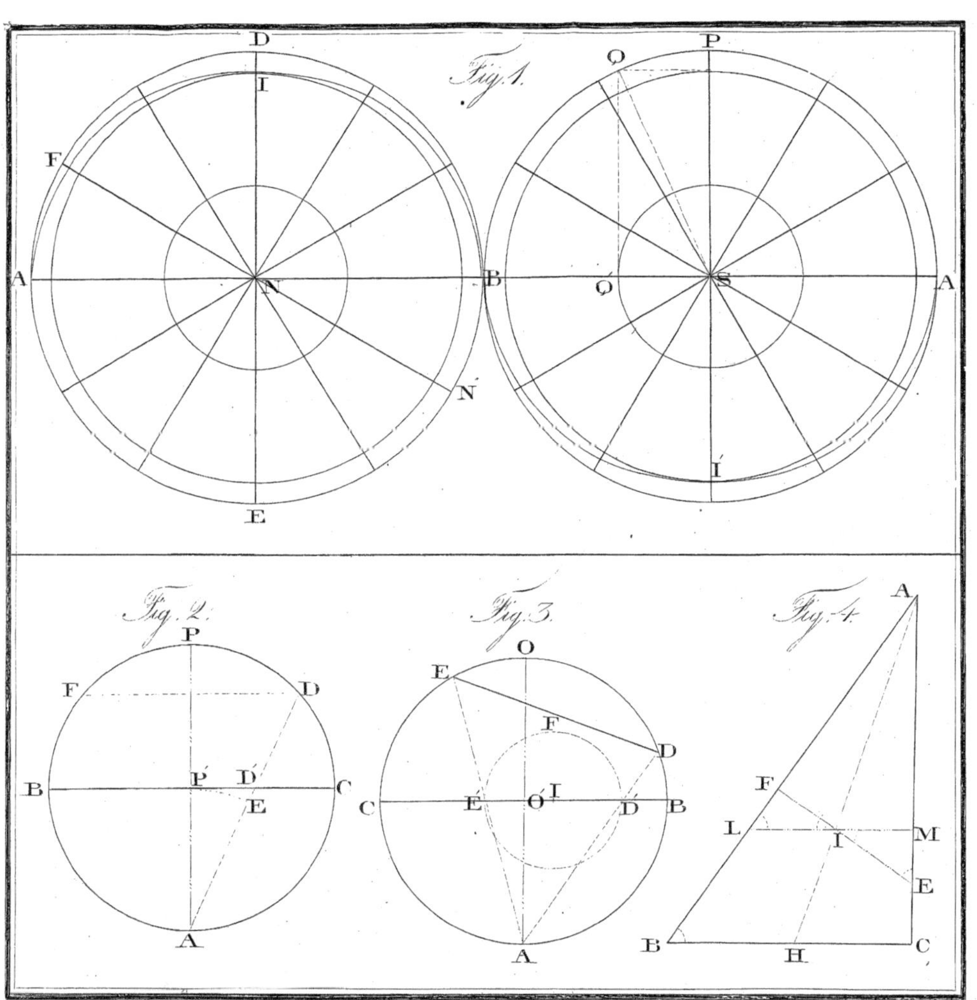
Fig. 1.
D
I
F
A
N
B
N′
E
Q
P
Q′
S
A
I′
Fig. 2.
P
F
D
B
P′
D′
C
E
A
Fig. 3.
O
E
F
D
C
E′
O′
I
D′
B
A
Fig. 4.
A
F
L
I
M
E
B
H
C

equal to ED′. But DE′, in space, is the hypothenuse of a triangle of which DE is the base and EE′ the perpendicular: D′E′ is the hypothenuse of a triangle of which D′E is the base and EE′ the perpendicular: as the bases of these right-angled triangles are equal and their perpendiculars the same line, it follows that their hypothenuses are equal. But DE′ is the tangent line in space, and D′E′ is its projection; therefore, the tangent line intercepted between the point of contact and the primitive plane is equal to its projection.

§ 200. Drawing another tangent at the point D, as DF, it will pierce the primitive plane at F, and its projection D′F is equal to itself. The angle E′DF, which the tangents make with each other in space, is equal to the angle E′D′F contained by their projections. For, in the triangles DE′F and E′D′F the side DE′ is equal to D′E′, DF to D′F, and the side E′F common; the two triangles are therefore equal, and the angle E′DF is equal to the angle E′D′F; that is, *the angle contained by the tangents in space is equal to the angle contained by their projections.*

§ 201. *If a right line be tangent to a circle of the sphere, the projection of the right line is tangent to the projection of the circle.* For, the projection of the circle is the intersection by the primitive plane of the cone of which the circle is the base and the eye the vertex; the projection of the right line is the intersection of the plane passing through it and the eye, with the primitive plane: but the plane which projects the line is tangent to the cone which projects the circle; their intersections with the primitive plane. are, therefore, tangent to each other.

§ 202. *The angle formed by the arcs of two circles intersecting on the surface of a sphere is equal to the angle contained by their projections.* For, the angle contained by two arcs intersecting on the surface of a sphere, is measured by the angle contained by two right lines drawn tangent respectively to the arcs at their point of intersection: the angle contained by the projections of these arcs is also measured by the angle of their tangents: but the projections of the tangents are tangent to the projections of the arcs (201); and the angle contained by the projections of the tangents is equal to the angle of the tangents in space: hence, the angle contained by the projections of the arcs is equal to the angle formed by the arcs on the surface of the sphere.

§ 203. If from the centres of the projections of two circles radii be drawn to the points in which their circumferences intersect, they will make the same angle with each other as the two tangents drawn to the circles at the same point, since they are respectively perpendicular to the tangents.

Hence, the radii drawn through either point in which the projections of circles intersect, make an angle with each other equal to that which the circles themselves formed on the surface of the sphere.

THEOREM IV.

The centre of the projection of a great circle is in the line of measures, at a distance from the centre of the primitive circle equal to the tangent of the inclination of the circles; and the radius with which the projection is described is equal to the secant of the inclination.

§ 204. Pl. 4. Fig. 1. Let ACA′B be a circle passed through the axis of the primitive circle and the axis of the circle to be projected, A the place of the eye, P‴BD′ the trace of the primitive plane, and ED the orthographic projection of the circle to be projected: P‴BD′ is its line of measures (176).

The point D is projected at D′, and the point E at E′; E′D′ is a diameter, and S, the middle of E′D′, the centre of the circle into which ED is projected. With S as a centre, and SE′ or SD′ as radius, let the circle be described in the primitive plane. Since all lines in the primitive plane are projected orthographically in P‴D′, they can only be presented to the eye by revolving the primitive plane to coincide with the plane of the paper. Let it be revolved around P‴D′: the points E′, S, and D′ remain fixed, being in the axis; the point directly over O falls at A′,

Plate 3.

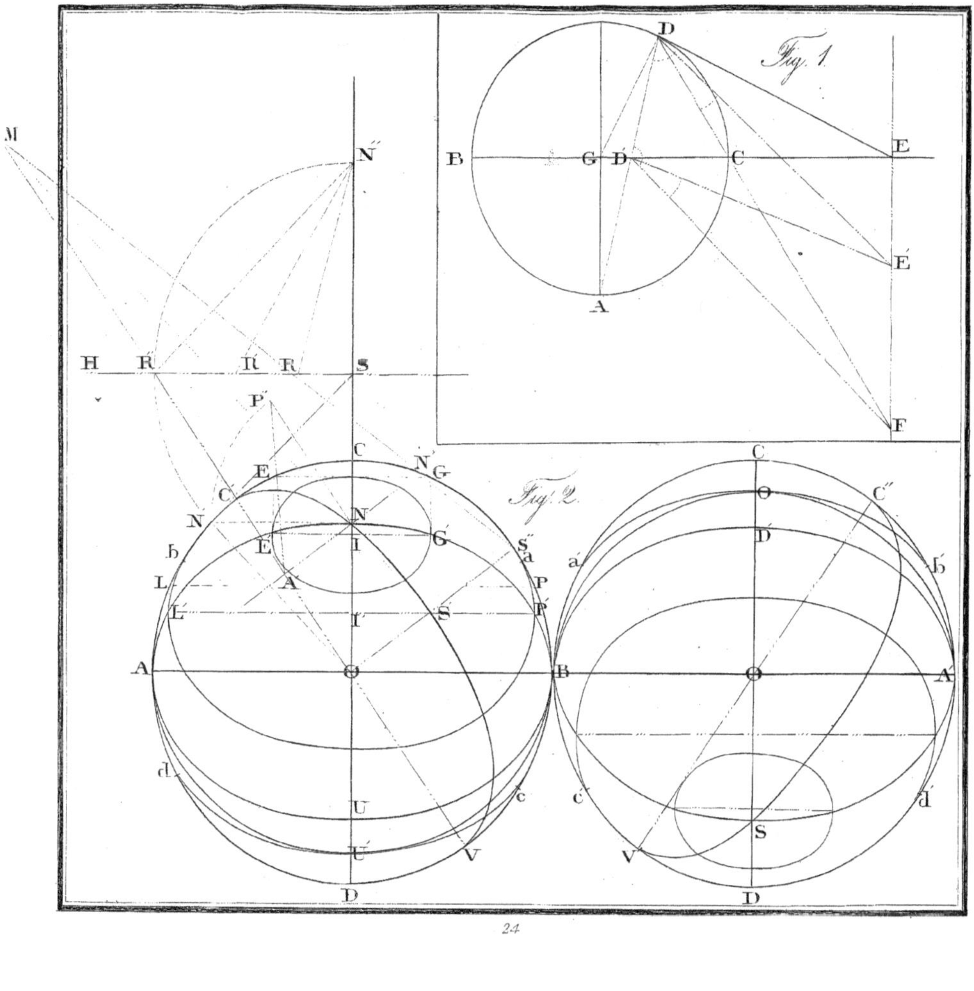

Fig. 1.

Fig. 2.

the primitive circle coincides with the circle ACA′B, and AD′A′ is the projection of the circle DE. As the primitive circle is its own projection, it follows that the angle SAO is equal to the inclination of the circles (203); that is, equal to the angle EOB. But OS is equal to the tangent of the angle SAO, to the radius of the sphere, and AS is its secant; therefore, the centre of the circle AD′A′ is in the line of measures at a distance from the centre of the primitive circle equal to the tangent of the inclination, and its radius is equal to the secant of the inclination.

THEOREM V.

The poles of a circle are projected in its line of measures; the one farthest from the eye, at a distance from the centre of the primitive circle equal to the semi-tangent of the inclination of the circles; the one nearest the eye, at a distance from the centre of the primitive circle equal to the semi-cotangent of the inclination.

§ 205. Since the axis of every circle of the sphere passes through the centre of the sphere, a plane can be drawn through the poles to be projected and the axis of the primitive circle. As this plane passes through the eye, the poles will be projected in its trace; that is, in the line of measures of the circle to which they belong (176).

Let DE (Pl. 4. Fig. 1) be the orthographic projection of a circle, PP′ its axis, P and P′ its poles, and AA′ the axis of the primitive circle. The pole P is projected at P″, and the pole P′ at P‴. The angle A′OP is equal to the inclination of the circles (175); and the angle A′AP is half this angle, being an angle at the circumference, and standing on the same arc A′P. But OP″ is the tangent of the angle P″AO; it is therefore the semi-tangent of A′P, or the semi-tangent of the inclination. The angle PAP′ is a right angle, being an angle in a semicircle; therefore, OAP‴ is the complement of OAP, or the complement of half the inclination of the circles: consequently, OP‴, the tangent of the angle OAP‴, or the cotangent of OAP″, is the cotangent of half the inclination of the circles, or semicotangent of their inclination.

Since the poles of a great circle and of a small circle parallel to it are the same, it is evident that the poles of a small circle are also projected in its line of measures, and at distances from the centre of the primitive circle equal to the semi-tangent and semi-cotangent of its inclination.

THEOREM VI.

The centre of the projection of a small circle perpendicular to the primitive plane is in the line of measures, at a distance from the centre of the primitive circle equal to the secant of the circle's polar distance, and the radius of the projection is equal to the tangent of the polar distance.

§ 206. Pl. 4. Fig. 2. Let ADEB, in the plane of the paper, be the circle in which the plane through the axis of the primitive circle and the axis of the lesser circle intersects the sphere, A the place of the eye, D′B the trace of the primitive plane, and ED the diameter of the lesser circle to be projected

The extremity D of the diameter is projected at D, the extremity E at E′, and E′D′ is a diameter of the projected circle. Bisect it at G, and suppose the circle to be described in the primitive plane. Let the primitive plane be revolved around D′B to coincide with the plane of the paper. The primitive circle will then coincide with the circle ADEB, and DE′ED′ is the projected circle thus revolved. The lines DO and DG, passing through D, the point in which the circumferences of the circles intersect, are perpendicular to each other, since the circles are at right angles in space (203); GD, therefore, is tangent to the circle ADEB. But CD is the polar distance of the small circle, GD is the tangent, and OG is the secant of this arc; therefore, the distance from the centre of the primitive circle to the centre of the projected circle is equal to the secant of its polar distance, and the radius with which it is described to the tangent of the polar distance.

THEOREM VII.

The extremities of a diameter of a small circle oblique to the primitive plane are projected in its line of measures, at distances from the centre of the primitive circle equal to the semi-tangent of the inclination plus the polar distance, and the semi-tangent of the difference between the inclination and polar distance; the projections of these extremities are on the same side of the centre of the primitive circle when the polar distance is less than the inclination, and on different sides when it is greater.

§ 207. Pl. 4. Fig. 3. Suppose the plane of the paper to pass through the axis of the primitive circle, and the axis of the circle to be projected; and let ABA′C be the circle in which it intersects the sphere. Let A be the position of the eye, AA′ the axis of the primitive circle, OP the axis of the circle to be projected, and HG its orthographic projection; PG is its polar distance, and PA′ its inclination.

The point H is projected in the line of measures at H′, a distance from the centre of the primitive circle equal to the semi-tangent of A′H; that is, the semi-tangent of A′P the inclination, plus PH the polar distance. The point G is projected at G′, a distance from the centre of the primitive circle equal to the semi-tangent of A′G; that is, the semi-tangent of the inclination A′P, minus the polar distance GP: G′H′ is a diameter of the circle into which the circle HG is projected.

For the second case, take a circle parallel to GH, and whose orthographic projection is DE. The polar distance PD of this circle is greater than PA′, its inclination. It is plain that the point D is projected at D′, and the point E at E′. The line OD′ is the semi-tangent of A′D; that is, of PD minus PA′: hence OD′ is equal to the semi-tangent of the polar distance minus the inclination. It is plain, that OE′ is equal to the semi-tangent of A′PE; that is, equal to the semi-tangent of the inclination A′P, plus the polar distance PE. In the second case, therefore, the extremities of that diameter which is in the line of measures correspond in their positions to the enunciation of the text.

§ 208. If the inclination of either of the circles, as DE, were equal to its polar distance, the point D would be at A′, and would be projected at O, the centre of the primitive circle. Hence, *the projections of all small circles whose polar distances are equal to their angles of inclination, pass through the centre of the primitive circle.*

§ 209. If the surface of an entire sphere were projected on the same plane, without changing the position of the eye, that part of it lying between the eye and primitive plane would be projected without the primitive circle; small circles near the eye would be projected into very large circles, and circles near the opposite pole would be projected into circles much less than themselves. Thus, the magnitudes of circles would bear little proportion to that of their projections; equal circles of the sphere would be unequal in projection, and the projection of the sphere made after this method would rather confuse than aid the mind in conceiving of its different parts. To remedy, in some degree, this defect of the stereographic projection, we generally project the hemisphere between the primitive plane and the pole opposite the eye; then revolve the other hemisphere 180° around a line tangent to the primitive circle, and suppose the eye to be removed parallel to the primitive plane, till it comes into the axis of this hemisphere after it is revolved: the hemisphere is then behind the primitive plane, and the eye in the pole of the primitive circle. If from this position the hemisphere be projected, we shall have the projection of the entire sphere on the same plane.

PROBLEM I.

To project the sphere on the plane of the equator.

§ 210. Let the eye be supposed at the south pole; the northern hemisphere will then be first projected.

Let FAGB (Pl. 4. Fig. 4) be the equator; the eye is in a perpendicular to the plane of the paper at N, and at a distance from it equal to the radius NA. The northern hemisphere lies behind the primitive plane. The north pole is projected at the centre N. Let A and B be the equinoctial points: AB is the line in which the plane of the ecliptic intersects the plane of the equator. The ecliptic passes through the points A and B, and makes an angle of $23\frac{1}{2}°$ with the equator; its line of measures is FG (176), which contains the centre of the circle into which it is projected (204). At the point A make the angle NAO equal to $23\frac{1}{2}°$; the line AO will pass through the centre of the circle into which the ecliptic is projected (203); O is, therefore, the centre of this circle. With this centre, and radius OA, let the arc AEB be described; this arc is the projection of that half of the ecliptic which lies north of the equator. The centre O might have been found by making NO equal to the tangent of $23\frac{1}{2}°$ (204).

The planes of the meridians, passing through the axis of the earth, must pass through the eye, and will consequently be projected into right lines (195); but, as they are great circles, their projections pass through the centre of the primitive circle (195). The projections of the meridians are, therefore, determined by laying off from A arcs equal to 15°, 30°, 45°, &c., and drawing diameters through their extremities. The line ANB is the projection of the equinoctial colure, and GNF of the solstitial colure; the projections of four other meridians are also drawn in the figure.

The parallels of latitude, being parallel to the primitive plane, the radii of their projections are equal to the semi-tangents of their polar distances (192). To project the arctic circle. Make the angle NFI equal to half of 23½°; NI is the semi-tangent of 23½° to the radius of the sphere. With NI as a radius and N as a centre, describe a circle; it will be the projection of the arctic circle. In like manner, making the angle NFD equal to half of 66½° determines ND, the radius of the circle into which the tropic of Cancer is projected. The projection of the tropic of Cancer is tangent to the projection of the ecliptic at E. The principles used in projecting the arctic circle and the tropic of Cancer are equally applicable in projecting any of the parallels of latitude.

Let the semi-sphere, which is in front of the primitive plane, be now revolved 180° around a line tangent to the primitive circle at B. The eye is supposed to be moved parallel to the primitive plane till it is projected at S. As the hemisphere, primitive plane, and eye have the same relative positions as they had in the projection which has just been made, it follows that the circles of the hemisphere will be projected in the same manner. The arc BE'A' is the projection of the half of the ecliptic corresponding to AEB; G'E'F' is the projection of the half of the solstitial colure corresponding to GF; BA' is the projection of the half of the equinoctial colure corresponding to AB; the small circles described about the centre S are the projections of the antarctic circle and tropic of Capricorn. The diameters passing through S are the projections of the meridians.

PROBLEM II.

To project the sphere on the plane of the equinoctial colure.

§ 211. Pl. 5. Fig. 1. Let SBNQ be the plane of the equinoctial colure, N the place of the north, and S the plane of the south pole: Q and B the equinoctial points.

Since the meridians pass through the poles, their projections pass through the projections of the poles N and S, and their planes intersect the primitive plane in the line SN. The line QBR, drawn through O, the centre of the primitive circle, per

Plate 4.

Fig. 1.
A′ P E P‴ B E O P″ S C D′ D P A
Fig. 3.
D A′ G P H B D′ O G′ H′ C E′ E A
Fig. 2.
E D′ G C E′ O B D A
Fig. 4.
G O A N I D B E F
G′ E′ S A′ F′

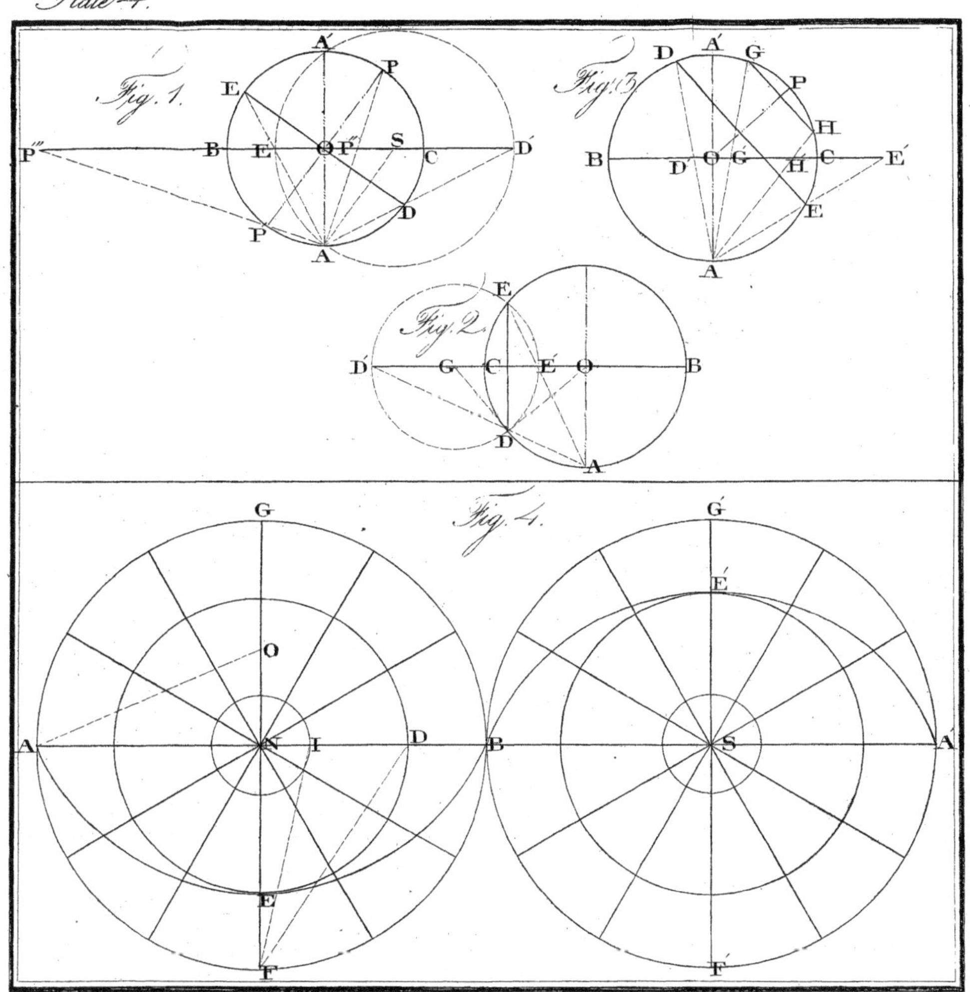

pendicular to NS, is the line of measures of all the meridians (176). To project any meridian, as the one, for example, that makes an angle of 30° with the primitive circle. At either pole, as S, lay off an angle OSD equal to 30°; the point D, in which the line SD meets the line of measures, is the centre of the projection of the meridian (203). With D as a centre and radius DS, let the meridian SEN be described. The centre D could also be found by laying off from O, in the line of measures, OD equal to the tangent of 30° the angle of inclination of the meridian with the primitive plane. After the same manner the other meridians are projected. The line SON is the projection of the solstitial colure. The equator passes through the eye, and its projection is the right line QOB. The ecliptic passes through the points Q and B, and makes an angle of $66\frac{1}{2}°$ with the primitive plane; NS is its line of measures. If, on the hemisphere which is behind the primitive plane, the ecliptic lies between the equator and south pole, lay off from O, in the direction ON, the tangent of $66\frac{1}{2}°$; with the extremity of this line as a centre, and the distance to Q as radius, describe the arc QFB, which will be the projection of that half of the ecliptic that lies behind the primitive plane. If, on the hemisphere behind the primitive plane, the ecliptic had been situated between the equator and north pole, the radius of its projection would have been laid off from O in the direction OS.

The parallels of latitude are perpendicular to the primitive plane, and SN is their line of measures. In projecting them, we shall begin with the arctic circle. From N lay off the arc N*f* equal to $23\frac{1}{2}°$; draw NC perpendicular to SN, join O*f*, and produce it to C. The line OC is the secant and NC the tangent of $23\frac{1}{2}°$ to the radius of the primitive circle. With O as a centre and radius OC describe the arc CC′; with C′ as a centre and radius equal to CN or C′*f* describe the arc *f*I; this arc is the projection of the arctic circle. We determine, by similar constructions, *ba* the projection of the tropic of Cancer, and *c*F*d*, the projection of the tropic of Capricorn (206).

Let the semi-sphere which is in front of the primitive plane be now revolved behind it, around a line tangent to the primi tive circle at B; the projections of its different circles can then be made by constructions entirely similar to those already given.

§ 212. The projection of the sphere on the plane of the solstitial colure, is made in the same manner as its projection on the plane of the equinoctial colure, excepting that the ecliptic, being perpendicular to the primitive plane instead of being oblique to it in an angle of $66\frac{1}{2}°$, is projected into a right line passing through the centre of the primitive circle, and making an angle of $23\frac{1}{2}°$ with the projection of the equator. Drawing the lines bOd and $d'b'$, making angles of $23\frac{1}{2}°$ with QR, the projection of the equator, and supposing the curve QFBR to be removed, the figure will represent the projection of the sphere on the plane of the solstitial colure.

PROBLEM III.

To project the sphere on the horizon of any place, that place, for example, the latitude of which is 45° north.

§ 213. Pl. 5. Fig. 2. Let AEBL be the plane of the horizon. Let the eye be supposed at the lower pole of the primitive circle; the upper hemisphere will then be first projected.

Assume A and B for the equinoctial points; AB is the line in which the plane of the equator intersects the horizon; the plane of the ecliptic and the plane of the equinoctial colure also intersect the horizon in the same line AB. The line EL, drawn through the centre D, perpendicular to AB, is the line of measures of the equator, ecliptic, and equinoctial colure. The equator makes an angle with the primitive plane equal to the complement of the angle which the axis of the earth makes with it; that is, an angle of 45°. The projection of the equator can therefore be described, and is the arc AFB. Suppose the ecliptic, on the upper hemisphere, to lie between the equator and north pole; it will, in that case, make an angle with the primitive plane greater by 23° than the angle made by the equator. The projection of the ecliptic can then be described.

it is the arc AGB. The equinoctial colure makes an angle of 45° with the primitive plane; and as DE is equal to the tangent of 45°, E is the centre, and the distance EA or EB the radius with which its projection ANB is described. The solstitial colure, being perpendicular to AB the intersection of the equator and equinoctial colure is, perpendicular to the primitive plane; its projection is therefore the diameter LDE. The point N, in which this line intersects the projection of the equinoctial colure, is the projection of the north pole. If the remaining part of the projection of the equinoctial colure be described, it will meet the line LE in another point, which point would be the projection of the south pole. If the distance intercepted between N and the projection of the south pole be bisected at E, and EH be drawn perpendicular to NE, EH will contain the centres of the circles which are the projections of the meridians. For, as the meridians pass through the poles, their projections will pass through the projections of the poles; therefore, the part of the axis intercepted between the projections of the poles is a common chord of the projections of the meridians; and the line EH, bisecting it perpendicularly, contains all their centres. To project any meridian, as the one, for example, making an angle of 30° with the equinoctial colure. At N lay off the angle ENH equal to 30°; the point H, in which NH intersects EH, is the centre of the projected meridian (203). With H as a centre and radius HN let the meridian H′NP be described. The projections of the other meridians drawn in the figure are made by similar constructions.

To project the parallels of latitude. These parallels are small circles, and being parallel to the equator have the same line of measures, and make the same angle with the primitive plane. To project the arctic circle. Its polar distance is $23\frac{1}{2}°$, and its inclination 45°. Lay off from L to g' $68\frac{1}{2}°$, that is, the polar distance $23\frac{1}{2}°+45°$ the inclination, and join g' and E. The line Dg is the semi-tangent of $68\frac{1}{2}°$. Let Lf be made equal to $45°—23\frac{1}{2}°=21\frac{1}{2}°$, and draw E$f$; D$f'$ is the semi-tangent of the inclination minus the polar distance. Let the distances Dg and Df' be laid off from D on the line of measures

EL; $f''g''$ is the diameter of the projection of the arctic circle (207). Let this diameter be bisected and the circle described. All other parallels of latitude are projected by similar constructions. The projection of the tropic of Cancer touches the projection of the ecliptic at G, and intersects the primitive plane at *a* and *b*. The tropic of Capricorn intersects the primitive plane at *d* and *c*. No part of the antarctic circle lies above the primitive plane.

Let, now, the lower hemisphere be revolved 180° around a line tangent to the primitive circle at B, and then project the different circles by the methods already explained. Their projections are easily recognised in the figure.

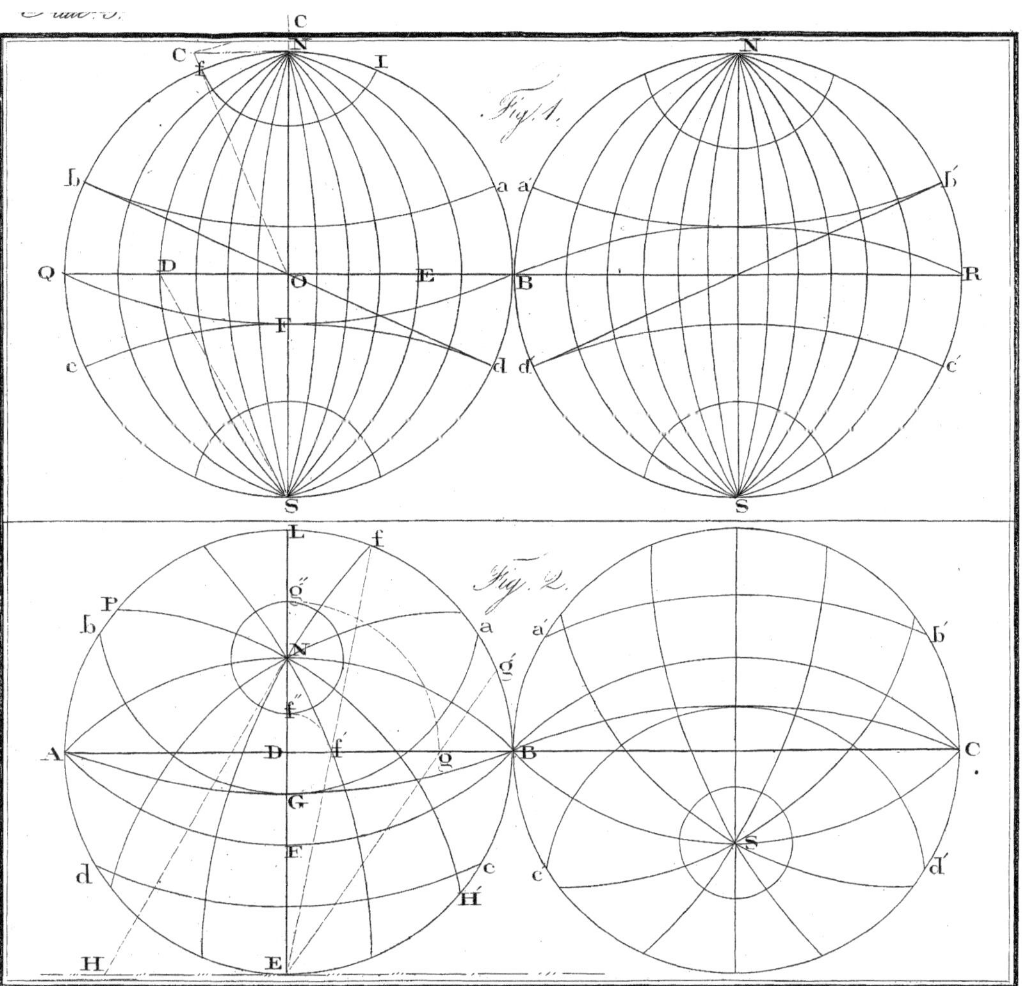
Fig. 1.
C
N
C
f
I
b
a
a′
b′
Q
D
O
E
B
R
F
c
d
d′
c′
S
S
Fig. 2.
L
f
g″
P
b
a
a′
b′
N
g′
f″
A
D
f′
g
B
C
G
F
S
d
c
c′
d′
H′
H
E

COMPLEMENT

OF

DESCRIPTIVE GEOMETRY.

WARPED SURFACES.*

§ 214. We have already defined Warped Surfaces to be those surfaces which may be generated by a right line moving in such a manner that its consecutive positions shall not be in the same plane (72). This class of surfaces is entirely distinct from the single-curved surfaces, though both are generated by a right line. In the single-curved surfaces, the consecutive positions of the generatrix are in the same plane; in the warped surfaces they are not; and although this difference in the manner of their generation may seem unimportant, yet it gives to the surfaces very different forms, and essentially different properties.

§ 215. This family of surfaces presents, perhaps, more varieties than any other; we shall examine only the most useful kinds, and begin with those whose properties are most simple.

§ 216. Of warped surfaces which have a plane-directer. Let there be supposed any two curves in space, and a line to move along these curves constantly touching them and continuing parallel to a given plane. Unless the curves have a particular position with each other, or with the given plane, the consecutive positions of the generatrix will not be in the

---

* A portion of this Complement is translated from *Vallée's* excellent *Traite de la Géométrie Descriptive.*

10

same plane: hence, the surface generated will be a warped surface. The plane to which the generatrix continues parallel is called the *plane-directer*, and the lines which it touches *directrices.*

§ 217. Pl. I. Let (AB, A′B′) and (CD, C′D′) be the linear directrices of a warped surface, and (OM, ON′) its plane-directer. *It is required to construct any element of the surface; the one, for example, passing through the point* (A, A′) *of the first directrix.*

If through this point, a plane be passed parallel to the plane directer, and the point in which it cuts the second directrix (CD, C′D′) determined, the line joining this point and the point (A,A′) will be the element required. We could thus determine the element passing through any point of either directrix; but, as drawing the planes and finding the points in which they cut the directrices is rather tedious, we give the following method for constructing the elements as more concise and elegant.

Draw in the plane-directer (MO, ON′) any right line, as (MN, M′N′). Intersect the plane-directer by a system of vertical planes, PM, Pa, Pb, &c. drawn through any point, P, of the trace OM: these planes cut the line (MN, M′N′) in the points (M,M′), (a,a'), (b,b'), &c.; the lines joining these points and the point (P,P′) are the intersections of the vertical planes with the plane-directer. Through the point (A,A′) draw a system of lines (Ar, A′r'), (Aq, A′q'), &c. respectively parallel to the lines (Pb, P′b'), (Pa, P′a'), &c. of the plane-directer; this system of lines forms a plane passing through (A,A′) parallel to the plane-directer; it is required to find the point in which this plane cuts the second directrix (CD, C′D′). The system of parallels through (A,A′) intersects the surface of the cylinder which projects the second directrix on the horizontal plane in a curve of which DCp is the horizontal projection; the vertical projection of this curve is found by drawing perpendiculars to the ground line through the points r, q, p, &c., and determining their intersections r', q', p', &c. with the vertical projections of the parallels through (A,A′); $r'q'p'$ is the vertical projection of the curve. The point in which this curve intersects the second directrix is the point in which the second directrix is cut by the plane passing through (A,A′) parallel to the plane-directer. The vertical projection of the point is in the curve D′C′, and also in the curve $r'q'p'$: hence, it is at C′, their point of intersection. Drawing through C′ a perpendicular to the ground line, determines C, the horizontal projection of the point. Therefore, (AC, A′C′) is the element of the surface passing through (A,A′). If we take any point, other than (A,A′), of either directrix, the element of the surface passing through it would be determined in a similar manner.

§ 218. *To find an element of the surface parallel to any line, as* (Pa, P′a'), *of the plane-directer.*

Through the several points (d,d'), (e,e'), (f,f'), (g,g'), &c. of either directrix, draw lines parallel to the given line (Pa, P′a'): they form the surface of a cylinder parallel to the line (Pa, P′a'); the element of this cylinder passing through the point in which the second directrix pierces its surface, touches both directrices, and is an element of the surface. This cylinder intersects the vertical cylinder which projects the second directrix on the horizontal plane in a curve of which kDp is the horizontal projection; its vertical projection is determined by finding the points k', i', j', h', &c. in which the perpendiculars to the ground line through the points k, i, j, h, &c. intersect the vertical projections of the parallels: $k'i'j'h'$ is the vertical projection of this curve. The point (D,D′), in which this curve intersects the second directrix, is the point in which the second directrix pierces the surface of the cylinder: hence, BD drawn parallel to Pa, and B′D′ drawn parallel to P′a', are the projections of the required element.

§ 219. If one of the directrices (AB, A′B′), (CD, C′D′) were a right line, the surface that would be generated belongs to a particular class of warped surfaces called *conoids*, because of the analogy existing between them and the surfaces of cones.*

* If all the points in which the elements touch the rectilinear directrix were brought together into one point, the elements still passing through the points in

If the directrix were perpendicular to the plane-directer, the conoid takes the name of *right conoid,* and the directrix the name of *the line of striction.**

If both the directrices are right lines, the surfaces generated, though a species of conoid, are called *hyperbolic paraboloids,* because the curves in which they are intersected by planes are either hyperbolas or parabolas. The rectilinear directrices are not in the same plane; for if they were, the generatrix would generate a plane, and not a warped surface.

§ 220. *The elements of a hyperbolic paraboloid divide the directrices proportionally.*

Let AC and A′C′ (Pl. 2. Fig. 1) be the directrices of a hyperbolic paraboloid; AA′, BB′, and CC′ three of its elements. Through A draw AD parallel to CC′; AD will be parallel to the plane-directer; and since AA′ is also parallel to the plane-directer, it follows that the plane A′AD is parallel to the plane-directer and may be taken for it. Demit from the points B′, C′, C, and B the perpendiculars B′*b*′, C′*c*′, C*c*, and B*b* on the plane A′AD. Since BB′ and CC′ are elements of the surface, they are parallel to the plane-directer, and consequently to the plane A′AD; therefore, C′*c*′=C*c*, and B′*b*′=B*b*: by drawing the lines A′*b*′*c*′ and A*bc* two similar triangles are formed, which give

$$Cc : Bb :: CA : BA, \text{ and } C'c' : B'b' :: C'A' : B'A';$$

but, on account of the equality of the terms of the first couplets, we have

$$CA : BA :: C'A' : B'A';$$

and by division,

$$CB : BA :: C'B' : B'A';$$

that is, the directrices CA and C′A′ are divided proportionally by the element BB′.

---

which they touch the second directrix, the surface becomes a conic surface. And if the vertex of a cone be moved along a right line, and lines be drawn from its different positions to the points of its base, such lines being parallel to a given plane, the surface thus formed is a conoid.

* It takes this name because it contains the shortest distance between the elements, so that the surface is, as it were, cramped or compressed along this line.

§ 221. Reciprocally, *if the lines* AA′, BB′, *and* CC′ *of a warped surface divide the rectilinear directrices* AC *and* A′C′ *into proportional parts, they will be parallel to the same plane, and consequently elements of a hyperbolic paraboloid of which that plane is the plane-directer.*

Let AD be drawn parallel to CC′, and demit the perpendiculars C*c*, B*b*, C′*c*′, and B′*b*′ on the plane A′AD. Drawing A*bc* and A′*b*′*c*′, we have

$$\text{AB} : \text{AC} :: \text{B}b : \text{C}c;$$

and

$$\text{A}'\text{B}' : \text{A}'\text{C}' :: \text{B}'b' : \text{C}'c';$$

but, by hypothesis,

$$\text{AB} : \text{BC} :: \text{A}'\text{B}' : \text{B}'\text{C}'.$$

By composition,

$$\text{AB} : \text{AC} :: \text{A}'\text{B}' : \text{A}'\text{C}';$$

therefore,

$$\text{B}b : \text{C}c :: \text{B}'b' : \text{C}'c'.$$

But the line CC′ being parallel to AD is parallel to the plane A′AD; therefore, C*c* is equal to C′*c*′, and consequently B*b* is equal to B′*b*′. All lines, therefore, which divide the directrices proportionally are parallel to the same plane, and consequently the surface generated by a right line moving with this law is a hyperbolic paraboloid.

§ 222. *If any two elements, as* AA′ *and* CC′ *of a hyperbolic paraboloid be taken as directrices, and a plane-directer be assumed parallel to* AC and A′C′, *the directrices in the first case, the surface generated by a right line moving on the new directrices and parallel to the new plane-directer, is the same surface as is generated by a right line touching* AC, A′C′, *and continuing parallel to the plane* A′AD. The surfaces are named respectively *the hyperbolic paraboloid of the first and second generation.*

We shall show that these surfaces are the same, by proving that all points of any element of the second generation are points of an element of the first generation, and reciprocally; that is, that the paraboloid of the second generation has all its points common with the paraboloid of the first generation: if this be proved, they are evidently the same surface.

Let *mn* (Pl. 2. Fig. 2) be any element of the second generation. In this generation the plane-directer is parallel to AC, A'C', and AA', CC' are the directrices. Draw from the points C and C' the lines C*c* and C'*c'* parallel to *mn*; and suppose *c* and *c'* the points in which they pierce the plane AA'D, drawn parallel to CC'. Let A*c* and A'*c'* also be drawn, and join the points *c* and *c'*: this line is the intersection of the plane AA'D with the plane passed through the element CC' and the parallels C*c*, *mn*, and C'*c'*; it therefore contains the point *n*, in which *mn* intersects AA'. Take, now, upon *mn* any point, as O, and conceive a plane to be drawn through this point parallel to AA'D; that is, parallel to the plane-directer of the first generation (220). This plane will cut the directrices AC and A'C', of the first generation, in two points B and B'; the line BB' is therefore an element of the first generation. It is now to be proved that O is a point of the element BB', and therefore a point of the surface of the first generation. Let the lines B*b* and B'*b'* be drawn parallel to *mn*, and as C*c* and C'*c'* are also parallel to *mn*, it follows that B*b* and B'*b'* will pierce the plane AA'D in the lines A*c* and A'*c'*. The triangles AB*b* and AC*c* are therefore similar, as also the triangles A'B'*b'* and A'C'*c'*:

therefore, AB : AC :: A*b* : A*c*;

and A'B' : A'C' :: A'*b'* : A'*c'*.

But (220), AB : AC :: A'B' : A'C';

therefore, A*b* : A*c* :: A'*b'* : A'*c'*.

Since the lines B*b* and C*c* are parallel to B'*b'* and C'*c'*, and since the four lines are all parallel to the plane-directer of the second generation, the plane of the triangle AC*c* is parallel to the plane of the triangle A'C'*c'*, and therefore their intersections A*bc* and A'*b'c'* with the plane AA'D are also parallel. But as these intersections are divided proportionally at *b* and *b'*, it follows that the points *b*, *n*, and *b'* are in the same right line: hence, the plane of the parallels B*b* and B'*b'* contains the lines BB' and *mn*; therefore, the point O of the element *mn* of the second generation is a point of the element BB' of the first generation. It may be proved in a similar manner, that any point of an element of the second generation is also a point of an element of the first generation: hence, the hyperbolic paraboloid is susceptible of two generations, as enunciated in the text.

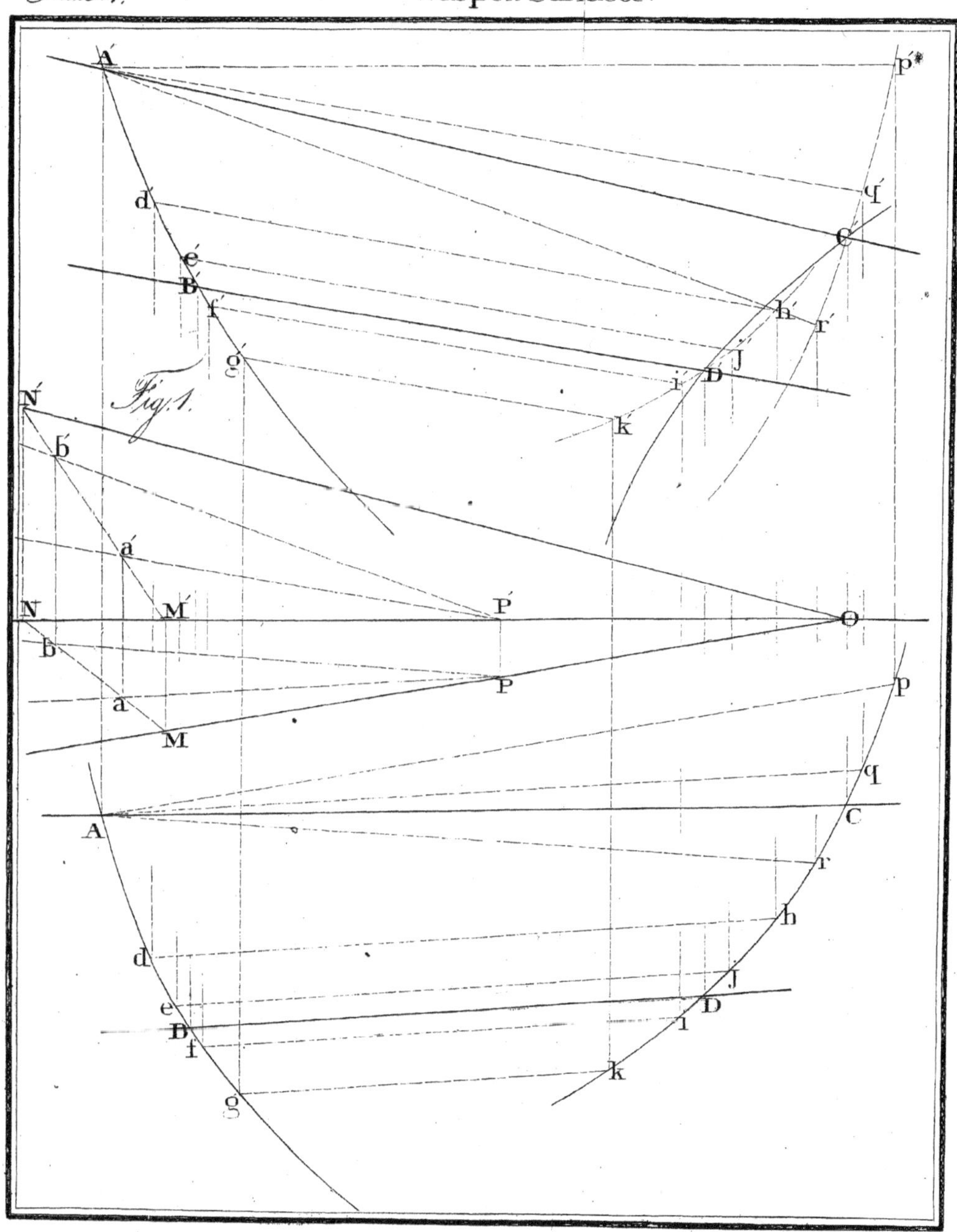
Fig. 1.
A′
p′
d′
q′
e′
C
B′
f′
h′
r′
g′
J
i
D
k
N′
b′
a′
N
M′
P′
O
b
P
a
M
p
q
A
C
r
h
d
J
e
D
B
i
f
k
g

§ 223. From what has preceded we conclude, that *if we take any two elements of the first generation and a plane parallel to its directrices, these lines and this plane are the directrices and plane-directer of the second generation; and, conversely, if we take two elements of the second generation and a plane parallel to its directrices, these lines and this plane are the directrices and plane-directer of the first generation.*

§ 224. Of warped surfaces which have three directrices. If we subject the generatrix to the condition of touching a third directrix, instead of continuing parallel to a plane-directer, the surface generated is still a warped surface, provided the directrices have such positions with each other that the consecutive elements of the surface are not in the same plane.

Let (AB, A′B′), (CD, C′D′), and (EF, E′F′) (Pl. 3) be the three directrices of a warped surface; and let it be required to find the element passing through any point of either directrix say the point (M,M′) of the directrix (AB, A′B′).

Suppose (M,M′) to be the vertex of a cone of which the second directrix (CD, C′D′) is the base. If the point (N,N′), in which the third directrix (EF, E′F′) pierces the surface of this cone, be determined, the line joining (M,M′) and (N,N′) will touch the three directrices, and consequently be an element of the surface. To find this point, take in the second directrix a series of points (D,D′), (a,a'), (b,b'), (c,c'), &c.; through these points and the vertex (M,M′) draw the elements (MD, M′D′), (Ma, M′a'), &c., and construct the points in which these elements pierce the vertical cylinder which projects the third directrix on the horizontal plane: these points are (F,H), (i,i'), (j,j'), (k,k'), &c., and H$i'j'k'l'm'n'$G is the vertical, and F$ijklmn$E is the horizontal projection of the curve in which the cone intersects the cylinder: the point (N,N′), in which this curve intersects the third directrix, is the point in which the third directrix pierces the surface of the cone: (MN, M′N′) is therefore a line which touches the three directrices, and is, consequently, an element of the surface. We can construct in a similar manner any number of elements, by means of which we can determine the contour and projections of the surface.

§ 225. If the three directrices are right lines, the surface generated belongs to a particular class of warped surfaces called *hyperboloids of one nappe.* Of this family of surfaces we shall discuss the most useful and interesting variety, viz. *the hyperboloids of revolution of one nappe.**

Before generating the hyperboloid of revolution of one nappe by a generatrix constantly touching three right lines having a particular position with each other, we shall generate it by a right line moving around another right line as an axis, and then show that this surface can also be generated by a right line touching three linear directrices. Let the horizontal plane be taken perpendicular to the line which is used as an axis, and the vertical plane parallel to the generatrix in any one of its positions.

Let (A,A′B′) (Pl. 2. Fig. 3) be the axis, and (CD, C′D′) the generatrix. The generatrix is to move around the axis in such a manner that each point of it shall describe a horizontal circle whose centre is in the axis (A,A′B′). Conceive a line to be drawn perpendicular to the axis and generatrix (60). Since the axis is perpendicular to the horizontal plane, this line will be parallel to it: hence, its horizontal projection is equal to

---

* If the hyperbola CFp' (Pl. 6. Fig. 7. Des. Geom.) be revolved around its conjugate axis, which is perpendicular to FB at E, it will generate the surface of a *hyperboloid of revolution of one nappe.* The convexity of this surface is turned towards the axis. If the hyperbolas CFp' and C′BC′ be revolved around the transverse axis FB, they will generate two distinct surfaces, but having the same axis FB; the two surfaces are called a *hyperboloid of revolution of two nappes.* If at either vertex of the transverse axis, as F, a line IFI′ be drawn tangent to the curve, and the parts FI and FI′ be each made equal to EO, the semi-conjugate axis, the lines CI′C′ and C′EH drawn through their extremities and the centre C, are called *asymptotes.* The asymptotes continually approach the curves CFp' and C′BC′, but never intersect them. If at any point of either curve, as G, a line HGN be drawn tangent to the curve, the part HG intercepted between the point of contact and one asymptote is equal to the part GN intercepted between the point of contact and the other asymptote. These properties of the asymptotes and tangent are demonstrated in conic sections, and are mentioned here only that they may be borne in mind in discussing the properties of the surface generated by a right line touching three rectilinear directrices.

itself and perpendicular to CD, the horizontal projection of the generatrix (51). The line AL is the horizontal and L′ the vertical projection of this perpendicular. When the generatrix (CD,C′D′) is revolved around the axis (A, A′B′), the line (AL,L′) continues perpendicular to it and to the axis: hence, the projections of the generatrix, from its different positions, are perpendicular to the projections of (AL,L′) from its different positions; that is, perpendicular to the extremities of the radii of a circle described with the centre A and radius AL. Hence, the horizontal projections of the elements of this surface are tangent to the circle *iqo*L, which is the smallest of the circles described by the points of the generatrix, and is called *the circle of the gorge.* The consecutive elements of this surface are not parallel, for if they were their horizontal projections would be parallel (30); but the horizontal projections are not parallel, since they are tangent to the circle *iqo*L. Neither do the consecutive elements intersect each other; for their points which are in the same horizontal plane are separated by arcs of horizontal circles. The surface, therefore, is a *warped surface*, and it is also a surface of revolution, since the sections by planes perpendicular to the axis are circles. Let C*k*G′EE′ be the circle described by the point C, as the element (CD, C′D′) moves around the axis; this is the circle in which the horizontal plane intersects the surface.

Through D draw the line (DC, D″C″) parallel to the vertical plane, and making the same angle with the horizontal plane as is made by the line (CD, C′D′): these lines intersect at the point (L,L′), and the perpendicular (AL,L′) to the one, is also perpendicular to the other. If the plane of the two lines be carried around the right cylinder whose axis is the axis of the surface, and whose base is the horizontal circle *oqi*L, each of the lines will generate the same surface; for, if a plane be drawn perpendicular to the axis (A,A′B′) it will cut the lines in points equidistant from the axis, and in the revolution of the lines these points describe the same horizontal circle: the point in which the lines intersect, describes the circle of the gorge. But if two surfaces have the same axis, and if all sections made in them by planes perpendicular to this axis are respectively equal, the two surfaces coincide throughout and are the same surface: hence, the surface we are discussing can be generated by either of two right lines at the same distance from the axis and making the same angle with a plane perpendicular to it.

§ 226. *If one of the generatrices remain fixed and the surface be generated by the other, the fixed generatrix will intersect the moving one in all its positions.* Let the generatrix (DC, D″C″) remain fixed, and suppose the surface to be generated by (CD, C′D′). When the point C is at any point of the circle CG′ED, as E, the horizontal projection of the generatrix is determined by drawing E*o*G tangent to the circle *oqi*L (225). Its vertical projection is determined by projecting E into the ground line at *e*, and *o* into the vertical projection of the circle of the gorge at *o*′, and drawing *eo*′*g*. The horizontal projections of the generatrices intersect at *n*, and *no* is equal to *n*L, since the lines are tangent to the same circle. But the points (L,L′) and (*o*,*o*′) are in the plane of the circle of the gorge, and the generatrices make equal angles with this plane: hence, the parts of the generatrices of which *no* and *n*L are the projections are equal. The points of the two generatrices of which *n* is the horizontal projection are, therefore, at the same distance above the plane of the circle of the gorge, and consequently above the horizontal plane; but their vertical projections are contained in a perpendicular to the ground line through *n* (13): hence, they are the same point *n*′, and therefore the generatrices intersect in space (44), and (*n*,*n*′) is their point of meeting. This point is above the circle of the gorge, and at an infinite distance from it, when the generatrix (EG, *eg*) becomes parallel to the vertical plane. When the generatrix (CD, C′D′) takes the position (E′G′, E″G″), it intersects the generatrix (DC, D″C″) at (*m*,*m*′), a point of the surface below the circle of the gorge. In the same manner it may be shown, that if the generatrix (CD, C′D′) remain fixed, and the generatrix (DC, D″C″) be revolved, (CD, C′D′) would, in all its positions, intersect (CD, C″D″): hence, we conclude that *the generatrix of the first generation intersects all the elements of the second generation.*

and that the generatrix of the second generation intersects all the elements of the first generation. If, therefore, any three elements of the first generation be assumed, and a right line drawn touching them, this line is the generatrix of the second generation; and if three elements of the second generation be chosen, a right line touching them is the generatrix of the first generation.

We have now shown that the surface generated by the revolution of a right line about an axis which it does not intersect, may also be generated by a right line touching constantly three rectilinear directrices. We should remark, however, that these directrices must have the same relative position as three elements of the surface generated by the other method; that is, they are at the same perpendicular distance from a fourth line, and the perpendiculars measuring this distance are contained in the same plane.

§ 227. *To show that this surface is the surface of a hyperboloid of revolution of one nappe.*

Pl. 2. Fig. 4. Let the axis of the surface be perpendicular to the horizontal plane at A, and let *d*A*c* be the trace of a meridian plane to which the vertical plane of projection is taken parallel. It will be proved that this meridian plane intersects the surface in hyperbolas, and that the projections of the generatrices (CD, C′D″) and (DC, D′C″) on this plane are asymptotes of the curves.

The vertical projections of the generatrices are the lines C′D″ and D′C″; (*ab*, *a′b′*) is the line in which the meridian plane intersects the circle of the gorge: this line is the transverse axis, and (*a*,*a′*) and (*b*,*b′*) the vertices of the curve in which the meridian plane intersects the surface. To find other points of the curve, let the surface be intersected by horizontal planes; these planes will intersect it in horizontal circles, and the meridian plane in right lines; the points in which these lines intersect the circles are points of the required curve. Let *h′*H′G*m′* be the vertical trace of one of these planes; (H,H′) is the point in which it cuts the generatrix (CD, C′D″), and is therefore one point of the circumference of the horizontal circle in which it intersects the surface. With A as a centre and AH as a radius, let the semicircle *h*H*m* be described: this is the horizontal projection of a part of the circle in which the horizontal plane intersects the surface, and the points *h* and *m*, in which it meets the projection of the line of intersection of the horizontal and meridian planes, are the projections of two points of the required curve. The vertical projections of these points are *h'* and *m'*. The horizontal plane *f'*F'*n'* determines the points (*f*,*f'*) and (*n*,*n'*). Thus, by using horizontal planes above and below the circle of the gorge, we obtain as many points as are necessary to describe the curves *d'h'f'a'd''* and *c'm'n'b'c''*.

The lines C'D'' and D'C'' continually approach these curves. For, the distances F'*f'*, H'*h'*, D''*d'*, &c. are equal to the differences between the radii AF, AH, AD, &c. and their vertical projections EF', GH', and UD''. But these differences continually diminish; for the radii AF, AH, and AD make a less and less angle with the vertical plane as the cutting plane is removed from the plane of the gorge, and therefore the differences between them and their projections constantly diminish. If the horizontal cutting plane were taken at an infinite distance from the circle of the gorge, the radius AD would become parallel to the vertical plane; the points *d'* and D'' would then coincide, and L'D'' would become tangent to the curve. We see, therefore, that the line L'D'' continually approaches the curve *d''a'f'h'd'*, and becomes tangent to it at an infinite distance from *a'*; this is the property of a hyperbola and its asymptote. The same can be shown for the curve *c''b'n'm'c'* and the line D'C'', and also for the curves and lines below the circle of the gorge.

Let (QIO, Q'I'O') be any element of the surface intersecting the meridian plane *d*A*c* in the point (*p*,*p'*); (*p*,*p'*) is a point of the curve *c'b'c''*. The line drawn through (*p*,*p'*) tangent to the horizontal circle of the surface passing through this point, is perpendicular to the vertical plane, and is therefore a line of the plane which projects the element on the vertical plane. This projecting plane is consequently tangent to the surface at the point (p,p') (88): hence its intersection with the meridian plane is tangent to the meridian curve. But the vertical projection of this intersection is the same line as the vertical projection of the element; consequently, Q′O′, the vertical projection of the element, is tangent to the curve $c''b'c'$ at the point p'. But Ip and pO are equal; therefore their vertical projections I′p' and p'O′ are also equal; that is, the part I′O′ of the tangent intercepted between the lines L′C″ and L′C′ is bisected at p', the point of tangency: and as this may be shown for any other point, it follows that the curve is a hyperbola, and the lines C′D″ and D′C″ its asymptotes. The same can be shown for the other curve. If either of these hyperbolas be revolved around A′B as an axis, it will evidently generate the surface from which it has been obtained. We therefore conclude, that the surface generated by a right line revolving around another right line which it does not intersect, or by a right line constantly touching three right lines having a particular position with each other, is the same surface as is generated by the revolution of a hyperbola around its conjugate axis, and is therefore properly called a hyperboloid of revolution of one nappe.

§ 228. Of warped surfaces in general. It is easily perceived from what has preceded, that if a right line be moved along two curves so that the part of the right line intercepted between them shall be of a given length, or so that it shall make with a given plane a constant angle, or make a given angle with one of the directrices; or should we move it upon three surfaces, or upon a curve and two surfaces, or upon two curves and a surface, or upon two surfaces and making a constant angle with a given plane, either of these conditions imposed upon the generatrix would, in general, give a warped surface of a different kind.

§ 229. We shall now demonstrate a general property of warped surfaces. It is this: *every plane passing through any element* K *of a warped surface is, in general, tangent to this surface at some point of the element* K. Suppose the plane to have any position, and let K′, K″, K‴, &c. be elements of the surface on one side of the element K; and H, H′, H″, &c. elements of the surface on the other side of the element K; and let these elements be consecutive with each other, and situated on the surface in the order in which the letters are written. The plane through the element K will not, in general, be parallel to these elements; it therefore intersects them in a series of consecutive points k''', k'', k', h, h', h'', h''', &c. forming a curve $k'''k''k'hh'h''h'''$; but since the points k' and h are on different sides of the element K, the indefinitely small part $k'h$ of the curve intersects the element K in a point. Let this point be designated by k; we say that the plane through the element K is tangent to the surface at the point k. For, if at k a line be drawn tangent to the curve $k'''k''k'khh'h''h'''$, it will be contained in the plane of the curve (67); that is, in the plane passed through the element. the element also is tangent to the surface at the same point; the plane, therefore, containing these tangent lines is tangent to the surface at the point k of the element K (88).

§ 230. As the curve $k'''k''k'khh'h''h'''$ varies with the position of the plane through the element K, it is evident that if this plane be turned around K as an axis, the point of contact k will move along this element. From these properties we conclude, that every tangent plane to a warped surface is also a cutting plane: secondly, that if we wish a plane tangent to a warped surface, we have only to draw it through an element of the surface; and thirdly, that the point of contact is the point in which the element intersects the curve of intersection of this plane and the surface.

§ 231. There are, however, a few cases in which a plane through an element of a warped surface is not tangent to it. Suppose, for example, that the given surface has a plane-directer, and that the plane through the element were parallel to the plane-directer; all the elements being also parallel to this plane, the curve $k'''k''k'khh'h''h'''$ would not exist, and the plane through the element would not be tangent to the surface. We have not heretofore spoken of the manner of representing warped surfaces on the planes of projection. They are, like other surfaces, generally represented by the projections of their elements, and their intersections with one or the other of the planes of projection.

PROBLEM.

To draw a plane tangent to a hyperboloid of revolution at a given point of its surface.

§ 232. Pl. 2. Fig. 4. Let (A,A′B) be the axis of the surface, XDC its intersection with the horizontal plane, (*xa*L*b*, *a′b′*) the circle of the gorge, and v the horizontal projection of the point at which the plane is to be tangent. Its vertical projection cannot be taken at pleasure (93), but must be constructed.

Through v draw DvC tangent to the horizontal projection of the circle of the gorge; this tangent is the projection of two elements, either of which may pass through the point of which v is the horizontal projection, according as the point is above or below the circle of the gorge. The two elements make the same angle with the horizontal plane, and pierce it at the points D and C. Projecting the point of tangency L into the vertical projection of the circle of the gorge, and the points C and D into the ground line at C′ and D′, two points in the vertical projection of each element are determined, and their vertical projections C′L′D″ and D′L′C″ can be drawn. Drawing from v a perpendicular to the ground line, and noting its intersections v′ and v″ with the projections of the elements, we determine the vertical projections of the two points of the surface of which v is the horizontal projection; one point is above the circle of the gorge and vertically projected at v″, the other below it and vertically projected at v′: these points are evidently those in which a line perpendicular to the horizontal plane at v pierces the surface. Let the tangent plane be first drawn at the point (v,v′).

Through v let the line Tv*x*X be drawn tangent to the horizontal projection of the circle of the gorge; this tangent is the projection of an element of the surface passing through (v,v'): and as (v,v') is below the circle of the gorge, it pierces the horizontal plane at T. The plane containing this element and the element (DC, D'C'') is tangent to the surface at the point (v,v') (88): DT is its horizontal trace, and its vertical trace is easily found.

§ 233. If it were required to draw a tangent plane to the surface at the point (v,v'') above the circle of the gorge, it would only be necessary to determine the plane of the elements of the two generations which pass through this point. The element (CD, C'D'') pierces the horizontal plane at C; and since (v,v'') is above the circle of the gorge, the element of which TvX is the horizontal projection pierces it at X: hence, XC is the horizontal trace of a plane tangent to the surface at the point (v,v'').

§ 234. The traces DT and XC of the tangent planes are parallel. For, draw Av and produce it in both directions, since the chords DvC and TvX make equal angles with the diameter passing through their point of intersection, the chords joining their extremities are perpendicular to this diameter, and consequently are parallel. This is as it should be; for the meridian plane of which vA is the horizontal trace is perpendicular to both the tangent planes (105); and being also perpendicular to the horizontal plane, its trace is perpendicular to the traces of the tangent planes.

§ 235. We see, therefore, that to draw a plane tangent to the surface of a hyperboloid of revolution, it is only necessary to determine the elements of the two generations passing through this point; the plane of these elements is the tangent plane required. Or, find the element of either generation passing through the given point, and draw through this element a plane perpendicular to the meridian plane of the given point: this plane will be tangent to the surface.

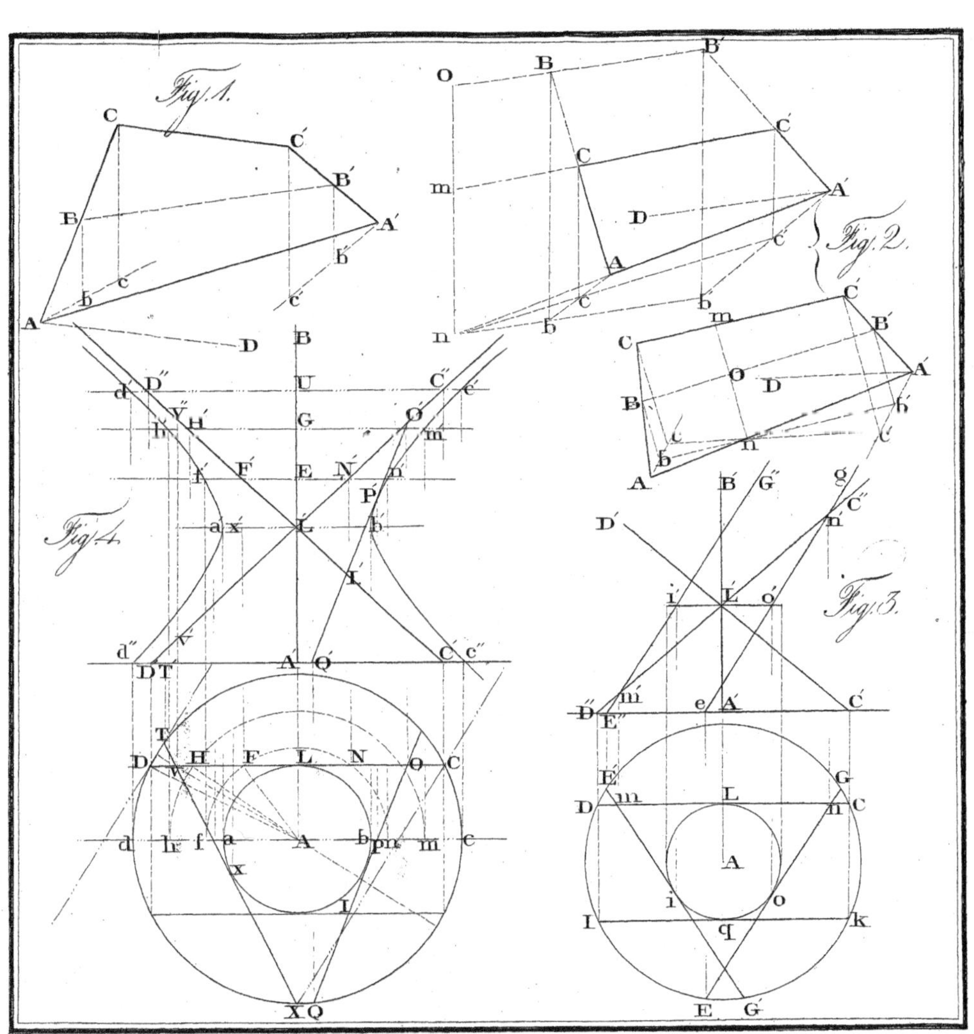
Fig. 1.
Fig. 2.
Fig. 3.
Fig. 4.

PROBLEM.

To pass a plane through a given right line, and tangent to a surface of revolution.

§ 236. Pl. 4. Let the surface be that of the ellipsoid. Let the transverse axis be perpendicular to the horizontal plane at A and A′B, its vertical projection; let the circle described with A as a centre and AE for a radius be the horizontal projection of the surface, and the ellipse A′G′E′BR′ its vertical projection; and let (CD, C′D′) be the given line.

Suppose the line (CD, C′D′) to revolve around (A,A′B) as an axis; it will generate the surface of a hyperboloid of revolution of one nappe. The hyperboloid thus generated, and the ellipsoid, having a common axis, a meridian plane of the one will be a meridian plane of the other. Let us suppose, for a moment, that the plane were drawn through (CD, C′D′) tangent to the surface of the ellipsoid, and that the point of contact were known.

Through the point of contact conceive a meridian plane to be passed; it will be perpendicular to the tangent plane (105), and will cut the line (CD, C′D′), which is an element of the hyperboloid, in a point. Since the tangent plane to the ellipsoid contains an element of the hyperboloid, it will be tangent to the hyperboloid at some point of the element (229). But the meridian plane passing through the point of. contact on the hyperboloid is perpendicular to the tangent plane: hence, the meridian plane which passes through the point of contact on the ellipsoid also contains the point of contact on the hyperboloid; therefore the point of contact on the hyperboloid is where this meridian plane cuts the given line (CD, C′D′). This meridian plane intersects the tangent plane to both surfaces in a line tangent to the two meridian curves. Suppose this meridian plane to be revolved about the common axis of the surfaces till it becomes parallel to the vertical plane of projection: the meridian curves of the hyperboloid would be projected into the

11

hyperbolas H′$f'''d$I′ and $f'c'o'$; these curves are the same as the sections made by a meridian plane parallel to the vertical plane, and may be determined as in Art. 227; the meridian section of the ellipsoid would be projected into the ellipse A′E′BR′, and the intersection of the tangent and meridian planes would be projected in a line tangent to these curves. But we can construct these curves without knowing the point of contact. If, then, we draw G′H′ tangent to the two curves, (H,H′) and (G,G′) are the revolved positions of the points at which the tangent plane touches the two surfaces. But the point (H,H′), in its true position in space, is a point of the line (CD, C′D′); in the counter revolution of the meridian plane this point describes the arc (H*h*, H′*h*′) of a horizontal circle, and the point (*h*,*h*′), in which this arc intersects the line (CD, C′D′), is the point at which the plane is tangent to the hyperboloid. The meridian plane A*gh* contains the point at which the plane is tangent to the surface of the hyperboloid, and also the point at which it is tangent to the surface of the ellipsoid. The point (G,G′), in the counter revolution, describes the arc (G*g*, G′*g*′) of a horizontal circle, and the point (*g*,*g*′), in which it intersects the meridian plane A*gh*, is the point at which the plane through the line (CD, C′D′) is tangent to the ellipsoid. Through the point of contact (*g*,*g*′) let a line be drawn parallel to the line (CD, C′D′): the point *m*, at which it pierces the horizontal plane, is a point of the horizontal trace; but C is another point; therefore PC*m*N is the horizontal trace of the tangent plane. The line drawn through (*g*,*g*′) pierces the vertical plane at *n* hence, *n*PQ is the vertical trace of the tangent plane.

If we consider the tangent L′I′, we perceive that it also gives a point of contact (*l*,*l*′) on the surface of the ellipsoid. The traces of the plane tangent at this point are found in the same manner as were the traces of the tangent plane in the other case. We see, therefore, that two planes can be drawn through a given line and tangent to a surface of revolution. The figure shows the manner in which the hyperbolas in the vertical plane are constructed.

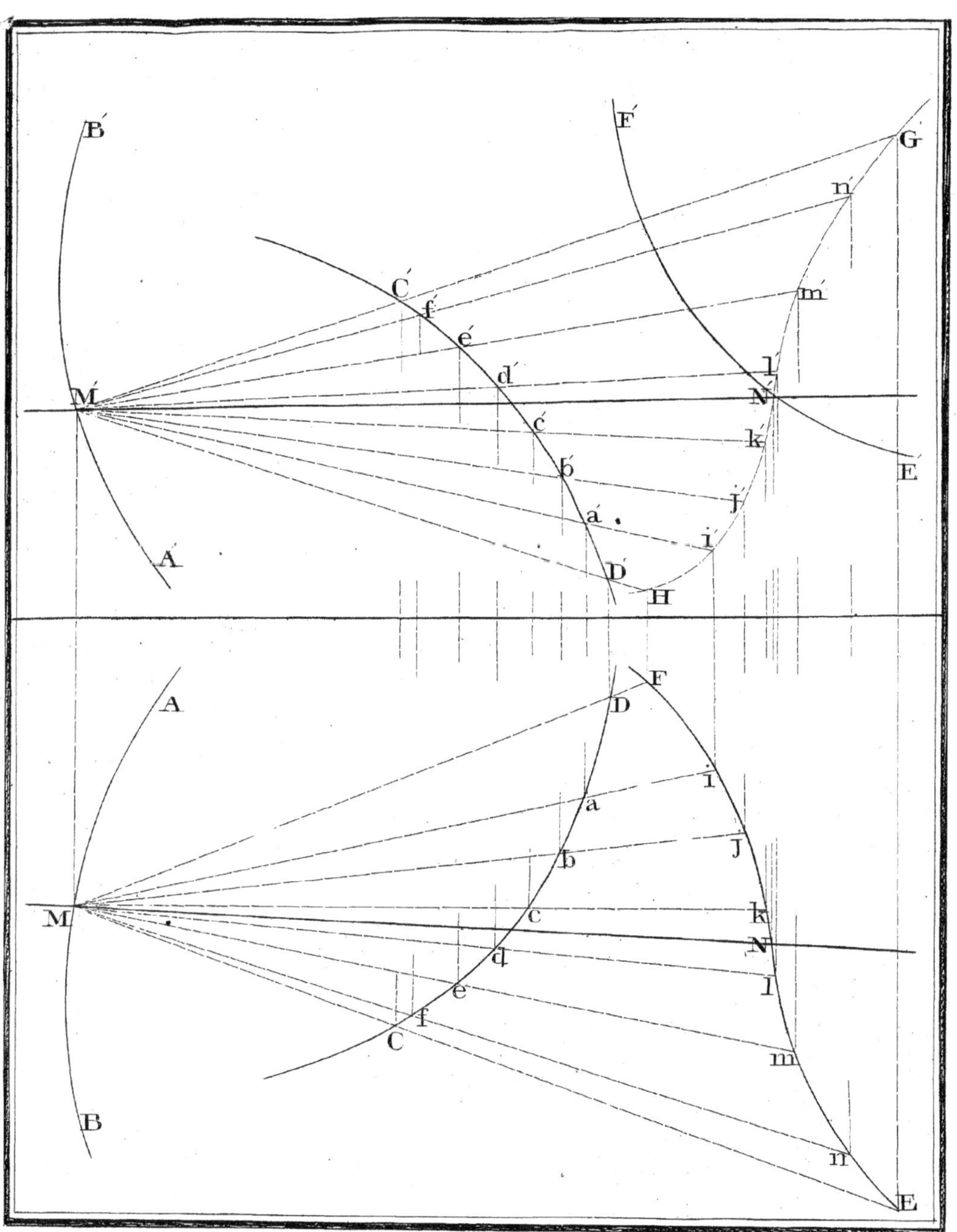

B'
F'
G'
n'
C'
f'
m'
e'
d'
l'
M'
N
c'
k'
b'
E'
J'
a'
i'
A'
D'
H
A
F
D
i
a
J
b
M
c
k
N
d
l
e
f
C
m
B
n
E

PROBLEM.

To find the intersection of a hyperboloid of revolution of one nappe with a given plane; to draw a tangent to the curve, and to find the curve in its own plane.

§ 237. Pl. 5. Let the horizontal plane be taken perpendicular to the axis of the surface; let A be the horizontal projection of the axis, and A′B its vertical projection. Let (CD, C′D′) be the generatrix, (*cots*, *c′t′*) the circle of the gorge, and (FE, FG″) the cutting plane.

Through the axis of the surface and perpendicular to the cutting plane let a plane be drawn; the intersection of these planes determines the transverse axis of the curve, and the points in which the transverse axis intersects the curve are the vertices. The line AE, drawn perpendicular to FE, is the horizontal trace of the meridian plane. The line of intersection of this plane and the cutting plane (FE, FG″) meets the axis of the surface at the point in which the axis pierces the cutting plane; that is, at the point (A,A″) (43); therefore AE is the horizontal and E′A″ the vertical projection of the line of which the transverse axis of the curve forms a part.

The points in which this axis pierces the surface are next to be found. If the line (EA*d*, E′A″*d*′) be revolved around the axis of the surface, it will generate the surface of a right cone with a circular base; (A,A″) is the vertex of this cone, and the circle described with A as a centre and radius AE is its intersection with the horizontal plane. But the cone and hyperboloid, having a common axis, intersect in circles, the planes of which are perpendicular to this axis; and the points in which the line (*d*AE, *d*′A″E′) pierces the surface are the points which describe these horizontal circles of intersection; the circles therefore contain the vertices of the axis. To find the radii of these circles, it will be sufficient to find the two points in which any element of the hyperboloid pierces the surface of the cone, since all the elements pierce the surface of the cone in the horizontal circles in which the two surfaces intersect. Let us find the points in which the element (CD, C′D′) pierces the surface of the cone. Draw a plane through the element (CD, C′D′) and the vertex of the cone; this plane will intersect the surface of the cone in two right-lined elements; the points in which the element of the hyperboloid intersects these elements, are points of the horizontal circles. To draw this plane. Through the vertex (A,A″) of the cone let a line be drawn parallel to the element (CD, C′D′) of the hyperboloid; its projections are parallel to CD and C′D′, and it pierces the horizontal plane at *a*: hence, N*a*CL is the horizontal trace of a plane containing the element of the hyperboloid and vertex of the cone. This plane intersects the cone in two elements, of which the horizontal projections are AL and NA*p*; the points *r* and *p*, in which these projections intersect CD, the projection of the element of the hyperboloid, are the horizontal projections of the two points, one in each of the circles, in which the hyperboloid and cone intersect; and as the circles are horizontal, A*r* and A*p* are the radii of their projections. But as the horizontal projections of the vertices are in the line E*d* as well as in the horizontal projections of the circles, they are at *q* and *d*, the points in which the line E*d* intersects the arcs described with the centre A and radii A*r* and A*p*. The vertical projections of these vertices are at *q′* and *d′*, in the vertical projection of the line (E*d*, E′*d′*). The vertex (*q*,*q′*) is below the circle of the gorge in the lower nappe of the cone, and the vertex (*d*,*d′*) is above the circle of the gorge in the upper nappe of the cone.

To find other points of the curve, intersect by horizontal planes between the points (*d*,*d′*) and (*q*,*q′*). Such planes will intersect the surface of the hyperboloid in horizontal circles, and the cutting plane in right lines parallel to its horizontal trace; the intersections of these right lines with the circles determine points of the curve. Let *h′b′* be the vertical trace of a horizontal plane; this plane cuts the element (CD, C′D′) in the point (v,v′), and intersects the plane (FE, FG″) in a line of which *bh*, parallel to FE, is the horizontal projection. The

Plate 4.

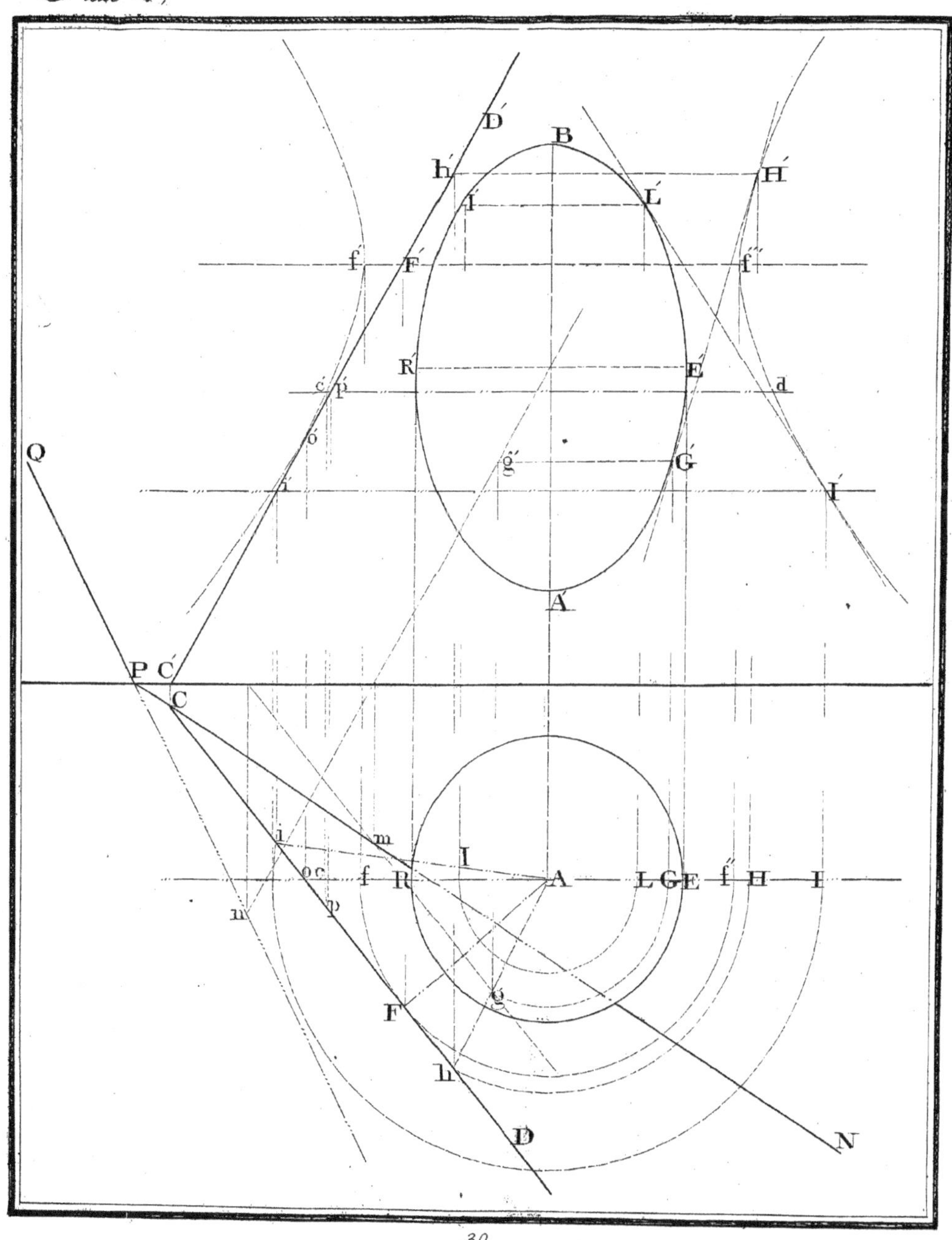

circle described with the centre A and radius Av is the horizontal projection of the circle in which the auxiliary plane intersects the surface of the hyperboloid. The points k and h, in which bh intersects this circle, are the horizontal projections of the two points of the curve determined by the auxiliary plane $h'b'$, and h' and k' are the vertical projections of these points. The points at which the horizontal projection of the curve is tangent to the horizontal projection of the circle of the gorge, are found by using the plane of the circle of the gorge as an auxiliary plane; they are the points o and s, and their vertical projections are o' and s'. Thus, having found any number of points, the projections of the curve can be described.

To draw a tangent line to the curve at any point, as (h,h'). Draw a plane tangent to the surface of the hyperboloid at this point (232); its intersection with the cutting plane is the tangent required (120). The line mnG is the horizontal trace of the tangent plane, and (Gh, gh') the tangent line.

Let the plane of the curve be now revolved around its vertical trace FG″; the points of the curve will fall in perpendiculars to this trace drawn through their vertical projections, and at distances from the trace equal to the hypothenuses of triangles whose bases are the distances from the vertical projections of the points to the trace FG″, and whose perpendiculars are equal to the distances of the horizontal projections of the points from the ground line. Having found the positions of the points, let the curve $q''h''Od''s''k''$ be described. The tangent line takes the position $G'h''$. In making the projections of the curve, we have supposed the part of the surface above the cutting plane to be removed; the horizontal projection of the curve is therefore made full. In the vertical projection, that part of the curve is made full which lies in front of the meridian plane nAt.

§ 238. We are next to consider the hyperbolic paraboloid, and shall begin by examining the manner of representing it on the planes of projection. If through any element of the surface a plane be drawn perpendicular to the horizontal plane (the surface being considered indefinite), the plane will be tangent to the surface at some point of this element (229); the line drawn through this point of contact perpendicular to the horizontal plane is tangent to the surface, and is therefore an element of the tangent cylinder which projects the surface on the horizontal plane. But the plane which is tangent to the surface is also tangent to the cylinder: hence, its horizontal trace is tangent to the base of the cylinder. But the horizontal trace of the tangent plane is the horizontal projection of the element through which the plane is drawn: hence, *the horizontal projection of every element of the surface is tangent to the base of the cylinder which projects the surface on the horizontal plane; that is, tangent to the curve which represents the projection of the surface.* By similar reasoning it may be shown, that the vertical projection of every element of the surface is tangent to the curve which represents the vertical projection of the surface. Therefore, if the projections of any number of elements be determined, and two curves be drawn respectively tangent to all the elements in each projection, these curves will represent the two projections of the surface. We will now show the easiest method of finding the projections of the elements.

§ 239. Pl. 6. Let (AB, A′B′) and (CD, C′D′) be the directrices of a hyperbolic paraboloid, and (FH, EG) the plane-directer. This plane cuts the directrix (AB, A′B′) in the point (1,1), and the directrix (CD, C′D′) in the point (1,1); therefore, the line joining 1 and 1 in the horizontal plane is the horizontal projection of an element of the surface, and the line joining 1 and 1 in the vertical plane is the vertical projection of the same element. Let now a plane be drawn parallel to the plane-directer, and at any distance from it: LN and L′N′ are the traces of such a plane; it cuts the directrix (AB, A′B′) at the point (2,2), and the directrix (CD, C′D′) in the point (2,2). If through these points a line be drawn, it will be an element of the surface; both its projections are made in the figure. If, now, a system of planes be drawn parallel to the plane (LN, L′N′), and at the same distance from each other as this plane is from the plane-directer; first, this system of planes being parallel

Plate 5.

B
O
d″
D′
h″
s′
G″
d′
q″
k″ c′
o′
s′ t′
c′
A′
h′
y′ k′
b′
E′ G′
q′
E′
g
F
C′
b
A′
e
L
k
G
C
r y
p
D
E
s
q
a
e
A
t
n
d
h
o
m
N

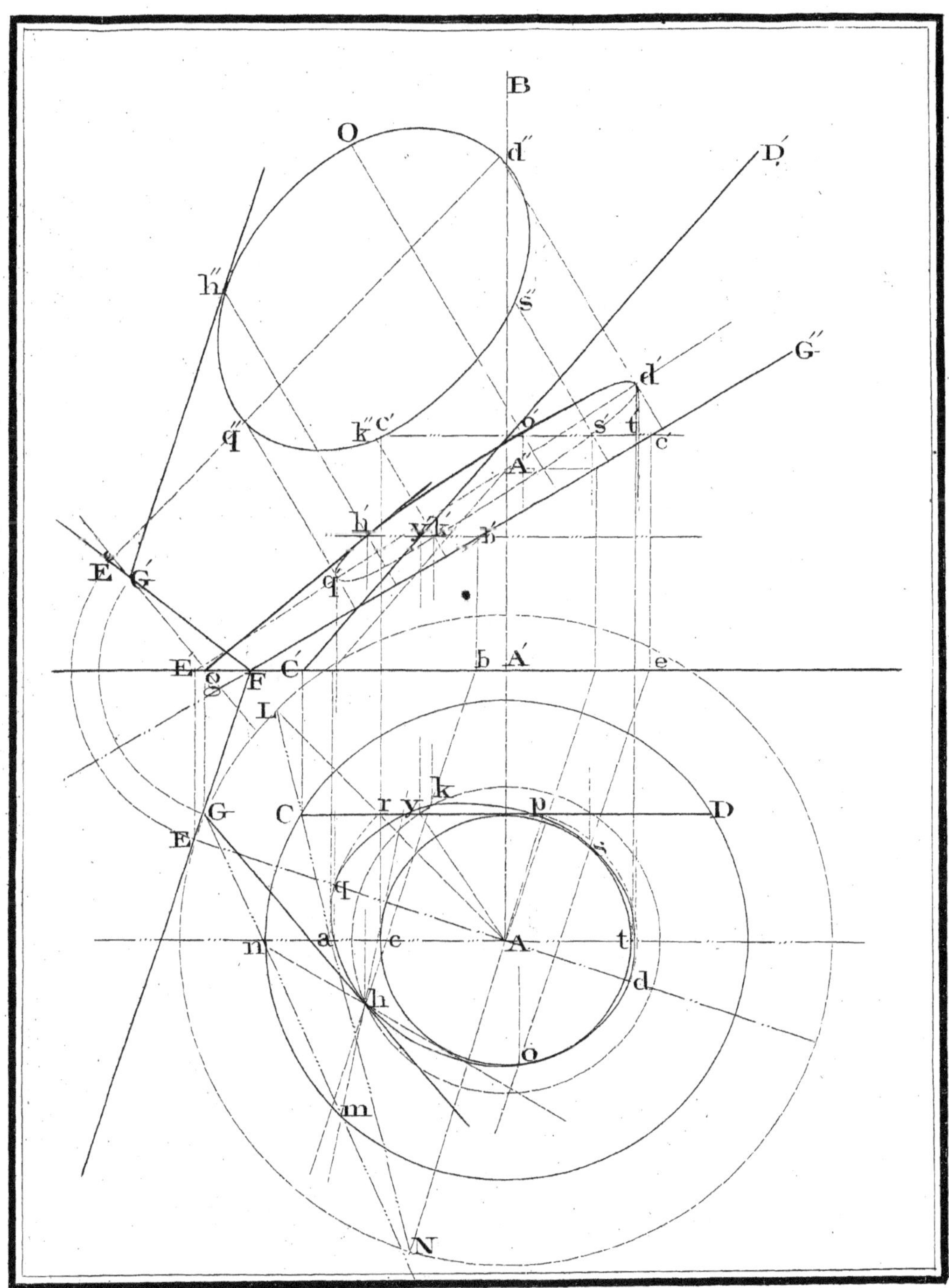

to the plane-directer, each plane will cut the directrices in two points, and the line joining them will be an element of the surface; secondly, since the planes are equidistant, the parts of the same directrix intercepted between any two of them which are adjacent will be equal, and the projections of these equal parts are also equal. If, therefore, on AB, the horizontal projection of one directrix, the parts from 2 to 3, from 3 to 4, from 4 to 5, &c. be each made equal to the part from 1 to 2; and on CD, the horizontal projection of the other directrix, the parts from 2 to 3, from 3 to 4, from 4 to 5, &c. be each made equal to the part between 1 and 2; the lines drawn through the corresponding points are the horizontal projections of elements of the surface. The vertical projections of the elements are determined either by finding the vertical projections of the points 1, 2, 3, 4, &c. in their corresponding directrices, and joining them; or by laying off on A′B′ the parts from 2 to 3, from 3 to 4, from 4 to 5, &c. each equal to the part from 1 to 2; and on C′D′ the parts from 2 to 3, from 3 to 4, from 4 to 5, &c. each equal to the part from 1 to 2: the lines joining corresponding points are the vertical projections of elements of the surface. The curve *fdcba*, drawn tangent to the horizontal projections of the elements, is the horizontal projection of the surface; and the curve *g′b′c′d′f′*, drawn tangent to the vertical projections of the elements, is the vertical projection of the surface.

In making the projections of the elements on either plane, the parts which are seen are made full, and the concealed parts dotted. With respect to the horizontal projection, it is evident that the part of each element which lies below the point at which the element touches the projecting cylinder, or at which the projecting plane of the element is tangent to the surface, is concealed, and the part which lies above this point is seen. Therefore, the horizontal projection of the element passing through 3 and 3 is made full from *a*, the element through 4 and 4 from the point at which it touches the curve, the element 7 and 7 from *c*, &c. With respect to the vertical projection, the part of each element which is in front of the point at which it touches the cylinder that projects the surface on the vertical plane is made full, and the part which is behind this point is dotted. Thus, the element passing through 2 and 2 is dotted to g', the element passing through 4 and 4 is dotted to b', &c. The directrices in either projection are seen when the elements which touch them are seen; but as they are important lines in the construction, they have been made full. The horizontal trace of the plane-directer, excepting the part F*b*, is concealed by the surface, and is therefore made broken; the vertical trace is also concealed by the surface, excepting the part 5G. It is easy to find the intersection of this surface with a given plane, since the points in which the elements pierce the plane are points of the curve. The horizontal plane of projection intersects the surface in the curve *ponml*: the element passing through the points (5,5) and (5,5) pierces it at *l*, the element through (6,6) and (6,6) at *m*, and similarly for the other points.

PROBLEM.

To draw a plane tangent to a hyperbolic paraboloid at a given point of the surface.

§ 240. Pl. 7. Let (GH, G'H') be the plane-directer, (AB,A'B') and (CD, C'D') the directrices, and *a* the horizontal projection of the point at which the tangent plane is to be drawn.

The vertical projection of the point cannot be taken at pleasure, but must be found by construction (93). The plane-directer cuts the directrix (AB, A'B') in the point (1,1), and the directrix (CD, C'D') in the point (1,1). Let any plane, as (EF, E'F'), be drawn parallel to the plane-directer; it cuts the directrix (AB, A'B') in the point (2,2), and the directrix (CD, C'D') in the point (2,2). By laying off the projections of the parts of the directrices intercepted between these two planes, and drawing lines through the corresponding points, we determine the projections of any number of elements.

At the point *a* conceive a line to be drawn perpendicular to

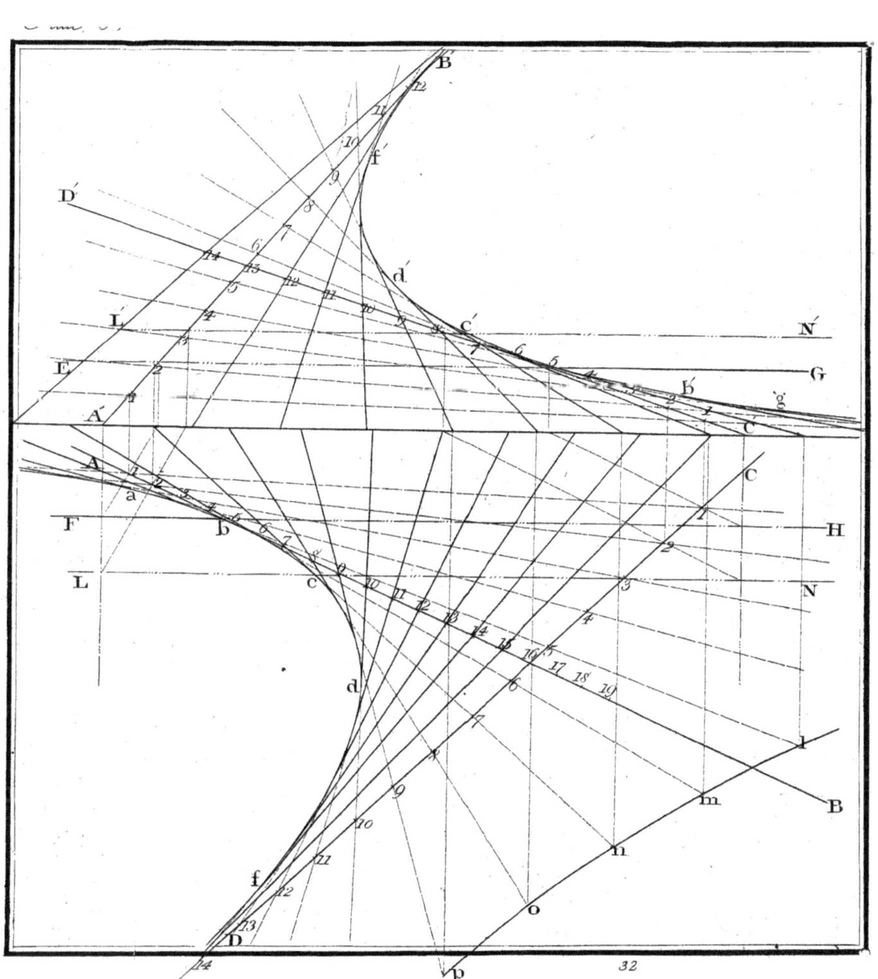

B
f′
D′
d′
L′
c′
N′
E
G
b′
g′
A′
C′
A
a
F
b
H
L
c
N
C
d
l
m
n
o
f
D
p
14
32

the horizontal plane; the point in which this perpendicular pierces the surface is the only point of the surface which is horizontally projected at *a*. Draw through this perpendicular the vertical plane (*cab*, *bb'*); this plane intersects the surface in a curve; the point in which the perpendicular meets this curve is the point in which it pierces the surface. This plane cuts the element drawn through (2,2) and (2,2) at the point (*d*,*d'*), it cuts the element drawn through (3,3) and (3,3) at the point (*f''*,*f'''*), the element drawn through (7,7) and (7,7) at the point (*e*,*e'*), and the element drawn through (9,9) and (9,9) at the point (*c*,*c'*); thus *d'f'''e'a'c'* is the vertical projection of the curve in which the vertical plane (*cab*, *bb'*) intersects the surface, and the point *a'*, in which this curve intersects the perpendicular to the ground line through *a*, is the vertical projection of that point of the surface which is horizontally projected at *a*. Having found the point (*a*,*a'*), if we draw through it an element of the first generation, it will be a line of the tangent plane (89); and if we draw through the point (*a*,*a'*) an element of the second generation, it will also be a line of the tangent plane (89): hence, the plane of these elements is the tangent plane required. To find the element of the first generation passing through the point (*a*,*a'*). Let a plane be drawn through this point parallel to the plane-directer, the point in which it cuts either of the directrices being joined with the point (*a*,*a'*) determines the element sought. Draw in the plane-directer, and through the same point, any two lines, as (*fg*, *f'g'*) and (*f*,*h*, *f'h'*), and as two lines determine a plane, a plane drawn through (*a*,*a'*) parallel to (*fg*, *f'g'*) and (*fh*, *f'h'*) will be parallel to the plane-directer. Drawing (*ai*, *a'i'*) parallel to (*fg*, *f g'*), its projections are parallel, and it pierces the plane which projects the directrix (CD, C'D') on the horizontal plane in the point (*i*,*i'*). Drawing (*at*, *a't*) parallel to (*fh*, *f h'*), this parallel pierces the plane which projects the directrix (CD, C'D) on the horizontal plane at the point (*t*,*t'*). But the lines (*ai*, *a'i'*) and (*at*, *a't'*) determine a plane passing through (*a*,*a'*) parallel to the plane-directer, and *t'i'* is the vertical projection of its intersection with the plane which projects (CD, C'D') on the horizontal plane:

hence, n' is the vertical projection of the point in which it cuts the directrix (CD, C'D'), and n is the horizontal projection of the same point. Therefore, $(an, a'n')$ is the element of the first generation passing through the point (a,a'), and the point L, in which it pierces the vertical plane, is one point of the vertical trace of the required tangent plane.

To find the element of the second generation passing through (a,a'). The plane-directer of the second generation is parallel to the directrices of the first generation (223). Therefore, if we draw through (a,a') a plane parallel to the directrices (AB A'B') and (CD, C'D'), and determine the point in which it cuts any element of the first generation, regarded as a directrix of the second generation, this point being joined with (a,a') deter mines the required element of the second generation. Take the element passing through (8,8) and (8,8) for one of the directrices of the second generation, and draw through (a,a') the lines $(aq, a'q')$ and $(ap, a'p')$ respectively parallel to the direc trices of the first generation; they determine a plane parallel to the plane-directer of the second generation (223). This plane intersects the plane which projects the directrix (88, 88) on the horizontal plane in a line of which $p'q'$ is the vertical projection; the point s', in which $p'q'$ intersects 88, is the vertical projection, and s is the horizontal projection of the point in which the plane passed through (a,a'), parallel to the plane-directer of the second generation, cuts the directrix (88, 88) of the second generation: hence, $(as, a's')$ is the element of the second generation passing through the point (a,a'). Having thus determined a second line of the tangent plane, a second point of its vertical trace is easily found, and the vertical trace LN can be drawn. The horizontal trace does not fall on the paper, but may be considered as found, since two lines of the plane are known.

Plate 1.

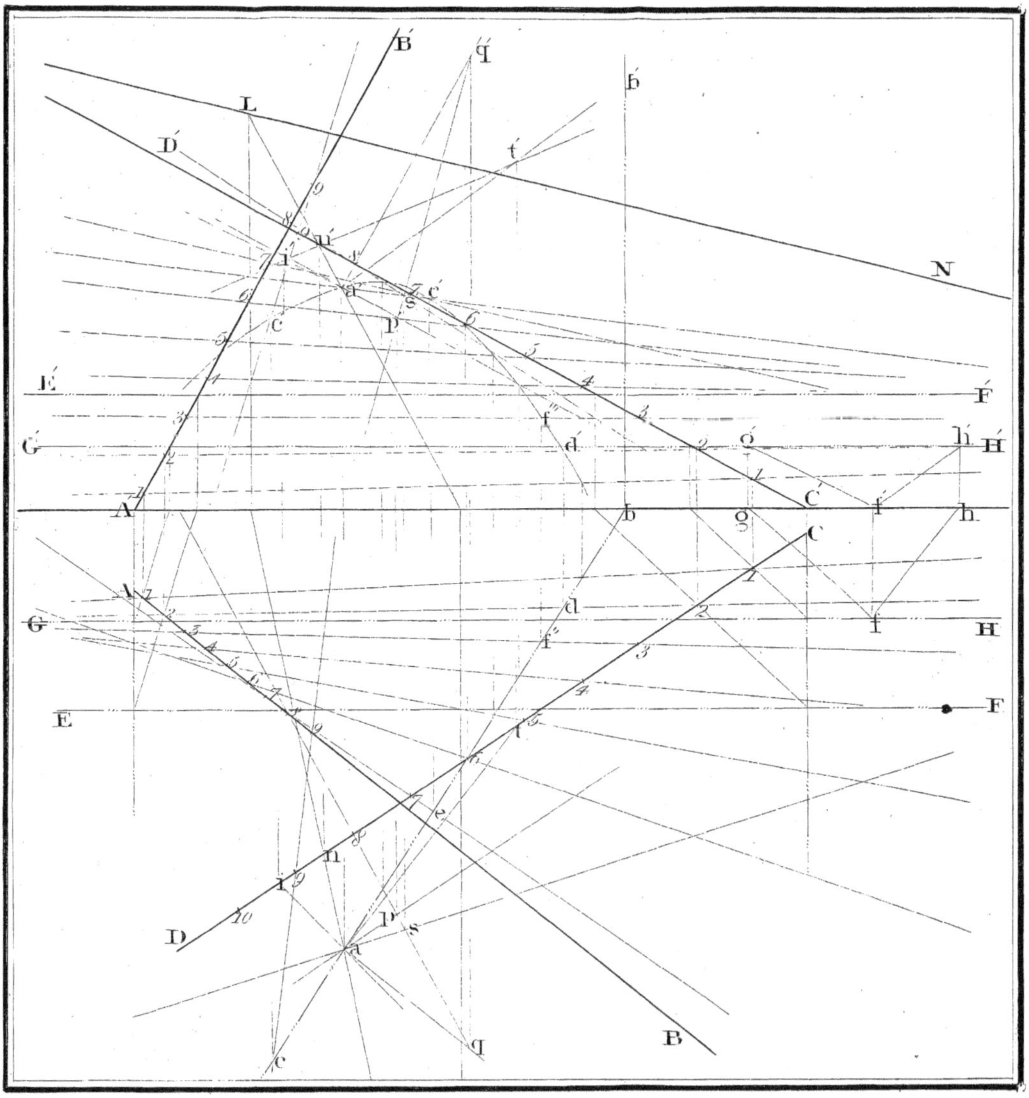

THEOREM.

If two warped surfaces, M *and* N, *have the same plane-directer, an element* E *common, and two tangent planes also common, their points of contact* m *and* m' *being on the element* E, *the surfaces will be tangent to each other throughout this element.*

§ 241. For, conceive any two secant planes P and P′ to be drawn through the points of contact m and m'. These planes intersect the surface M in the curves d and d', and the surface N in the curves f and f'. Since the surfaces are tangent to each other at the point m (85), the plane P intersects the tangent plane at this point in a line tangent to the curves d and f; consequently, these curves are tangent to each other at the point m. For similar reasons the curves d' and f' are tangent to each other at the point m'. If, now, we take the two curves d and d' for directrices, and the common plane-directer for a plane-directer, the elements of the surface M which pass through the consecutive points of tangency of the curves d and f and d' and f' are consecutive and belong also to the surface N. If any secant plane be drawn through a point of the element E, it will intersect the consecutive elements in consecutive points, and the curve of the surface M and the curve of the surface N will be tangent to each other, since they have two consecutive points common. Hence the surfaces themselves are tangent throughout the element E.

THEOREM.

Any two warped surfaces M *and* N *having an element* E *common and three common tangent planes, their points of contact* m, m', m'', *being on the element* E, *are tangent to each other throughout this element.*

§ 242. The demonstration of this theorem is very analogous to the preceding. Through the three points of contact m, m', and m'' conceive three secant planes to be pass... let d, d', and d'' be the curves in which they intersect the surface M, and f, f', and f'' the curves in which they intersect the surface N.

Since the surfaces are tangent to each other at the three points m, m', and m'', it is evident that the curves d and f, d' and f', and d'' and f'' are tangent to each other at the same points. Let the generatrix of the surface M move on the three curves d, d', and d'' as directrices; when indefinitely near the element E, it will pass through the consecutive points of tangency of the curves d and f, d' and f', and d'' and f'', and in this position it is consecutive with the element E: hence, the two surfaces have two consecutive elements common about the element E; therefore, the surfaces are tangent to each other along this element: for, if the surfaces be intersected by a plane through any point of the element E, the sections made in the surfaces will be tangent to each other.

PROBLEM.

A warped surface whose generatrix is parallel to a plane-directer being given, it is required to draw a tangent plane at a given point of this surface.

§ 243. Pl. 8. Take the vertical plane of projection for the plane-directer; let the curves ($abcf$, $a'b'c'f'$) and ($ghjm$, $g'h'm'j'$) be the directrices, and M the horizontal projection of the point at which the plane is to be tangent. The vertical projection of this point must be determined by construction. Draw a series of planes ag, bh, cj, &c. parallel to the vertical plane of projection; they cut the directrices in the points (a,a'), (b,b'), (c,c'), &c., and (g,g'), (h,h'), (j,j'), &c.; the right lines joining these points are elements of the surface. Having thus determined as many elements as are necessary, draw through the point M the vertical plane nMS; this plane cuts the elements before found in the points (n,n'), (o,o'), (q,q'), (i,i'), (s,s'), and the curve drawn through these points is the curve in which the plane intersects the surface. The point of which M is the horizontal projection being a point of the surface and of the secant plane nMS, is a point of the curve of intersection: hence, it is vertically projected in the curve $S'i'q'o'n'$; it is also vertically projected in a perpendicular to the ground line through M; therefore, M′ is the vertical projection of the point. Knowing the point of contact (M,M′), let a plane be drawn through it parallel to the vertical plane of projection; this plane cuts the directrices in the points (A,A′) and (B,B′), and the line (AB, A′B′), drawn through these points, is an element of the surface, and consequently a line of the required tangent plane. Now, of all the planes which can be drawn through (AB, A′B′), it is required to find the one which shall be tangent to the surface at the point M. To do this, let us use an auxiliary surface, the hyperbolic paraboloid. Through the points (A,A′) and (B,B′) draw the right lines (AC, A′C′) and (BD, B′D′) respectively tangent to the directrices (abf, $a'b'f'$) and (ghm, $g'h'm'$), and let us suppose a right line to move upon these tangents, continuing parallel to the vertical plane of projection; it is evident that it will generate the surface of a hyperbolic paraboloid containing the element (AB, A′B′); the hyperbolic paraboloid is tangent to the warped surface along the element (AB, A′B′). For, if through the tangent (AC, A′C′) and the element (AB, A′B′) a plane be drawn, it will be tangent to both surfaces at the point (A,A′); and if through the tangent (BD, B′D′) and the element (AB, A′B′) a plane be drawn, this plane will also be tangent to both surfaces at the point (B,B′). Hence, the surfaces are tangent to each other along the element (AB, A′B′) (241). If, now, a plane be drawn tangent to the hyperbolic paraboloid at the point (M,M′), this plane will also be tangent to the given surface, and consequently be the plane required.

§ 244. The vertical plane having been taken for the plane-directer, it was not necessary to construct the curve (noS, $n'o'$S′) in order to find the vertical projection of the point (M,M′); for, the point M being given, the plane AB, which contains the element of the surface in which the point (M,M′) is found, is determined, and projecting the points A and B into the vertical projections of the directrices determines A′B′, the vertical projection of the element; the point M′ is therefore known. It would not be thus if the plane-directer were not parallel to the vertical plane of projection; we should then have to use the first method to determine the vertical projection of the element.

THE END

Plate 8.

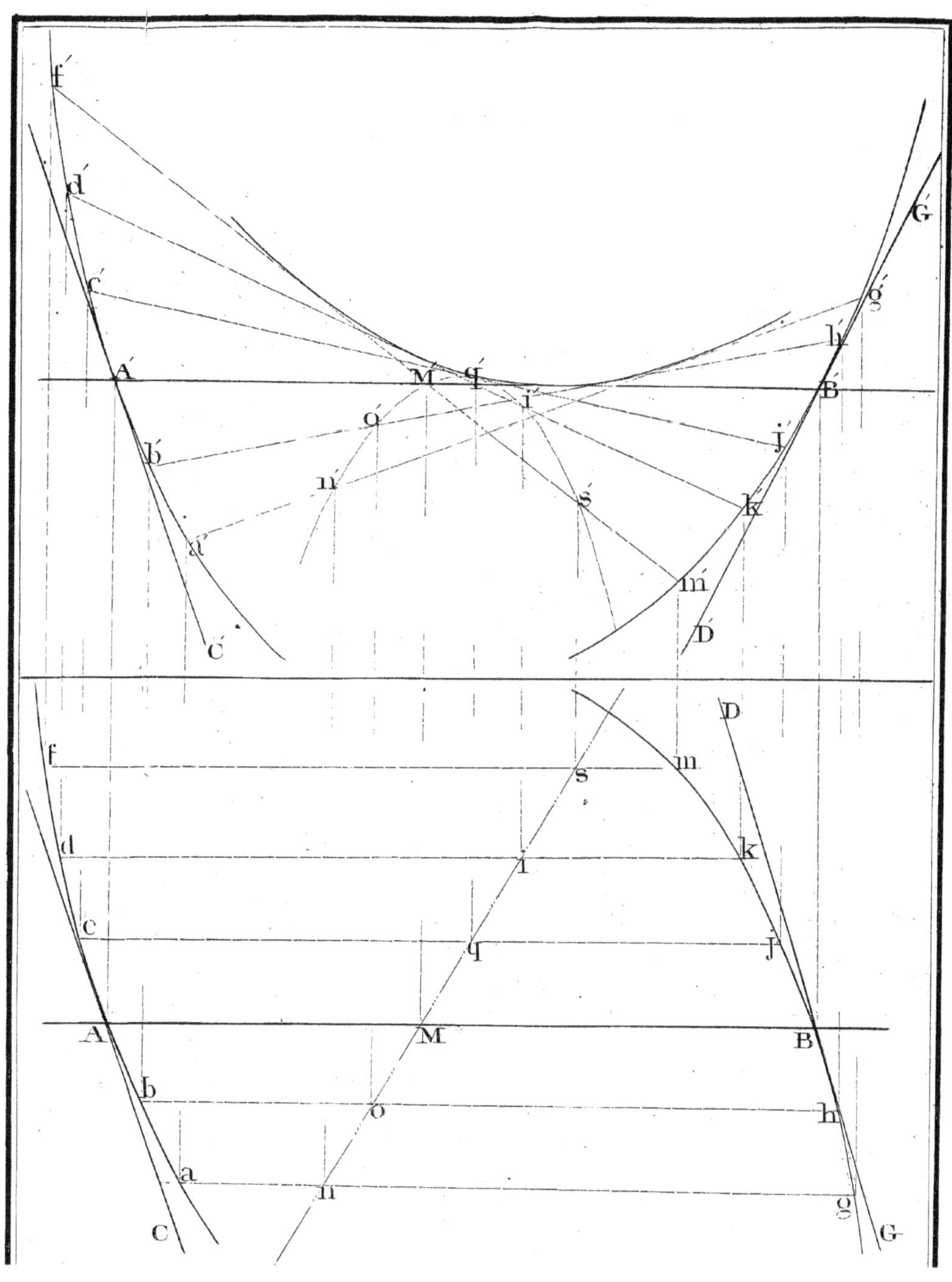

www.ingramcontent.com/pod-product-compliance
Lightning Source LLC
LaVergne TN
LVHW050522100826
845148LV00002B/415

* 9 7 8 1 4 2 5 5 2 1 1 4 1 *